This collection of essays presents many of the newer, innovative, and stimulating analytical approaches and methods that scholars use to study the history of American foreign relations. The essays highlight a variety of conceptual categories, including bureaucratic, dependency, and world systems theories, corporatist and national security models, culture, gender, and ideology.

Explaining the History of
American Foreign Relations

Explaining the History of American Foreign Relations

Edited by

MICHAEL J. HOGAN
The Ohio State University

THOMAS G. PATERSON
The University of Connecticut

CAMBRIDGE
UNIVERSITY PRESS

PUBLISHED BY THE PRESS SYNDICATE OF THE UNIVERSITY OF CAMBRIDGE
The Pitt Building, Trumpington Street, Cambridge CB2 1RP, United Kingdom

CAMBRIDGE UNIVERSITY PRESS
The Edinburgh Building, Cambridge CB2 2RU, United Kingdom
40 West 20th Street, New York, NY 10011-4211, USA
10 Stamford Road, Oakleigh, Melbourne 3166, Australia

First published 1991
Reprinted 1992, 1993, 1994, 1996

Printed in the United States of America

Typeset in Sabon

A catalogue record for this book is available from the British Library

Library of Congess Cataloguing-in-Publication Data is available

ISBN 0-521-40383-9 hardback
ISBN 0-521-407362 paperback

To
Lawrence E. Gelfand and
Ellis W. Hawley, and
to the memory of
Armin Rappaport

Contents

Preface

The history of American foreign relations, we have been told again and again, is a backwater of scholarly inquiry. According to the familiar indictment, addressed in some of the essays that follow, the study of American foreign relations has been dominated by an ethnocentric point of view, mired in detail, short on synthesis, and desperately in need of new directions. The tale of woe reminds us of the Maine farmer who was asked if a recent hurricane had damaged his barn. "Don't know," he answered. "Haven't found it yet." Not all is lost, however. In fact, historians of American foreign relations have been developing fresh topics, mining foreign archives, and applying new methods. Some scholars have sought to reconceptualize the field; others have explored new ways to think about older approaches.

The essays in this volume demonstrate the field's vitality. They are not intended to rehash old debates or to rebut specific critics. Nor are they designed as historiographical surveys of the literature. Instead, the essays present some of the new topics of inquiry and some of the innovative analytical approaches that have emerged in recent years. They point to the variety of ways scholars go about explaining the history of American foreign relations. And they are offered here in an effort to define the field, point research in fresh directions, and stimulate cross-disciplinary thinking, especially between historians and political scientists.

Numerous friends and colleagues helped us with this book and deserve special mention here. Many of the following essays first appeared in *Diplomatic History* and the *Journal of American History*. We want to thank the staffs of both journals for their assistance, especially David Thelen and Richard Blackett of the *Journal of American History* and Mary Ann Heiss and Toby D. Rosenthal of *Diplomatic History*. We are also indebted to Elizabeth Mahan and George Herring for their help with the project, and to the authors for taking the time to critique each other's work. In addition, thanks are due to Alexandra Nickerson for her work on the index, and to the Ohio State University and the University of

Connecticut Research Foundation for financial assistance and other forms of aid in advancing this volume to completion.

Earnings from the sale of this book are being contributed to the Society for Historians of American Foreign Relations in support of its journal, *Diplomatic History*. The society has established a fund for this purpose in the name of Armin Rappaport, the first editor of *Diplomatic History*. We invite others to contribute to this fund. We especially thank Scholarly Resources Inc., the *Journal of American History*, and the authors in this volume for making their own contribution to the Armin Rappaport Journal Fund by waiving the usual republication fees.

We are very pleased to dedicate this volume to Lawrence E. Gelfand and Ellis W. Hawley, and to the late Armin Rappaport. As our graduate directors many years ago, they first introduced us to the exciting ways of thinking about the history of American foreign relations and its relationship to other fields.

MJH
Columbus, Ohio
TGP
Storrs, Connecticut

The Authors

J. GARRY CLIFFORD is professor of political science at the University of Connecticut. He received his doctorate from Indiana University. His book *The Citizen Soldiers: The Plattsburg Training Camp Movement, 1913–1920* (1972) won the Frederick Jackson Turner Award of the Organization of American Historians. He has also written *The First Peacetime Draft* (1986, with Samuel R. Spencer, Jr.) and *American Foreign Policy: A History* (3d rev. ed., 1988, with Thomas G. Paterson and Kenneth J. Hagan) and edited *Memoirs of a Man: Grenville Clark* (1975). Professor Clifford's articles have appeared in the *Journal of American History, Diplomatic History,* and *Peace and Change,* among other journals. His current research centers on FDR and American entry into World War II.

ALAN K. HENRIKSON is associate professor of history at the Fletcher School of Law and Diplomacy, Tufts University, and counselor on Canadian Affairs at the Center for International Affairs, Harvard University. Professor Henrikson has written extensively on the history of American foreign policy and on current issues involving the North Atlantic Treaty Organization, political geography, and international relations. He is the editor of *Negotiating World Order: The Artisanship and Architecture of Global Democracy* (1986).

MICHAEL J. HOGAN is professor of history at the Ohio State University and editor of *Diplomatic History.* His articles have appeared in several journals, including the *Journal of American History,* the *American Historical Review,* and *Diplomatic History.* He is also the author of *Informal Entente: The Private Structure of Cooperation in Anglo-American Economic Diplomacy, 1918–1928* (1977) and *The Marshall Plan: America, Britain, and the Reconstruction of Western Europe, 1947–1952* (1987). Professor Hogan is the recipient of the Stuart L. Bernath Lecture and Book prizes of the Society for Historians of American Foreign Relations, the Quincy Wright Book Prize of the International Studies Association, and the George Louis Beer Prize of the American Historical Association.

OLE R. HOLSTI is George V. Allen Professor of International Affairs in the Department of Political Science at Duke University. Since receiving his doctorate at Stanford University, he has taught at Stanford, the University of British Columbia, and the University of California (Davis). In addition to many journal articles, his publications include *Enemies in Politics* (1967), *Content Analysis for the Social Sciences and Humanities* (1969), *Unity and Disintegration in International Alliances* (1973), and *American Leadership in World Affairs: Vietnam and the Breakdown of Consensus* (1984, with James N. Rosenau). Professor Holsti, a former president of the International Studies Association, has received the Nevitt Sanford Award from the International Society of Political Psychology.

MICHAEL H. HUNT received his doctorate from Yale University and has taught at the University of North Carolina at Chapel Hill since 1980. His most recent book is *Ideology and U.S. Foreign Policy* (1987). His earlier award-winning work on Sino-American relations includes *Frontier Defense and the Open Door* (1973) and *The Making of a Special Relationship* (1983). Professor Hunt has also written on the history of Chinese foreign relations, and he is currently examining the Chinese Communist party's views of, and policies toward, the United States from the 1920s to the 1950s.

RICHARD H. IMMERMAN is professor of history at the University of Hawaii. He received the Stuart L. Bernath Book Prize from the Society for Historians of American Foreign Relations for *The CIA in Guatemala: The Foreign Policy of Intervention* (1982) and was the 1990 winner of the Stuart L. Bernath Lecture Prize. He has coauthored *Milton S. Eisenhower, Educational Statesman* (1983), collaborated on *How Presidents Test Reality: Decisions on Vietnam, 1954 and 1965* (1989), and edited *John Foster Dulles and the Diplomacy of the Cold War* (1990). His articles have appeared in *Political Science Quarterly*, the *Journal of American History*, *Diplomatic History*, and other journals. From 1987 to 1989, Professor Immerman was an SSRC/MacArthur fellow in International Peace and Security Studies. He is currently writing a book on foreign and national security policy during the Eisenhower administration.

AKIRA IRIYE, professor of history at Harvard University, is a past president of both the Society for Historians of American Foreign Relations and the American Historical Association. Professor Iriye's publications include *Across the Pacific: An Inner History of American–East Asian Relations* (1967), *Power and Culture: The Japanese-American*

War, 1941–1945 (1981), and *The Origins of the Second World War in Asia and the Pacific* (1987). He is now preparing a book on ideas of war and visions of peace in the twentieth century.

MELVYN P. LEFFLER is professor of history at the University of Virginia. He is the author of *The Elusive Quest: America's Pursuit of European Stability and French Security, 1919–1933* (1979) and *A Preponderance of Power: National Security, the Truman Administration, and the Cold War, 1945–1952* (forthcoming). His articles have appeared in the *American Historical Review*, the *Journal of American History*, *Diplomatic History*, and *International Security*. As a Council on Foreign Relations fellow, Professor Leffler served in the Office of the Secretary of Defense, International Security Affairs. He is a recipient of the Gilbert Chinard Incentive Award and the Stuart L. Bernath Lecture and Article prizes.

THOMAS J. MCCORMICK is professor of history at the University of Wisconsin-Madison. He received his Ph.D. degree from the University of Wisconsin, where he studied with Fred Harvey Harrington and William Appleman Williams. He is the author of *China Market: America's Quest for Informal Empire, 1893–1910* (1967) and other works. His most recent publication is *America's Half-Century: United States Foreign Policy in the Cold War* (1989). Professor McCormick is currently working on a study of America's wars for Asian integration, 1941–75.

ROBERT J. MCMAHON is associate professor of history at the University of Florida. He is the author of *Colonialism and Cold War: The United States and the Struggle for Indonesian Independence, 1945–49* (1981). He is also the editor of *Major Problems in the History of the Vietnam War* (1990) and *The Origins of the Cold War* (3d ed., 1991, with Thomas G. Paterson). Professor McMahon's articles have appeared in the *Journal of American History*, *Political Science Quarterly*, *Pacific Historical Review*, and *Diplomatic History*. The winner of the 1991 Stuart L. Bernath Lecture Prize of the Society for Historians of American Foreign Relations, he is currently completing a book on U.S. relations with India and Pakistan, 1947–65.

THOMAS G. PATERSON, professor of history at the University of Connecticut, has written *Soviet-American Confrontation* (1973), *On Every Front: The Making of the Cold War* (1979), *Meeting the Communist Threat* (1988), and *American Foreign Policy* (3d rev. ed., 1991, with J. Garry Clifford and Kenneth J. Hagan). He has also edited and contributed to a book of original essays, *Kennedy's Quest for Victory* (1989). His articles have appeared in the *Journal of American History,* the *American Historical Review,* and *Diplomatic History,* among other journals. Professor Paterson is a past president of the Society for Historians of American Foreign Relations.

STEPHEN PELZ is professor of history at the University of Massachusetts at Amherst, where he has taught since receiving his doctorate from Harvard University. A specialist in U.S. relations with Asia, he has written *Race to Pearl Harbor: The Failure of the Second London Naval Conference and the Onset of World War II* (1974) and a number of articles, including "A Taxonomy for U.S. Diplomatic History," in the *Journal of Interdisciplinary History* (1988), and "Systemic Explanation in International History," in the *International History Review* (1990).

LOUIS A. PÉREZ, JR., is graduate research professor of history at the University of South Florida. He has published articles in the *Hispanic American Historical Review,* the *Journal of Latin American Studies,* ar.d the *Journal of American History,* among other journals. Professor Pérez has written a number of books, the most recent of which, *Cuba and the United States: Ties of Singular Intimacy, 1780s–1980s,* was published in 1990.

EMILY S. ROSENBERG is professor of history at Macalester College. She has written *Spreading the American Dream: American Economic and Cultural Expansion, 1890–1945* (1982), *World War I and the Growth of United States Predominance in Latin America* (reprinted, 1986), and *In Our Times: America since World War II* (3d ed., 1987, with Norman L. Rosenberg). She serves on the board of the Minnesota Humanities Commission and is a past vice-president of Women Historians of the Midwest. Professor Rosenberg's articles have appeared in the *Journal of American History,* the *Journal of Inter-American Studies and World Affairs, Diplomatic History, Business History Review,* and other journals. Currently, she is engaged in research on dollar diplomacy in the early twentieth century.

MELVIN SMALL is professor of history at Wayne State University. Since receiving his doctorate at the University of Michigan, he has written *Was War Necessary?* (1980), *International War* (2d ed., 1988), and *Johnson, Nixon, and the Doves* (1988), winner of the Warren Kuehl Prize of the Society for Historians of American Foreign Relations. He is also coauthor, with J. David Singer, of *The Wages of War* (1972) and

Resort to Arms (1982). Professor Small's articles have appeared in *Peace and Change,* the *Journal of Conflict Resolution,* and *Diplomatic History,* among other journals. A member of the editorial boards of *Peace and Change* and *International Interactions,* he is currently studying the anti–Vietnam War movement and the media.

1

Introduction

MICHAEL J. HOGAN AND
THOMAS G. PATERSON

World War I helped to spawn the first generation of specialists in the history of American foreign relations, most of whom had been trained originally as political historians. Influenced by that training, as well as by the war, these scholars soon created two distinct approaches to the study of American foreign policy. The nationalist perspective of Samuel Flagg Bemis and Dexter Perkins stressed the continuities in American diplomacy. These scholars celebrated the growth of American power and the creation of an American diplomatic tradition marked by such hallowed principles as those embodied in the Monroe Doctrine. Although not indifferent to the domestic influences on American policy, they concentrated primarily on state-to-state relations, placed American diplomacy in an international, usually European, setting, and often conducted research in foreign archives that established a high standard for subsequent scholars.[1]

From the start, however, Charles Beard and other progressive historians challenged the nationalist perspective.[2] The scholars in this school were less enamored of multiarchival research and less inclined to focus

1 For overviews of the field, from which this essay borrows, see Alexander DeConde, *American Diplomatic History in Transformation* (Washington, 1976); John Higham, *History: The Development of Historical Studies in the United States* (Englewood Cliffs, 1965); Charles Neu, "The Changing Interpretive Structure of American Foreign Policy," in *Twentieth-Century American Foreign Policy*, ed. John Braeman, Robert H. Bremner, and David Brody (Columbus, 1971), 1–57; and Jerald A. Combs, *American Diplomatic History: Two Centuries of Changing Interpretations* (Berkeley, 1983). We are also indebted to Michael Hunt for allowing us to benefit from his unpublished paper, "The New U.S. Diplomatic History." For the nationalist perspective see Bemis, *A Diplomatic History of the United States* (New York, 1936); idem, *The Diplomacy of the American Revolution* (New York, 1935); idem, *John Quincy Adams and the Foundations of American Foreign Policy* (New York, 1949); Perkins, *The Monroe Doctrine, 1823–1826* (Cambridge, MA, 1927); and idem, *The Monroe Doctrine, 1826–1867* (Baltimore, 1933).
2 See Charles A. and Mary R. Beard, *America in Midpassage* (New York, 1939). For further discussion of the progressive school, as well as citations to the literature, see Neu, "Changing Interpretive Structure," 16–21.

on state-to-state relations. They searched instead for the intellectual assumptions that guided American policymakers and for the domestic political, economic, and regional forces that shaped their diplomacy. Because these forces varied with historical circumstances, the progressive historians saw change rather than continuity, conflict rather than consensus, as major features in the history of American foreign relations.

The two approaches of these early scholars influenced later generations, as did such international developments as the rise of Fascist aggression and the outbreak of World War II, the Holocaust in Germany and the atomic bombings of Japan, the Cold War and the nuclear arms race. These dramatic developments contributed to a pervasive sense of disillusionment, to a pessimism about the future, and to a tragic view of life in an age dominated by war, revolution, and the prospect of nuclear annihilation. These themes were commonplace in intellectual circles generally and even began to influence the thinking of Bemis, Perkins, and other scholars among the founding generation of diplomatic historians. Although their writing on early American diplomacy had often been marked by an unbridled optimism, they grew increasingly disillusioned with the unfolding record of American foreign policy in the twentieth century. They also became more critical of the influence that public opinion and partisan politics exerted on policymaking, and more pessimistic about the ability of decision-making elites to understand, let alone to control, an international system that was increasingly complex and dangerous.

This critical, sometimes pessimistic, tone became one of the hallmarks of the realist historians who dominated the writing on American foreign relations in the 1950s and into the 1960s. Led by George F. Kennan, Hans J. Morgenthau, and others, realist historians, much like the nationlist school of an earlier day, were concerned primarily with the state, with state policymaking elites, and with the use of power to advance the national interest.[3] Their work tended to downplay the internal sources of American diplomacy that had preoccupied the progressive historians, although it did not ignore the influence of public opinion, partisan politics, and misguided idealism. The realists, in fact, often heaped the blame for failed policies on the shifting moods of an uninformed public, on partisan rivalries, and on befuddled legal and moral precepts that blinded political leaders to the nation's real interests. Informed by these failures, realist historians touted the need for policymaking by professional elites

3   For a sample of the original works of the realist scholars see Kennan, *American Diplomacy, 1900–1950* (Chicago, 1951); Morgenthau, *Politics among Nations: The Struggle for Power and Peace* (New York, 1948); and idem, *In Defense of the National Interest* (New York, 1951).

who stood above the crowd, who were unimpeded by the pressures of electoral politics, and who were guided instead by a disinterested expertise. These elites, argued the realists, were more likely to understand the architecture of global balances, contending alliances, and competing national interests that marked the world after 1945. They were also more likely to devise rational strategies that ensured the nation's security and fulfilled its weighty responsibilities as a world power.

The tendency of realist historians to celebrate elite management, draw lessons from the past, and write in prescriptive terms made their work particularly appealing to official Washington, as did their celebration of power and their focus on geopolitics and grand strategy. As Stanley Hoffmann pointed out, realism provided American leaders in the early Cold War with an "intellectual compass." It helped them to "excoriate isolationism," to "justify a permanent and global involvement in world affairs," and to "rationalize the accumulation of power, the techniques of intervention, and the methods of containment." What the realists offered, Hoffmann concluded, "the policy-makers wanted."[4]

Yet the realist historians also made important contributions to the study of American foreign relations. To be sure, they were largely indifferent to the sources of foreign policy that were rooted in the domestic American system and to the role played by trade unions, multinational corporations, and other nonstate actors. But the realists did focus renewed attention on certain issues intrinsic in the field, such as national security, national interest, balances of power, and grand strategy; and they introduced a critical point of view that continues to characterize more recent studies. In addition, many historians who worked within the realist framework added significant new dimensions of their own. In a series of monographs, for example, Ernest R. May rivaled Bemis's research in foreign archives. Not only did May place American diplomacy in an international setting, he went beyond Bemis in using multiarchival research to write multinational history.[5] Other historians delineated the influence of key individuals on American diplomacy or explored the intellectual and ideological assumptions that guided policymakers.[6] These lines of analysis would broaden and deepen in the 1960s, producing such works as those

4 Hoffmann, "An American Social Science: International Relations," *Daedalus* 106 (Summer 1977): 47–48.
5 A sample of May's work would include *World War I and American Isolation, 1914–1917* (Cambridge, MA, 1959), *Imperial Democracy: The Emergence of America as a Great Power* (New York, 1961), and *The Making of the Monroe Doctrine* (Cambridge, MA, 1975).
6 See, for example, Howard K. Beale, *Theodore Roosevelt and the Rise of America to World Power* (Baltimore, 1956); and Felix Gilbert, *To the Farewell Address: Ideas of Early American Foreign Policy* (Princeton, 1961).

by Arno J. Mayer and N. Gordon Levin on the ideological and social forces that shaped Wilsonian diplomacy.[7]

At the same time, however, the works by Mayer and Levin highlighted a renewed interest in the internal sources of American diplomacy. Emphasized by Beard and the progressive historians but slighted by the realists, these sources became the special concern of William Appleman Williams and many other revisionists of the 1960s and 1970s.[8] The revisionists placed primary emphasis on American ideas and on the American system of liberal capitalism. As they saw it, American leaders had embraced an ideology of expansionism founded on the principle of the Open Door. They had sought foreign markets to relieve domestic economic and political crises, and had forged in the process an overseas empire that violated the best principles of the nation. Although they surveyed the whole record of American diplomacy, the revisionists focused special attention on the Cold War. Finding that American policy in this era was more purposeful than the realists would admit, they also deviated from the realists in assigning the United States, rather than the Soviet Union, primary responsibility for the breakdown of the wartime coalition and for the years of unremitting tension that followed. Influenced by these events and by the wrenching experience of the Vietnam War, the revisionists were particularly critical of American policy toward developing countries. In the Third World, they argued, American officials had linked the United States to decaying colonial regimes, jeopardized their nation's best interests, and betrayed its basic commitment to the principle of self-determination.

The revisionists helped other historians shift their attention away from Europe and the great powers to the developing world. By shining a Beardian light on the economic forces that influenced decision making, they also brought more clearly into view the important role played by actors outside the state, especially organized business and financial interests. They reminded their readers of the significant linkages between state and society and of how social structure can shape foreign policy. In addition, the revisionists reemphasized the importance of ideas and

7 See Mayer, *Political Origins of the New Diplomacy, 1917–1918* (New Haven, 1959); idem, *Politics and Diplomacy of Peacemaking: Containment and Counterrevolution at Versailles, 1918–1919* (New York, 1967); and Levin, *Woodrow Wilson and World Politics: America's Response to War and Revolution* (New York, 1968).
8 Williams launched New Left revisionism with *The Tragedy of American Diplomacy* (Cleveland, 1959). He explained the development of his thinking in "A Historian's Perspective," *Prologue* 6 (Fall 1974): 200–203. See also William Appleman Williams, "Open Door Interpretation," in *Encyclopedia of American Foreign Relations: Studies of the Principal Movements and Ideas,* ed. Alexander DeConde, 3 vols. (New York, 1978), 2:703–10.

ideology in the history of American foreign relations and lent new credence to the view of American leaders as rational policymakers who sought to control events, calculate the national interests, and pursue a coherent, if misguided, vision.

At the same time, however, critics complained that revisionism was monocausal in its emphasis on economic motives, failed to differentiate between competing domestic interests, and ignored the influence of legitimate national security concerns and of the actions of other states on American diplomacy.[9] Reacting to these criticisms, some historians in the last two decades have sought to replace revisionist assumptions with those more characteristic of realism. Typified by John Lewis Gaddis, these postrevisionist scholars have refocused attention on the state as the principal actor, on decision-making elites, on the strategic and geopolitical determinants of policy, and on such traditional notions as national security, national interest, and the balance of power. Postrevisionists have generally discovered success in America's diplomatic record, especially in the early Cold War. When critical of American policy, their criticism tends to echo the older realist complaints about the deleterious effects on decision making of bureaucratic struggles, misplaced ideals, public opinion, and party politics. In addition, although postrevisionist historians accord economic diplomacy some room in their studies, they treat it as an instrument of grand strategy driven by geopolitical concerns, not by domestic pressures. If American leaders were empire builders, as these scholars admit in a nod to revisionism, the empire grew by invitation from abroad rather than from imperatives rooted in the American system. It was a defensive empire erected in the context of the Cold War, for which the Soviets were primarily responsible.[10]

Postrevisionism is neither a new method of analyzing American foreign relations nor a coherent synthesis of older approaches. In contrast to revisionism, in whose shadow it emerged, postrevisionism reasserts the primacy of geopolitical considerations over internal forces in American foreign policy. Taken together, the two schools recapitulate a division that has marked the study of American foreign relations from its inception, and that also runs through many of the essays in this volume. But ongoing differences over the primacy of causal forces have not deterred the current generation of historians from exploring new avenues of re-

9 For one of the many critiques of revisionism see Bradford Perkins, " 'The Tragedy of American Diplomacy': Twenty-five Years After," *Reviews in American History* 12 (March 1984): 1–18.
10 The case for postrevisionism is made in John Lewis Gaddis, "The Emerging Postrevisionist Synthesis on the Origins of the Cold War," *Diplomatic History* 7 (Summer 1983): 171–90.

search, reconceptualizing older approaches, and charting fresh directions. On the contrary, as the essays in this book suggest, the historical study of American foreign relations has been undergoing a fertile transformation in recent years.

The current ferment in the field, like earlier transformations, has been influenced by developments in the United States and abroad. The debate in the 1970s and 1980s over the proper role of the United States in world affairs stimulated scholarly and popular interest in the history of American foreign relations, much as the Vietnam War had done earlier.[11] The fracturing of the Cold War consensus and a succession of new crises in Iran, Nicaragua, and elsewhere helped to sustain that interest. So did a growing concern with the natural environment, an awareness of how the earth had been despoiled in the past, and international efforts to protect the land, air, and water. In addition, the tremendous increase in the flow of information, made possible by a remarkable revolution in the means of communication, has enabled greater numbers of Americans to become more aware of how foreign policy can impinge on their personal lives. Something similar can be said of the debate over the relative decline of America's economic power, with some scholars attributing that decline to massive spending on the military establishment and to the nation's burdensome commitments around the world.[12] One can only imagine how popular thinking and historical scholarship will be influenced by developments in the 1990s, including the fading of the Cold War and the seismic changes in the Soviet Union and the rest of Asia and Europe.

The availability of new sources and the development of new interpretative frameworks have also enlivened the field. The declassification of large numbers of documents in the United States and abroad has forced historians of events since the 1940s to rethink old conclusions and to explore new topics. Those records available in foreign archives have lent new perspectives to American foreign policy and have encouraged a trend toward international history that builds on the scholarship of Bemis, May, and others. Works by Michael H. Hunt and Michael J. Hogan, to name two scholars represented in this volume, fit into this category. So does the scholarship of Akira Iriye, who has done more than most to

---

11   For the wounded condition of the foreign policy consensus after the Vietnam War see Ole R. Holsti and James N. Rosenau, *American Leadership in World Affairs: Vietnam and the Breakdown of Consensus* (Boston, 1984); and idem, "Consensus Lost. Consensus Regained? Foreign Policy Beliefs of American Leaders, 1976–1980," *International Studies Quarterly* 30 (December 1986): 375–409.

12   See, for example, Paul Kennedy, *The Rise and Fall of the Great Powers: Economic Change and Military Conflict from 1500 to 2000* (New York, 1988); and David P. Calleo, *Beyond American Hegemony: The Future of the Western Alliance* (New York, 1987).

promote international history. In addition, specialists in the history of American foreign relations have responded to criticism that portrays their field as parochial, ethnocentric, and hidebound.[13] Besides exploring international history, they have borrowed insights from scholars in related disciplines. The cross-fertilization with political science and other social sciences has been particularly fruitful. It has led diplomatic historians to reexamine such topics as public opinion, bureaucratic politics, and geography and to explore such new avenues of analysis as those offered by dependency theory, world-systems models, and cognitive psychology. At the same time, specialists in the history of American foreign relations have learned from scholars in other fields of American history. If social historians are showing renewed interest in political history, diplomatic historians, long immersed in political history, are now giving greater attention to corporatism and to culture, gender, and other topics associated with the new social history.

Many of the latest trends and reconsiderations are summarized in the essays in this book. Taken as a whole, these essays offer an overview of the current state of scholarship on the history of American foreign relations. They do not systematically review recent literature, detail all topics worthy of inquiry, or summarize all methods and interpretative frameworks, especially the seasoned schools of thought outlined in this introduction. They seek instead to define the state of the field, to outline new analytical models, to show how familiar topics and methods are being rethought, and to reveal the usefulness of questions raised by other disciplines and other fields of American history. These chapters illustrate many of the challenging ways of approaching the study of American foreign relations and highlight the healthy ferment and rich diversity that now mark the field.

13 This criticism is discussed and assessed in the subsequent essays by Robert J. Mc-Mahon, Emily S. Rosenberg, and Thomas G. Paterson.

Part One

The History of American Foreign Relations: Defining the Field

The essays in this section seek to assess and to define the historical study of American foreign relations. Scholarship in the field has been roundly criticized in recent years, particularly by Charles S. Maier, Christopher Thorne, Sally Marks, and other advocates of what they call "international history." According to these scholars, the history of American foreign policy is only one dimension of a global story that should be told from many perspectives. Specialists in the history of American foreign relations have not ignored this criticism. Many have benefited from biarchival and multiarchival research, made an effort to place American diplomacy in a global setting, and written what amounts to international and comparative national history. Indeed, there is a long tradition of such scholarship in the field, from Samuel Flagg Bemis, through Ernest R. May, to Akira Iriye, whose emphasis on international history as cultural history is summarized in Part Two of this volume.

Still, this scholarship has not gone far enough to satisfy the advocates of international history. Their criticisms are summarized and evaluated in the following essays. Robert J. McMahon reminds us that American foreign policy can properly be treated as one aspect of the national experience of the United States. Emily S. Rosenberg points out that an international perspective is not a guarantee against parochialism in historical scholarship. Both authors use the criticism leveled by international historians as the springboard to a larger assessment of the field, including suggestions for interdisciplinary research, for greater efforts to connect with scholarship in other fields of American history, and for new studies on such issues as culture, gender, and global capitalism. In his contribution to this section, Thomas G. Paterson identifies the core questions in the study of American foreign relations and elaborates the levels of analysis that have marked the field. He also summarizes some of the field's well-developed subjects, suggests topics deserving greater study, and notes how work in the field might be improved.

2

The Study of American Foreign Relations: National History or International History?

ROBERT J. McMAHON

"It was the best of times. It was the worst of times." Dickens's classic statement about prerevolutionary France might serve as an equally apt observation about the current state of American diplomatic history. Signs of robust health abound. The last several annual meetings of the Society for Historians of American Foreign Relations (SHAFR) each attracted more than two hundred participants, extraordinary figures for any sub-field and the highest since the organization's first national meeting in 1975. The work published in *Diplomatic History* grows more sophisticated with each issue, and the number of article submissions continues to mount. University and commercial publishers actively solicit manuscripts on diplomatic history, some of which even manage to attract an enthusiastic readership outside academe, as demonstrated most recently by Paul Kennedy's runaway best-seller, *The Rise and Fall of the Great Powers.*[1] At the undergraduate level, courses in American foreign relations register impressive enrollments. A growing number of American diplomatic historians, moreover, teach courses on the Vietnam War that rank among the most popular at their respective universities.

Yet indications of stagnation and malaise coexist in paradoxical tension with signs of vitality. For more than a decade American diplomatic historians have found themselves swimming against the strongest currents of professional scholarship. In a discipline now dominated by the methods and concerns of social history, diplomatic historians and the problems they address have been "marginalized," to use one of the social historians' favorite terms, by many of their Americanist colleagues. In most U.S.

Another version of this essay originally appeared in the Fall 1990 issue of *Diplomatic History*, copyright 1990 by Scholarly Resources Inc. It is printed here by permission of Scholarly Resources Inc.

1 Kennedy, *The Rise and Fall of the Great Powers: Economic Change and Military Conflict from 1500 to 2000* (New York, 1987).

history graduate programs one can receive a Ph.D. without ever taking a course—or even reading a book—on foreign relations. In an influential article, Thomas Bender recently called for a new synthesis for American history. Decrying the fragmentation of the discipline, he argued that it was time to integrate into a whole, integrative narrative the findings of the various new subspecialties that exploded during the 1970s and 1980s. Significantly, he made no mention of diplomatic history.[2] It would be preaching to the converted to tell students of U.S. foreign relations that the external projection of American power and influence must be an essential element of that story. Still, the ease with which so many professional scholars can dismiss or ignore the work of diplomatic historians sets the necessary context within which all recent critiques of the field should be read and assessed.

Those critiques have proliferated, issued as often as not by diplomatic historians themselves. Two prominent historians of European diplomacy recently leveled a series of stinging attacks on their Americanist counterparts. In order to judge the soundness and ultimate consequences of a policy, complained Sally Marks, it must be weighed against the real world, not just the world as perceived by policymakers in Washington. Yet the failure of most U.S. diplomatic historians to consult foreign archives or to master the necessary foreign languages perpetuates a one-sided perspective that tends to repeat, rather than critically examine, the assumptions of American officials. Accusing Americanists of typically "looking at only one side of a multifaceted problem," she implored them to "enlarge their horizons" by breaking out of "the less than splendid isolation in which the practice of twentieth-century American diplomatic history has incarcerated itself."[3] Christopher Thorne similarly blasted the ethnocentric bias that he said plagued so much of the field, resulting in a "regrettable" "national, cultural, and disciplinary parochialism." Is it not time, he asked, to consider a fundamental reconceptualization of the field?[4]

Marks and Thorne have not, of course, been the only eminent Europeanists to raise troubling questions about American diplomatic history. Back in 1980, Charles S. Maier surveyed the historiography of international relations and found it languishing, suggesting that it had become a "stepchild" at some remove from "the cutting edge of scholarship."

2   Bender, "Wholes and Parts: The Need for Synthesis in American History," *Journal of American History* 73 (June 1986): 120–36.

3   Marks, "The World According to Washington," *Diplomatic History* 11 (Summer 1987): 265–67, 281–82.

4   Thorne, "After the Europeans: American Designs for the Remaking of Southeast Asia," *Diplomatic History* 12 (Spring 1988): 206–8.

He identified the principal problems as a lack of theoretical rigor and an absence of methodological innovation. "Narrowly cast inquiries, parochial perspectives, and unfamiliarity with foreign languages and sources have limited not the best, but still too many works."[5]

Many of those criticisms have been repeated, and broadened, by two of the most highly respected diplomatic historians. In 1988, at an American Historical Association session devoted to an examination of the state of the art, John Lewis Gaddis offered a scathing critique of diplomatic history as the academic equivalent of a "self-replicating automaton." "We are said to occupy, in the academic world," he commented acidly, "something like the position in nature filled by the crocodile, the armadillo, and the cockroach: we have been around for a long time and are in no immediate danger of extinction; but we are still pretty primitive and, for that reason, not very interesting." His blast centered on the field's lack of methodological sophistication, manifested in three distinct ways: a tendency to seek synthesis through reductionism; an inclination to exaggerate America's influence on other nations; and a cultural and temporal parochialism that assumes the uniqueness of the American national experience. His prescription: more liberal borrowings from related disciplines, especially international relations and political science, to impart greater methodological and theoretical sophistication to studies of American foreign relations and to give them greater "predictive utility."[6]

At the same session, Michael H. Hunt suggested another path. Graduate training for the next generation of diplomatic historians, he urged, should be broadened to emphasize the development of linguistic skills, frequent foreign travel, and immersion in non-American cultures. Sensitive to the complaint repeated by Thorne that Americans rarely "enter into the texture of a foreign society,"[7] Hunt recommended that students of American foreign relations develop an expertise in at least one nation or region equal to their expertise in American history and culture. They should, in short, become not just historians of U.S. diplomacy but also area specialists.[8]

These scholars see American diplomatic history as a deeply flawed field

5 Maier, "Marking Time: The Historiography of International Relations," in *The Past before Us: Contemporary Historical Writing in the United States*, ed. Michael Kammen (Ithaca, 1980), 355–56.
6 Gaddis's paper was later published as "New Conceptual Approaches to the Study of American Foreign Relations: Interdisciplinary Perspectives," *Diplomatic History* 14 (Summer 1990): 403–25.
7 Thorne, "After the Europeans," 207.
8 Hunt, "New Conceptual Approaches to the Study of United States Foreign Relations: International Perspectives" (Paper delivered at the 103d Annual Meting of the American Historical Association, Cincinnati, Ohio, 28 December 1988).

in need of far-reaching changes. Although the charges run the gamut from narrowness to insularity to ethnocentrism, at the risk of oversimplification the prescriptions boil down to two principal ones: (1) we should all become international (rather than simply American) historians; (2) we should all adopt interdisciplinary approaches. Each prescription has undeniable appeal. If more diplomatic historians adopted the perspectives afforded by international history and the theories and methods associated with interdisciplinary analysis, the study of American foreign relations could be enriched. Yet dangers also inhere in these prescriptions, especially if they mean to condemn traditional approaches as intrinsically inferior. Before we rush to abandon traditional methods, we must first examine what questions about America's external behavior can be addressed more effectively through international or interdisciplinary history. The value of any new approach must ultimately rest on its ability to answer the most significant questions about the subject at hand.

In this respect, the value of the international history approach for students of American foreign affairs derives, as Marks noted, from its ability to illuminate two critical questions: What has been the impact of American policy? How do we judge the relative effectiveness of that policy? One simply cannot discuss with any degree of authority the *impact* of American policies on France or the Soviet Union or Japan or Brazil unless one is familiar with the histories and cultures of those areas. It would be equally inexcusable to ignore any available archival records in those countries that might shed light on the issue. Marks, in short, makes an excellent point. American diplomatic historians too often assume influence without demonstrating it. If American actions and policies have truly made a difference on other nations and peoples, as so many specialists in American foreign relations assert, then diplomatic historians must begin to devote at least some of the attention traditionally accorded to the formulation of policy to the consequences of policy, and they must utilize or develop methods appropriate to the task.

Likewise, area expertise coupled with binational or multinational research can contribute in a significant manner to policy evaluation, a subject invariably tackled in studies of U.S. diplomacy. No diplomatic historian worth his or her salt writes about a bilateral or regional relationship or an international crisis without offering some thoughts on the relative wisdom of American actions. Yet a historian whose sources are exclusively American is at a great disadvantage here. Without alternative sources of information about the world as it really was, to use Marks's terminology, the historian tends to recreate "the world according to Washington" and to judge policy against the standards, values, and assumptions of American decision makers. Even the most painstaking research in American documents about nation X will reveal little if erroneous preconceptions, ill-informed reporting, and cultural blinders prevented officials from comprehending what was actually occurring in that nation. To take a recent example, complete access to all of the documents produced by the American government with regard to Iran before the 1978 revolution would probably tell the interested researcher an enormous amount about U.S. perceptions but remarkably little about the seething discontent that was transforming Iranian society.[9] If we consider policy evaluation an essential part of American diplomatic history, and wish to go beyond the banal generalization that policy did or did not work, then a greater familiarity with foreign cultures and a more systematic examination of available foreign sources are indispensable tools.

The advantages of area expertise and non-American sources appear greatly exaggerated, however, when one turns to the two broad issues that have consumed the vast bulk of attention. Stated most simply, they are why and how. Why has the United States followed the international course that it has? How have important policy decisions been reached? Those are American-centered questions that demand expertise in the history, political culture, and social structure of the United States along with a mastery of American archival sources. Research in foreign archives can illuminate the issue of policy formulation only at the margins.

The centrality of the why and how questions to most American diplomatic historians probably derives in large measure from the origins of this area of inquiry as a subfield of American history. Most historians of American foreign relations identify themselves first and foremost as historians of the United States. Their writing and teaching have thus focused principally on America's external behavior as a reflection of American perceptions, values, and interests; their larger purpose, for the most part, has been to elucidate the broader contours of the American national experience. It is this self-identity as U.S., rather than international, historians that lies at the heart of so many of the complaints and misgivings expressed by advocates of internationalism.

But American diplomatic historians need not apologize for the orientation of their scholarship. The questions they have traditionally asked remain essential not only to American history but, given the leading world role played by the United States throughout the twentieth century, to the larger international arena as well. "The present world system," Walter LaFeber has perceptively pointed out, "to a surprising extent, has been

---

9   For the inability of American officials to comprehend Iranian dynamics see especially Gary Sick, *All Fall Down: America's Tragic Encounter with Iran* (New York, 1985).

shaped not by some imagined balance-of-power concept but by the initiatives of Woodrow Wilson and his successors. The United Nations, multilateral trade institutions, ideas about self-determination and economic development, determining influences on international culture, and strategic military planning have sprung from the United States more than from other actors in the global theater."[10]

For scholars concerned with the wellsprings of American policy, the motivations of U.S. officials, and the relative significance of internal and external determinants on governmental decisions, foreign archives hold minimal allure. It may be objected that American sources do not always explicate fully the external environment that the United States must react to and within, but because American decisions are invariably predicated upon perceptions of reality rather than upon reality itself (if the latter can ever accurately be gauged) that complaint appears hollow. If we wish to explain why U.S. officials responded in the way they did to Soviet postwar expansion, research trips to London, Paris, Bonn, even Moscow, can provide only marginal assistance. If we wish to understand the origins of the Cold War in a wider international compass, examine the role played by other powers, evaluate the consequences of American actions, or test U.S. assumptions and perceptions against the "real world," then such sources would become critical. But those are different questions that require different research strategies. Neither set of questions should be seen as intrinsically more important; neither research strategy should be viewed as inherently superior. Sally Marks's conclusion that American diplomatic historians work primarily with American records because they are "so much cheaper, quicker, and easier to explore" is not just uncharitable but also wrongheaded.[11]

Indeed, to the extent that some scholars rely on European archives to understand American behavior they risk a grave distortion of the motivations of U.S. officials. The recent utilization of British sources to help explicate American Cold War initiatives provides a case in point. Several British scholars have argued, based largely on documents from the Public Record Office, that London strongly influenced Washington's actions in postwar Europe. Some go so far as to suggest that foreign secretary Ernest Bevin should be credited as the true originator of the containment doctrine, the Marshall Plan, and the North Atlantic Treaty Organization.[12]

10   LaFeber, "Responses to Charles S. Maier's 'Marking Time: The Historiography of International Relations,' " *Diplomatic History* 5 (Fall 1981): 326.
11   Marks, "The World According to Washington," 281.
12   See, for example, R. Frazier, "Did Britain Start the Cold War? Bevin and the Truman Doctrine," *Historical Journal* 27 (September 1984): 715–27; D. C. Watt, "Britain, the United States and the Opening of the Cold War," in *The Foreign Policy of the*

Yet their evidence derives almost entirely from British Foreign Office and Cabinet papers; and the obvious satisfaction that some take in restoring Britain to center stage in the historiography of the Cold War suggests that national pride may be playing some role in this scholarly trend. The specific merits of their case concern me less here than its inadequate and illogical evidentiary base. If one seeks to prove the influence exerted by country X over country Y, the more relevant documentation must be found in country Y, the country presumably being influenced. The records of country X will reveal little more than what that country thinks the impact of its actions has been.

The indictment against U.S. diplomatic history issued by Marks, Thorne, Maier, Hunt, and others distorts the field in another respect as well. In order to advance their prescriptions for the future, they sketch a portrait of American diplomatic history that is more caricature than accurate representation. The nonspecialist might be surprised after reading their broadsides to learn that many scholars of American foreign relations do read foreign languages, work with non-American sources, and have more than a passing acquaintance with the histories and cultures of the lands encompassed by their research interests.

To be sure, even the sternest critics acknowledge exceptions to their complaints, but they appear unwilling to accept the extent and significance of those exceptions. Yet Samuel Flagg Bemis, in many respects the godfather of modern American diplomatic history, was writing from a multiarchival, international perspective generations ago. His account of the diplomacy of the American Revolution, for all its nationalist bias, still stands as a model of the genre. Ernest R. May's magisterial account of U.S. entry into World War I, published over thirty years ago, gained much of its power from the multinational perspective the author's exploitation of British and German sources shed on Wilson's decisions. Akira Iriye's first book, *After Imperialism,* now over twenty years old, still impresses with its mastery of the archival sources and languages of half a dozen nations. David M. Pletcher's carefully researched account of American expansion in the 1840s draws on unpublished documents in Mexico, Spain, France, and Great Britain as well as those in the United States. Lloyd C. Gardner's recent studies of the Anglo-American response to revolutionary upheaval squarely belong to that tradition.[13] The point

British Labour Governments, 1945–51, ed. Ritchie Ovendale (Leicester, England, 1984), 43–60; and Martin H. Folly, "Breaking the Vicious Circle: Britain, the United States, and the Genesis of the North Atlantic Treaty," *Diplomatic History* 12 (Winter 1988): 59–77.

13 Bemis, *The Diplomacy of the American Revolution* (1935; reprint, Bloomington, 1957); May, *The World War and American Isolation, 1941–1947* (Cambridge, MA,

is that each of these authors, and the examples could easily be multiplied, chose topics that required a broad, multinational focus; the success of their efforts does not render other approaches obsolete or inferior.

Contrary to the critics' charges, the study of American foreign relations has also attracted an increasing number of genuine area specialists. Many historians of inter-American relations have long functioned precisely as the area experts that Hunt seeks to train. Most teach Latin American history as comfortably as the history of the United States, travel throughout the region as often as time and money permit, possess language fluency, and utilize Latin American archival records wherever possible. In recent years, the history of American-Asian relations has been energized by the growing number of scholars who, although trained primarily as U.S. diplomatic historians, function as regional specialists as well. Michael Hunt provides an excellent example of how one can successfully straddle two distinct fields. But he is not alone; Warren I. Cohen, Stephen E. Pelz, Roger Dingman, Nancy Bernkopf Tucker, and of course Akira Iriye also spring to mind. In addition, American diplomatic history is proud to include within its fold those, like Bruce Cumings, who have moved from their Asianist roots into the study of U.S. foreign policy; his challenging work on the Korean War provides a model of how one can simultaneously advance the study of two different national histories while also illuminating the interactive process.[14] Nor are historians of European-American relations as insulated as the strictures of the field's critics imply. To take but a few examples, the work of Melvyn P. Leffler, Frank C. Costigliola, and Douglas Little for the interwar period has been informed by a familiarity with European developments, as have the studies of the postwar era by Lawrence S. Wittner, James Edward Miller, and Michael J. Hogan.[15]

1959); Iriye, *After Imperialism: The Search for a New Order in the Far East, 1921–1931* (Cambridge, MA, 1965); Pletcher, *The Diplomacy of Annexation: Texas, Oregon, and the Mexican War* (Columbia, MO, 1973); Gardner, *Safe for Democracy: The Anglo-American Response to Revolution, 1913–1923* (New York, 1984); idem, *Approaching Vietnam: From World War II through Dienbienphu, 1941–1954* (New York, 1988).

14 See especially Bruce Cumings, *The Origins of the Korean War: Liberation and the Emergence of Separate Regimes, 1945–1947* (Princeton, 1981).

15 Leffler, *The Elusive Quest: America's Pursuit of European Stability and French Security, 1919–1933* (Chapel Hill, 1979); Costigliola, *Awkward Dominion: American Political, Economic, and Cultural Relations with Europe, 1919–1933* (Ithaca, 1984); Little, *Malevolent Neutrality: The United States, Great Britain, and the Origins of the Spanish Civil War* (Ithaca, 1985); Wittner, *American Intervention in Greece, 1943–1949* (New York, 1982); Miller, *The United States and Italy, 1940–1950: The Politics and Diplomacy of Stabilization* (Chapel Hill, 1986); Hogan, *The Marshall Plan: America, Britain, and the Reconstruction of Western Europe, 1947–1952* (New York, 1987).

To the extent that the internationalist critics are prodding American diplomatic historians to widen their angle of vision and broaden their evidentiary base, the attacks on the field, however overdrawn, are welcome. A more widespread utilization of foreign archives and internationalist perspectives may not resolve all of the scholarly debates that have for so long enlivened the study of American foreign relations, but they may well elevate some of them to a new level of sophistication while introducing salient new issues. The net result, for the field as a whole, could prove enriching. To the extent that the advocates of internationalism are trumpeting a superior method of studying foreign relations and urging the abandonment of traditional methods and questions, however, their agenda should be challenged. If one believes that the internal determinants of policy are at least as important as the external determinants, and the issue of policy formulation in its broadest context at least as significant as the issue of impact, then much of U.S. diplomatic history will, and should, remain a subfield of American history. It should continue to be influenced, informed, and broadened by the methods and insights of international history, but it must not allow itself to be transformed by them.

The same caveats must be raised about the transformative potential of interdisciplinary approaches. The work of John Lewis Gaddis demonstrates eloquently how interdisciplinary perspectives can open up new conceptual vistas. His analyses of the international system as system, especially his provocative essay on "the long peace," use international relations concepts to cast postwar diplomacy in a different light.[16] The theoretical literature on international relations and decision making has direct relevance for diplomatic history, as Ole R. Holsti's contribution to this volume points out. Recent articles by Gaddis, Pelz, and William O. Walker III have usefully outlined some of the specific ways in which diplomatic historians can adopt those theoretical constructs to add nuance and rigor to their work.[17] At the macro level, they can help us gauge the relative weight of systemic variables on America's external behavior; at the micro level, they can help us probe the role of cognition and bureaucratic structures in decision making.

Political scientists and historians have opened a long overdue dialogue

16 Gaddis, *The Long Peace: Inquiries into the History of the Cold War* (New York, 1987).
17 Gaddis, "Expanding the Data Base: Historians, Political Scientists, and the Enrichment of Security Studies," *International Security* 12 (Summer 1987): 3–21; Pelz, "A Taxonomy for American Diplomatic History," *Journal of Interdisciplinary History* 19 (Autumn 1988): 259–76; Walker, "Drug Control and the Issue of Culture in American Foreign Relations," *Diplomatic History* 12 (Fall 1988): 365–82.

in recent years that should benefit both disciplines. Among the more significant manifestations of this trend are the inclination of a growing number of international relations theorists to use archival evidence and the willingness of at least some diplomatic historians to employ social scientific theories in their work. The pages of *International Security* in particular testify to the rich possibilities of such cross-fertilization.

More borrowing from the social sciences should be encouraged in the hope that "bumping" against related disciplines, to use Gaddis's word, will encourage innovation. Greater attention to the theoretical underpinnings of our work cannot help but lend rigor to our analyses. But the concepts and theories of the social sciences can no more be embraced as diplomatic history's salvation than the techniques and perspectives of international history. They can, to be sure, deepen our understanding of the complex dynamics of decision making in modern bureaucratic structures and sharpen our awareness of the systemic forces that shape and limit the actions of any state in the international arena. But international relations and decision-making theories cannot by themselves provide the answers we seek about the core purposes of American foreign relations. Historians interested in probing the interplay between the internal and external determinants of American policy by explicating the relative importance of and interrelationships among economic, strategic, political, geopolitical, and ideological forces must continue to look elsewhere.

Neither international nor interdisciplinary perspectives, moreover, speak to the root concern that almost certainly prompted the critiques in the first place: the widespread perception among so many professional scholars that diplomatic history has become a retrogressive field—old-fashioned, dull, unimaginative, perhaps even irrelevant. A marriage with political science would likely intensify those misgivings. Reconceptualizing the field as a branch not of American history but of international history, as if the international system existed as an autonomous entity, would almost surely further the isolation from other Americanists that diplomatic historians already experience. We should recognize, in sum, that these proposed solutions to diplomatic history's presumed inadequacies may actually exacerbate the field's marginalization within the larger professional world.

The present unenviable status of diplomatic historians can be ascribed in great measure to the combination of intellectual, ideological, and technological forces that together have transformed the study of history over the past two decades. Diplomatic history, of necessity, focuses primarily on elites at a time when much of the profession has turned to the study of nonelites. Diplomatic historians typically serve as analysts of, rather than advocates for, the individuals they study; in contrast, most historians of women, blacks, minorities, workers, ethnics, and immigrants—all growth fields during the 1970s and 1980s—actively sympathize with the groups they examine. In seeking to give a voice to the formerly voiceless, many social historians thus embrace an ideological agenda as well as a scholarly one. Much of their pioneering work has of course been made possible by the computer, which permits the systematic analysis of aggregate data so indispensable to the new social and political histories. Other than word-processing, the computer revolution has created hardly a ripple in diplomatic history circles. In addition, the social scientific methodologies and theories most useful to social and political historians have thus far afforded precious few insights to specialists in American foreign relations. Those broad scholarly trends served to distance diplomatic historians from their professional colleagues at the same time that common approaches and commitments were creating strong bonds among otherwise disparate historians of social, political, cultural, and economic developments.

Other factors as well contribute to the view, held by diplomatic and nondiplomatic historians alike, that the study of foreign affairs is different, separate, distinct. Scholarship has been shaped to an unusual degree by presentist concerns. Work is overwhelmingly on the contemporary period; indeed, a recent estimate revealed that over half of SHAFR's members specialize in the post–1941 era. Only a minuscule proportion of social and political historians write within that same time frame. Further, many of the most exciting new works in diplomatic history have been spurred more by archival openings or discoveries than by conceptual, methodological, or theoretical breakthroughs. The reverse is certainly the case for social and political historians. As so many of us rush to exploit the newly available records, the percentage of diplomatic historians left toiling in the vineyards of the eighteenth and nineteenth centuries decreases. Because those are precisely the periods that have seen the most important and challenging historical works outside of diplomatic history, the opportunities for dialogue are diminished.

For all of these reasons, diplomatic history has become both isolated and marginalized. There is plenty of blame for this regrettable state of affairs to spread around. Some social historians have viewed diplomatic history as the enemy, as Stephen G. Rabe's 1989 Stuart L. Bernath Lecture reminded us.[18] If events are mere dust, in Fernand Braudel's memorable phrase, then surely an event-driven field like diplomatic history must seem dangerously anachronistic. Its preoccupation with a universe in-

---

18 Rabe, "Marching Ahead (Slowly): The Historiography of Inter-American Relations," *Diplomatic History* 13 (Summer 1989): 297–316.

habited predominantly by white, male, Anglo-Saxon elites undoubtedly strikes many practitioners of the "new" history as an unfortunate relic of the "old."

But diplomatic history's outsider status cannot be attributed purely to the short-sightedness of others. Diplomatic historians have often failed to make their findings as germane as they might to those genuinely concerned with the broader contours of American history. They have not always presented their work in its widest context, thus neglecting opportunities to connect with the scholarship produced in related areas. Diplomatic historians have, in addition, participated willingly in the fragmentation and specialization that has characterized so much of academic discourse in recent years. Indeed, the very success of SHAFR reflects this phenomenon. There are sufficient professional rewards and responsibilities attached to SHAFR now—ranging from offices to awards to committee assignments to the opportunity for presenting papers at its annual meeting and publishing articles and reviews in *Diplomatic History*—that it alone can provide ample professional sustenance for many a career. We simply do not have to interact with the larger professional world of which we are a part. But our colleagues suffer from our failure to engage them, we suffer, and American history as a whole suffers.

If one of the chief challenges of American historiography as we enter the 1990s is to provide a fresh synthesis for American history, as many of the discipline's luminaries have advocated, then a major task for diplomatic historians must be to integrate our work and our perspectives into that larger story. A number of scholars have taken social historians to task for their failure to deal effectively with elites and with the exercise of power—subjects that have traditionally been among diplomatic history's strengths.[19]

At its best, the work of diplomatic historians examines fundamental questions about the configuration of power in American society. How have elites attained, maintained, and exercised power? What have been the internal, or systemic, sources of the nation's external behavior? To what end have public and private elites interacted? Certainly any effort to present a holistic view of the American national experience that ignores those cardinal questions would be fatally flawed.

---

19 On this point see especially Elizabeth Fox-Genovese and Eugene Genovese, "The Political Crisis of Social History: A Marxian Perspective," *Journal of Social History* 10 (Winter 1976): 205–9; Lawrence Stone, "The Revival of Narrative: Reflections on a New Old History," *Past and Present* 85 (November 1979): 3–24; Alan Brinkley, "Writing the History of Contemporary America: Dilemmas and Challenges," *Daedalus* 113 (Summer 1984): 121–41; and William Leuchtenberg, "The Pertinence of Political History: Reflections on the Significance of the State in America," *Journal of American History* 73 (December 1986): 585–600.

To ensure that diplomatic history attains its necessary place in any new synthesis, to guarantee that its concerns, questions, and debates become an essential part of the graduate training of all future American historians, to seek common ground and dialogue with Americanists—those goals should top diplomatic historians' professional agenda for the 1990s. To be sure, more diplomatic historians should explore interdisciplinary perspectives. More of them should follow the counsel of Marks, Thorne, and others and recognize that foreign archives and international perspectives can often yield fresh insights. There is much to be learned from both approaches. Competing modes of analysis should be as welcome as the critical self-examination that diplomatic historians engage in periodically. They are signs of health, not stagnation. But let us also remember that most American diplomatic historians are by training and inclination historians of the United States, an identification that carries its own set of responsibilities for the future.

3

Walking the Borders

EMILY S. ROSENBERG

Over the past decade, a number of scholars have suggested that U.S. diplomatic history is too narrowly cast, that it fails to reach out to international scholars or to other disciplines. Charles S. Maier and Sally Marks, for example, have charged American diplomatic history with parochialism and stressed the importance of transnational research and perspectives.[1] Christopher Thorne has recently criticized studies of the "America and" genre and joined the call for "international history."[2] Akira Iriye, Charles R. Lilley, Michael H. Hunt, and William O. Walker III have also argued for an "international history" that would encompass social and cultural issues.[3] The desire to "fix" old historical frameworks also surfaces in recent methodological works, such as Stephen E. Pelz's attempt to mesh all disparate investigations within an all-encompassing "taxonomy" of domestic and international factors.[4] When posed as an antidote to narrowness, international history seems an irresistible agenda.

But what is "international history"? E. H. Carr likened such categories to a blank check in which "the printed part consists of abstract words, ... valueless until we fill in the other part."[5] International history is not a methodological prescription but, to switch the metaphor, a vast empty

Another version of this essay originally appeared in the Fall 1990 issue of *Diplomatic History*, copyright 1990 by Scholarly Resources Inc. It is printed here by permission of Scholarly Resources Inc.

1   Maier, "Marking Time: The Historiography of International Relations," in *The Past before Us: Contemporary Historical Writing in the United States,* ed. Michael Kammen (Ithaca, 1980), 355–87; Marks, "The World According to Washington," *Diplomatic History* 11 (Summer 1987): 265–82.
2   Thorne, "After the Europeans: American Designs for the Remaking of Southeast Asia," *Diplomatic History* 12 (Spring 1988): 201–8. See also idem, *Border Crossings: Studies in International History* (Oxford, 1988), esp. pt I.
3   Iriye, "The Internationalization of History," *American Historical Review* 94 (February 1989): 1–10; Lilley and Hunt, "On Social History, the State, and Foreign Relations: Commentary on 'The Cosmopolitan Connection'," *Diplomatic History* 11 (Summer 1987): 243–50; and Walker, "Drug Control and the Issue of Culture in American Foreign Relations," ibid. 12 (Fall 1988): 365–82.
4   Pelz, "A Taxonomy for American Diplomatic History," *Journal of Interdisciplinary History* 19 (Autumn 1988): 259–76.
5   Edward Hallett Carr, *What Is History?* (New York, 1962), 105–6.

plain with undetermined borders and topography that must be sketched by the historian-guide. Is this empty plain the remedy for parochialism?

Historical works cannot literally mirror the texture of reality; at some level any history is structured. Which issues get emphasized over others in the structure? Into what frameworks are human actions compressed? From whose vantage point are the implicit analytical questions asked?[6] Sally Marks dismisses American historians as hopelessly narrow and contrasts them with European historians for whom, she claims, "it is axiomatic that one must look at all elements in the situation."[7] But what does "all" mean? Who determines all the relevant elements in Marks's international history or Pelz's taxonomy? One person's international history may be another's parochial vision, depending upon where boundaries get drawn, what categories of analysis are privileged over others, and where the viewer is situated. Unless we are going to write forever, choices about coverage and presentation must be made. To me, issues related to what choices are available and to how fields of vision get defined, rather than some abstract call to see it whole, open the best opportunities for fruitful discussions.

Consider Christopher Thorne's barbs at the "America and" formula which, he writes, "places the United States at the center and draws out from there simply a series of bilateral links, like spokes of a rimless wheel."[8] There are projects in which such a pattern would be inappropriate and ethnocentric. As Thorne's own scholarly work shows, there are also projects for which such a U.S.-centered approach makes perfect sense. The issue lies not in the abstract validity of the "America and" approach as opposed to international history, but in the historical context and perspective of the work itself.

Barbara Stallings's recent *Banker to the Third World,* for example, places the United States at the center of two waves of bilateral lending that washed into Latin America during the twentieth century. She frames her particular investigation in this way not because she writes ethnocentric or parochial history but because financial forces in the United States were, in fact, central to the lending process. Moreover, she models the historical questions she asks upon a previous body of scholarship that took the "Britain and" form in shaping investigations of the nineteenth-century international financial order. Surely few would dub parochial the body of British histories that analyzed British capital flow in the nine-

---

6   Thorne effectively explores the issue of inevitable subjectivity in *Border Crossings*, chap. 2.
7   Marks, "World According to Washington," 280.
8   Thorne, "After the Europeans," 206.

teenth century and the central role it played in the world economy.[9] The
point here is not to defend "United States and" history or "Britain and"
history. Rather, it is to point out the limitations of abstracted propositions
about the kinds of work that historians should or should not write.

Another issue relating to fields of vision and the definition of international history may be illustrated by an exchange over Jon Jacobson's
essay, "Is There a New International History of the 1920s?" which sought
to carry out Charles Maier's call for international history by identifying,
for the 1920s, "some of the elements of an integrated analysis." Jacobson
synthesized European and North American scholarship, connecting the
domestic histories of several countries to their international relations and
interrelating military, political, financial, and economic concerns. In a
subsequent comment, however, Mira Wilkins objected to the appellation
"international history" for an analysis that she thought was, in fact, quite
narrowly scoped. She charged that Jacobson neglected the major international economic and business histories of the period and, unlike such
truly international works, dealt "exclusively with the history of Western
Europe and the United States."[10]

Wilkins's point deserves serious consideration. Can an international
history of the 1920s address only the North Atlantic, paying no attention
at all to the global frameworks suggested by, say, Charles P. Kindleberger,
Mira Wilkins, Paul Bairoch, and Immanuel Wallerstein, or to the many
scholars associated with dependency analysis? Postwar stabilization efforts were, after all, a worldwide, not a European phenomenon. North
Atlantic political and economic stabilization, of course, could certainly
be studied on its own, but should it be termed international history? Is
Paul W. Drake's comparable study of the play of domestic and international, political and economic forces in the stabilization programs of
the Andean countries of Chile, Ecuador, Peru, and Bolivia during the
same period also international history?[11] The question raised is whether
the term international history describes methodology or scope or both
and in what mix.

The exchange over Jacobson's international history illustrates how
situation shapes definition. If U.S.-centered history seems parochial to
many Europeans, so metropolitan, North Atlantic–centered history may

9   Stallings, *Banker to the Third World: U.S. Portfolio Investment in Latin America,
    1900–1986* (Berkeley, 1987).
10 Jacobson, "Is There a New International History of the 1920s?" *American Historical
    Review* 88 (June 1983): 617–45; Wilkins, "Letter to the Editor," ibid. 89 (April
    1984): 586.
11 Drake, *The Money Doctor in the Andes: The Kemmerer Missions, 1923–1933* (Dur-
    ham, 1989).

appear parochial to scholars who have taken a global view of a world system or to scholars of the Third World who so often complain of invisibility. Again, the remedy to tunnel vision is not necessarily international history as an abstract proposition.

By highlighting ethnocentrism and parochialism, those calling for international history have rightly pointed to the political arrogance and cultural blindness that often characterize power centers. The perspectives of those on the periphery, in any power system, often remain largely invisible to those in the center. To counter narrow visions, it may help to walk the borders of global power, analyzing power systems from various perspectives situated on the periphery.

Walking the borders of power is not an easy task. Walter LaFeber, in a similar call for developing a peripheral perspective, pointed out one obvious difficulty: "It is a problem," he wrote, "to try to act as an outsider when one lives at the center of the system."[12] But there is, after all, no single system of power that arranges international affairs. Centers and peripheries will shift depending on the field of reference: Different systems of power can be framed along lines of nation-states, of economics, of class, of culture, of religion, of gender, of race, and so forth. Most of us are both insiders and outsiders, depending upon which structures of power we wish to analyze. A peripheral vantage is not only a geographic location but can be a habit of mind and a scholarly approach that can be nurtured by an awareness of our own positions as insiders or as outsiders or as would-be mediators on the margins of both. A peripheral view comes less from where we stand than from the critical questions we frame and who we choose to hear.

Studies, then, tend to be narrow not simply by some geographic or disciplinary criteria but by whether or not they seek to remove themselves from the discourse of the situation under examination. The concept of discourse, used in the sense that Michel Foucault and others developed it, is the structure of terms, categories, and institutions that constitute the presumably self-evident truths that organize and legitimate power relations in any particular historical context. Calls for a broad, international sweep will miss the mark unless they also adopt peripheral vision and challenge the abstract assumptions, such as progress, modernization, destiny, and internationalism, upon which dominant systems of power have rested. If borders are seen as frontier areas that delineate and separate lines of power and discursive fields, we should linger at the intersections, walking the borders to analyze things from the outside in.

12 LaFeber, "Responses to Charles S. Maier, 'Marking Time: The Historiography of International Relations,'" *Diplomatic History* 5 (Fall 1981): 362.

A rapidly growing body of scholarship concentrating on the role of culture in international relations, for example, is attempting to dissect the dominant discourses of U.S. power. Many of these interdisciplinary studies borrow from literary criticism, anthropology, and sociology in order to examine the workings of, as well as the resistance to, hegemonic ideologies and institutions. Robert W. Rydell's *All the World's a Fair* examines how scientific, professional, and business elites structured nationalistic and ethnocentric visions of the world in turn-of-the-century world fairs. Borrowing from Raymond Williams, Rydell analyzes the construction of the hegemonic ideology that both shaped and reflected the emerging socioeconomic order.[13] Michael Hunt's *Ideology and U.S. Foreign Policy* elaborates a similar critique of dominant paradigms, especially those related to race and revolution.[14] My *Spreading the American Dream* examines the discourses of American liberalism, particularly the faiths in free markets and free flow of information that masqueraded as universal truths but were selectively applied to bolster national advantage.[15] Richard Slotkin's *Fatal Environment* and Sam Gill's *Mother Earth* deal with the construction of the symbols and rhetoric—in the Custer myth and the myth of Mother Earth, respectively—that have appeared so often in America's assertions of nationalism.[16] Michael S. Sherry sets his fascinating history of American air power against a lengthy discussion of relevant myths and images in American culture.[17] William O. Walker III shows how the failure of U.S. narcotics diplomacy in the 1920s resulted, at least in part, from American cultural assumptions that were blind to the traditions of producer nations.[18]

Growing numbers of scholars are also examining the exportation of American popular culture abroad, the trend that Reinhold Wagnleitner colorfully describes as the shift "from the Monroe Doctrine to the Marilyn Monroe Doctrine."[19] In two pioneering works, *How to Read Donald Duck* and *The Empire's Old Clothes*, Ariel Dorfman examines the so-

13   Rydell, *All the World's a Fair: Visions of Empire at American International Expositions, 1876–1916* (Chicago, 1984).
14   Hunt, *Ideology and U.S. Foreign Policy* (New Haven, 1987).
15   Emily S. Rosenberg, *Spreading the American Dream: American Economic and Cultural Expansion, 1898–1945* (New York, 1982).
16   Slotkin, *The Fatal Environment: The Myth of the Frontier in the Age of Industrialization, 1800–1890* (New York, 1985); Gill, *Mother Earth: An American Story* (Chicago, 1987).
17   Sherry, *The Rise of American Air Power: The Creation of Armageddon* (New Haven, 1987).
18   Walker, "Drug Control."
19   Wagnleitner, "The Irony of American Culture Abroad: Austria and the Cold War," in *Recasting America: Culture and Politics in the Age of Cold War*, ed. Lary May (Chicago, 1989), 286.

cioeconomic messages contained in such pop culture exports as Disney comics, Lone Ranger stories, and *Reader's Digest* and indicts the values purveyed by American "cultural imperialism."[20] Dorfman, a Chilean, tried to put his theories about the dangers of American popular culture into action during the short-lived administration of Salvador Allende. Although many cultural historians are veering away from Dorfman's concepts of cultural domination toward response-oriented perspectives, the emphasis on close examination of cultural assumptions and inter-actions within particular contexts of time and place still emerges as a clear historiographical trend.

Cultural issues have become central particularly to recent histories related to U.S.-Asian relations. Warren I. Cohen, Randall E. Stross, Jane Hunter, Patricia Hill, Christopher Thorne, and John W. Dower, to name just a few, have probed a variety of American cultural assumptions and analyzed their intersections with particular societies and situations in the Far East.[21] Stanley Karnow, in his book and the accompanying television series *In Our Image,* has recently projected into popular history the importance of American ethnocentrism in shaping relations with the Philippines.[22]

All of these disparate works on ideology, symbols, popular culture, and cultural interchange may pertain to international history in some way, but many are largely domestic intellectual histories and others are bilateral or small-scale investigations of cultural contacts. The larger characteristics that bring these studies together relate to their implicit understanding that knowledge and truth are situational and to their attempts to get outside dominant foreign policy discourses in order to dissect them critically. Most of these works borrow interdisciplinary techniques from literary criticism, anthropology, and sociology to ex-amine the workings of, as well as the resistance to and interaction with, hegemonic ideologies.

---

20 Dorfman and Armand Mattelart, *How to Read Donald Duck: Imperialist Ideology in the Disney Comic,* trans. David Kunzle (New York, 1975); idem, *The Empire's Old Clothes: What the Lone Ranger, Babar, and Other Innocent Heroes Do to Our Minds* (New York, 1983).

21 Cohen, *The Chinese Connection: Roger S. Greene, Thomas W. Lamont, George E. Sokolsky and American-East Asian Relations* (New York, 1978); Dower, *War without Mercy: Race and Power in the Pacific War* (New York, 1986); Hill, *The World Their Household: The American Women's Foreign Mission Movement and Cultural Trans-formation, 1870–1920* (Ann Arbor, 1985); Hunter, *The Gospel of Gentility: American Women Missionaries in Turn-of-the-Century China* (New Haven, 1984); Stross, *The Stubborn Earth: American Agriculturalists on Chinese Soil, 1898–1937* (Berkeley, 1986); Thorne, *American Political Culture and the Asian Frontier, 1943–73* (London, 1988).

22 Karnow, *In Our Image: America's Empire in the Philippines* (New York, 1989).

As a number of these works illustrate, however, analyzing power systems from the outside implies more than international vantages within the system of nation-states. In charting the dimensions of international history, Akira Iriye has perceptively argued that "as long as we define the study of international history as interstate, interpower relations, we will have to agree that innovative techniques and methodological breakthroughs are unlikely."[23] More than nationality provides important borders delineating systems of power. Two of the other systems of power (and discourse), of the many that crosscut global affairs, might briefly be examined here: global capitalism and gender.

In world systems scholarship, in which global capitalism and markets, rather than nation-states per se, provide the organizing principles, peripheral vantage shifts the questions and frames of reference. Recently, world systems debates have moved away from economic structures in the metropolitan center toward the importance of the culture in peripheral areas. Focusing on workers in the mining areas of colonial Latin America, for example, Steve J. Stern has criticized Immanuel Wallerstein's work for overemphasizing trends emanating from the European core. World systems theory, he charges, has contributed to the "disappearance of agency, historical and intellectual" in peripheral areas. Stern proposes that local conditions and responses, particularized from cultural and historical circumstances, significantly shaped global capitalism. Indigenous communities in Latin America, he argues, were not simply passive pawns of global markets but actively affected, through decisions about work and resistance, historical dynamics of global economic networks. Writing in response, Wallerstein agrees, insisting that the dynamic interaction between structure and locality guided his assumptions all along.[24]

The Stern-Wallerstein exchange illustrates the extent to which debates over world systems and dependency theory are shifting away from broad, generalized, structural trends and toward the specific interactions of the structures with local cultural traditions. Absent from this discussion of the world system are the usual disputes over unequal exchange and other macroeconomic issues. Instead, there are extended explications of the behavior and perspectives of silver miners of Potosi and slaves in the Caribbean. As the central actors in these histories become less the traders, bankers, and politicians in London or New York and more the inhab-

---

23　Iriye, "Responses to Charles S. Maier, 'Marking Time: The Historiography of International Relations'," *Diplomatic History* 5 (Fall 1981): 360.
24　Stern, "Feudalism, Capitalism, and the World System in the Perspective of Latin America and the Caribbean," *American Historical Review* 93 (October 1988): 829–72; Immanuel Wallerstein, "Comment," and Stern, "Reply," ibid., 873–97.

itants of particular villages in Peru or plantations in the West Indies, the focus of the larger theoretical framework about the social construction of global capitalism changes. Viewing systems of power from the periphery helps to transcend grand abstract models of development or of underdevelopment and to recall the necessity of contextuality, both in terms of time and place.[25]

Global systems have also recently been reinterpreted by yet another kind of view from the periphery: feminism. In nearly every society, social systems and cultural discourse divide sharply along lines of gender, a situation that undermines many universalized formulations based solely on male experience. Feminism, as one kind of peripheral vision, has forced particularistic examinations of much historical discourse. Just as feminist historians revealed the blind spots of male-dominated histories by asking questions such as "was the Renaissance a renaissance for women," so feminist scholarship has similarly challenged some of the language and categories of male-dominated analyses of global issues.

For example, what has development (or underdevelopment) meant for women? Using gender as a framework, an entire subfield of development studies has emerged in the last decade. Most theorists of development and modernization, as well as most theorists of underdevelopment associated with the dependency school, previously neglected women. In terms of global production, however, women have provided most of the agricultural labor, the reproductive tasks, and the goods and services offered in the informal sector. Labor demands upon the time of women have frequently been more intense than those upon men. If the divisions of labor by gender have, historically, provided fundamental organizing principles for most economic systems, how can gender be omitted from economic calculation or historical analysis of economic trends?

As scholars have begun looking at national development through the lens of gender difference, it has became clear that rapid changes in land-use patterns, technology, agricultural practices, communications, sanitation, availability of factory work, and the like have affected practices of "men's work" and "women's work" in substantially different ways. In a number of pathbreaking early studies on the impact of development efforts, liberal feminists charged that particular programs had, by omitting any consideration of women's work, often failed entirely or resulted in greater exploitation of women. Radical feminists, who viewed most development programs as tools of economic domination anyway, often

25 See also the critique of Wallerstein by Theda Skocpol in "Wallerstein's World Capitalist System: A Theoretical and Historical Critique," *American Journal of Sociology* 82 (March 1977): 1075–90.

found evidence of further subordination of women, especially where male-run international markets supplanted localized, often women-controlled, systems of production and exchange. Despite different emphases and interpretations, works on historic shifts in the global economy that consider gender-related divisions of labor have begun to transform the meaning of development. Thus, development (or underdevelopment), like other abstractions, needs to be grounded in a specific time, place, and cultural condition.[26]

Many other international phenomena besides development may affect men and women differently, making gender a relevant category of analysis.[27] Examination of gendered overtones of so much foreign policy language and symbolism can provide fresh, provocative insights into the wellsprings of policy formulation and public legitimation. In some historical contexts, for example, cultural definitions of masculinity and bellicose assertions of national power appear to be linked. There have likewise been historical ties between feminism and pacifism.[28]

Ideas about natural hierarchies and dependence that are embedded in general imagery at the turn of the twentieth century, for example, were part of a pervasive cultural milieu that supported foreign policies of domination. The subtle psychological and discursive linkages between attitudes regarding gender, race, and foreign policy have received recent attention in cultural studies such as Michael Paul Rogin's *Ronald Reagan, the Movie* and Richard Drinnon's *Facing West*.[29] Women, nonwhite races, and tropical countries often were accorded the same kinds of

26 Major studies include Ester Boserup, *Women's Role in Economic Development* (New York, 1970); Irene Tinker and Michele Bo Bramsen, eds., *Women and World Development* (New York, 1976); Eleanor Leacock and Helen I. Safa, eds., *Women's Work: Development and the Division of Labor by Gender* (South Hadley, MA, 1982); June C. Nash and Maria Patricia Fernandez-Kelly, eds., *Women, Men, and the International Division of Labor* (Albany, 1983); and Lourdes Beneris and Martha Roldan, *The Crossroads of Class and Gender* (Chicago, 1987).
27 For a discussion of theoretical issues see Joan W. Scott, "Gender: A Useful Category of Historical Analysis," *American Historical Review* 91 (December 1986): 1053–75; idem, *Gender and the Politics of History* (New York, 1988); and Mary E. Hawksworth, "Feminist Rhetoric: Discourses on the Male Monopoly of Thought," *Political Theory* 16 (August 1988): 444–67.
28 Barbara J. Steinson, *American Women's Activism in World War I* (New York, 1982); Harriet Alonso, *The Women's Peace Union and the Outlawry of War, 1921–42* (Knoxville, 1989).
29 Rogin, *Ronald Reagan, the Movie and Other Episodes in Political Demonology* (Berkeley, 1987); Drinnon, *Facing West: The Metaphysics of Indian-Hating and Empire-Building* (Minneapolis, 1980). Although it deals with the British Empire, a model essay linking images and foreign policies with issues of race and gender is Elizabeth Schmidt, "Patriarchy, Capitalism, and the Colonial State: An Alliance to Control African Women in Southern Rhodesia, 1890–1939," *Signs: Journal of Women in Culture and Society* (forthcoming).

symbolic characterization from white, male policymakers: emotional, irrational, irresponsible, unbusinesslike, unstable, childlike. These naturally dependent peoples could be expected to exhibit the same kinds of natural responses to patriarchal tutelage. They were assumed, if behaving properly, to be loving, grateful, happy, and appreciative of paternal protection. Concepts of dependency, both in the domestic family order and in the international order, reinforced and helped legitimate each other.

At particular times in the United States's relations with weaker nations, gendered imagery helped convert stories about foreign affairs into mythic tales, often with the form and structure of popular romance novels.[30] Romantic formulas helped articulate and justify policies of dependence, portraying a courtship in which the disorganized but alluring (feminine) tropics ultimately succumbed to the outward thrust of manly organizers of civilization. Gendered imagery abounds in popular portrayals of international relationships: the noisy and muscular parting of Mother Earth in Panama; the fiery engines of progress that penetrated virgin land in the American West and then in Latin America; the North American financial advisers who continually proclaimed the man-sized jobs they were undertaking in financially insolvent countries. Michael Hunt observes that when North Americans "saw themselves acting benevolently, they liked to picture the Latino as a white maiden passively awaiting salvation or seduction." Annexationist rhetoric during the Mexican War thus sought to bring the "Spanish maid" into the Yankee's "valiant arms"; in 1898, Cuba frequently became encoded as an alluring damsel in distress.[31]

These kinds of gendered images did not make arguments justifying creation of zones of dependence; but, as powerful rhetorical devices, they *exemplified* the presumed naturalness of the hierarchical arrangements and helped to make arguments unnecessary. Mythical, transhistorical narratives embedded in metaphorical images, as Richard Slotkin has argued in a different context, transcended policy argumentation, persuading by symbolic association.[32]

A growing body of literature explores the connections between gender, ideology, and war.[33] Outbursts of a bellicose rhetoric about manliness

---

30 Amy Kaplan, "Romancing the Empire" (Paper presented at the American Studies Association Convention, November 1987, in possession of author).

31 Hunt, *Ideology and U.S. Foreign Policy*, 60–61. J. Michael Hogan, *The Panama Canal in American Politics* (Carbondale, 1986), while not addressing itself specifically to gendered metaphors, nonetheless provides an intriguing discussion of the construction of a romanticized "history" of the canal.

32 Slotkin, *Fatal Environment*.

33 Diverse perspectives on this issue from various disciplines include Margaret Randolph Higonnet et al., eds., *Women, War, and History* (New Haven, 1986); Jean Bethke

in foreign relations seem historically related to domestic feminist challenges to male power.[34] Similarly, although gender systems have often bent when men were away fighting, the nationalism and violence of war may ultimately have worked to constrict women's boundaries. During World War II, despite new employment opportunities for women, for example, the broader exaltation of family (reinforced by images of the nation as a family) and of male bonding in an environment of danger and violence may have ultimately widened the gulf between social constructions of male and female.[35]

During the Cold War period, the wartime symbols of gender difference persisted, narrowing opportunities for women while simultaneously suffusing the discourse in which foreign relations were often expressed. Cold War containment, Elaine Tyler May's *Homeward Bound* suggests, structurally dovetailed with the "containment" of women in the domestic sphere.[36] Richard J. Barnet and Carol Cohen have elaborated how defense intellectuals of the period had, above all, to be tough and manly in their recommendations; feminine symbolism became a code for weakness, defeat, and even treason.[37] The Vietnam War, argues Susan Jeffords, was part of an effort to "remasculinize" American culture.[38]

Here, comparative dimensions may be useful. George Mosse and Klaus Theweleit have explored complex connections between male experience and nationalistic action in German history. Theweleit finds Freikorps literature of the interwar period obsessed with communism as a red

---

Elshtain, *Women and War* (New York, 1986); Jean Bethke Elshtain and S. Tobias, eds., *Thinking about Women, Militarism, and War* (New York, 1987); Betty A. Reardon, *Sexism and the War System* (New York, 1985); Peggy Sanday, *Female Power and Male Dominance: On the Origins of Sexual Inequality* (New York, 1981); and Cynthia Enloe, "Feminists Thinking about War, Militarism, and Peace," in *Analyzing Gender: A Handbook of Social Science Research*, ed. Beth B. Hess and Myra Marx Ferree (Beverly Hills, 1987), 526–47.

34 Peter G. Filene, *Him/Her/Self: Sex Roles in Modern America* (New York, 1974), 104–27; Susan Jeffords, "Debriding Vietnam: The Resurrection of the White American Male," *Feminist Studies* 14 (Fall 1988): 525–43.

35 Sonya Michel, "American Women and the Discourse of the Democratic Family in World War II," in *Behind the Lines: Gender and the Two World Wars*, ed. Margaret Randolph Higonnet et al. (New Haven, 1987), 154–67.

36 May, *Homeward Bound: American Families in the Cold War Era* (New York, 1988); idem, "Cold War—Warm Hearth: Politics and the Family in Postwar America," in *The Rise and Fall of the New Deal Order, 1930–1980*, ed. Steve Fraser and Gary Gerstle (Princeton, 1989), 153–81.

37 Barnet, *Roots of War: The Men and Institutions behind U.S. Foreign Policy* (New York, 1971), 109–10; Cohen, "Sex and Death in the Rational World of Defense Intellectuals," *Signs: Journal of Women in Culture and Society* 12 (Summer 1987): 687–718.

38 Jeffords, *The Remasculinization of America: Gender and the Vietnam War* (Bloomington, 1989).

woman (a whore, an engulfing tide) contrasted with the vision of the white woman (mother, wife, nurse). Seeing how the thoughts and actions of the Freikorps so thoroughly intertwined international and gender imagery points toward other historical investigations of how private gender identities conditioned public policy execution.[39] Jeffords's *The Remasculinization of America* and Robin Morgan's *The Demon Lover* elaborate similar themes in different contexts.[40]

The discourse of twentieth-century international relations, then, is packed with terms and images that represented gender differences. Sensitivity to how such divisions encoded power relationships of all kinds can prompt new analytical questions and different histories than those that would emerge from supposedly gender-blind examination. Views from the periphery of power, within many fields of vision, can transform conventional categories and interpretations.

Understanding the parochial perspective of power centers of all kinds (national, economic, and cultural) ought to be a constant concern of historians. Calls for something as contested and as abstract in meaning as international history, however, present no guaranteed remedy for narrow analyses. The term international history may describe a broad and largely empty field, but it should not be mistaken for a specific methodology or an automatic antidote to parochialism in the writing of U.S. foreign relations.

This essay suggests the importance of "walking the borders" of a variety of global power systems to see how things might look from different peripheries. This cannot be done according to any prescriptive taxonomy, nor should scholars strive to create international history in some Olympian sense. Universalized systems and supposed objectivity have worked, in the past, to create the discourses of hegemonic power; the language of critique, as a result, may need to be localized, partial, and contextual. Perhaps nonparochial history can emerge out of the term *international history*, but it can also be built by small, carefully situated glimpses.

39 Mosse, *Nationalism and Sexuality: Respectability and Abnormal Sexuality in Modern Europe* (New York, 1985); Theweleit, *Male Fantasies: Volume One—Women, Floods, Bodies, History*, trans. Stephen Conway (Minneapolis, 1987).
40 Jeffords, *The Remasculinization of America;* Morgan, *The Demon Lover: On the Sexuality of Terrorism* (New York, 1989). See also Helen Caldicott, *Missile Envy: The Arms Race and Nuclear War*, rev. ed. (New York, 1986). For visual and textual material on the changing imagery of American nationalism as expressed through female forms in statuary, art, and posters from the late nineteenth century through World War I see Martha Banta, *Imaging American Women: Idea and Ideals in Cultural History* (New York, 1987), 562–70.

4

Defining and Doing the History of American Foreign Relations: A Primer

THOMAS G. PATERSON

This "primer" seeks to define the field of the history of *American* foreign relations (what are we trying to do?), identify some of the well-explored topics in the field (what are we doing successfully?), suggest two subjects in the field that receive inadequate attention (what might we be doing that we are not doing?), and recommend some steps for improving performance (what can we do?).[1]

All foreign relations historians are engaged in explaining over time the interaction of states, peoples, and cultures in the international system, or, to use other popular phrases, the global village, the earth system, and the world society.[2] Historians of American foreign relations are curious primarily about the impact at home and abroad of American foreign policies, as well as about the variety of relations that Americans have had with other peoples and nations. They attempt to explain what, if

Another version of this essay originally appeared in the Fall 1990 issue of *Diplomatic History*, copyright 1990 by Scholarly Resources Inc. It is printed here by permission of Scholarly Resources Inc. The author thanks Elizabeth Mahan, J. Garry Clifford, Dennis J. Merrill, Stephen Streeter, Frank Costigliola, Douglas Little, John Offner, William O. Walker III, and Stephen G. Rabe for reading drafts of this essay and for making excellent suggestions for its improvement, and he especially expresses his appreciation to Professor Mahan of the University of Connecticut for her help on international communications issues. The University of Connecticut Research Foundation has been generous in supporting his scholarship.

1 This essay is not intended to be comprehensive, but rather suggestive in its citations to the vast literature in foreign relations history. Recent representative studies are emphasized.

2 "Foreign relations" makes more sense than other definitions. "Foreign policy" focuses on the process in government of making a decision and on the policy decision itself, and "diplomacy" emphasizes negotiations between states (or statecraft). "International history" is so broad a term that is loses its usefulness. "Foreign relations" can be used to explain the totality of interactions – economic, cultural, political, and more – among peoples and states. For the problem of definition see "What Is Diplomatic History?" *History Today* 35 (July 1985): 33–41.

anything, is peculiarly *American* about U.S. behavior in the international system. Are there any constants? Is there anything unique about American foreign relations? What is distinctive, and when is it so? Is it true, as Theodore H. von Laue has written, that the United States for much of its history enjoyed "a uniquely privileged existence," an "exceptionality" that eroded after 1945?[3] This is not the place to debate such factors as the richness of natural resources, the abundance of fertile land, immigration, ethnic diversity, religion, political ideology, form of government, "free security," the strengths and weaknesses of neighboring nations, and socioeconomic structure. Historians of *American* foreign relations try to study the combination of factors that has produced an *American* foreign policy, an *American* participation in the world system.[4]

To proceed in this way does not mean to ignore those many characteristics that the United States has shared with other nations. On the contrary, finding the similarities through comparative history is essential to discovering differences. Nor does it mean ripping America out of its broad international context, inspecting it narrowly. To study American foreign relations is not to assume that the United States has been responsible for every change or problem in the world, that U.S. power is unlimited, or that weaker nations do not possess some countervailing power.[5] Nor does this study mean uncritical acceptance of the notion of American exceptionalism. Rather, it is to ask why Americans have believed and often acted as if they were exceptional and when, if ever, U.S. power has in fact been exceptional.[6] Critics have charged that some

3   Theodore H. von Laue, *The World Revolution of Westernization: The Twentieth Century in Global Perspective* (New York, 1987), 152, 166.
4   Here I am disagreeing with Akira Iriye. He has written that "to confirm local, national, or cultural distinctions is counter to the ideal of internationalization. To the extent that we seek to internationalize history, it would be unfortunate if our work merely nationalized it in the sense of stressing the uniqueness of each country's historical development. Sometimes, it may be necessary to try to denationalize history in order to internationalize it." Although I appreciate his call for the study of "international history," I do not find the exploration of a peculiarly American foreign relations at odds with this call—as the discussion that follows shows. See Iriye, "The Internationalization of History," *American Historical Review* 94 (February 1989): 4.
5   For these complaints against American diplomatic historians see James A. Field, Jr., "American Imperialism: The Worst Chapter in Almost Any Book," *American Historical Review* 83 (June 1978): 644–68; and John Lewis Gaddis, "New Conceptual Approaches to the Study of American Foreign Relations: Interdisciplinary Perspectives," *Diplomatic History* 14 (Summer 1990): 403–25.
6   One journalist sets us to thinking about this question because he believes that Americans are and have been quite exceptional in their individualistic values and pluralistic social system and that a return to traditional strengths could reverse the 1980s decline of U.S. power. See James Fallows, *More Like Us: An American Plan for American Recovery* (Boston, 1989).

historians of American foreign relations are ethnocentric, by which the
critics apparently mean that American historians evince an uncritical
preference for their own culture in judging the past or suffer a one-sided
perspective because of a national bias. But such criticism sometimes con-
fuses the study of what Washington has said and done with fawning and
celebrating. Historians must study rigorously and critically what U.S.
leaders have uttered and decided in order to explain *American* foreign
relations. We have come a considerable way, after all, since the days of
the "nationalist" school of Samuel Flagg Bemis, whose 1961 presidential
address to the American Historical Association equated U.S. expansionism with the "blessings of liberty" and discussed white migration through
an "empty continent" without mentioning the harsh removal of native
Americans.[7]

Historians of American foreign relations ideally go about their work
by analyzing their subject at four levels: international, regional, national,
and individual. A comprehensive understanding of Americans and their
foreign relations requires an analysis of all four parts and of their inter-
relationship, although emphasis can rest with a topic lodged in one level
only. There should be no tension among the levels. No one level of
analysis seems inherently superior to the others.[8] One theme runs through
all four levels and is thus central to the study of foreign relations history
itself: the competition for power among individuals, interest groups,
governments, economic systems, cultures, images, ideas, and more. Like
other historians, foreign relations historians are asking the question "who
or what has power?" That is, who or what has the power to create, to
set agendas, to control, to shape, to condition, to dominate—and to
cooperate?

First, let us consider the *international* level of analysis. Studies at this
level most commonly treat state-to-state relations, comparative history,
balance of power, nonstate actors, the world economy, cultural links,
crossnational images, and global environmental issues. At this level the
historian seeks to understand U.S. foreign policy by identifying the characteristics of the international system and by comparing U.S. behavior
with that of other nations. How is power distributed—along multipolar,
hegemonic, or bipolar lines? What are the major sources of conflict, which
states are the key actors, and which instruments of power do they use?
How prevalent and influential are alliances, cultural linkages, multilateral

---

7   Bemis, "American Foreign Policy and the Blessings of Liberty," *American Historical
    Review* 67 (January 1962): 291–305.
8   A point made by Stephen E. Pelz, although he has identified different categories, in "A
    Taxonomy for American Diplomatic History," *Journal of Interdisciplinary History* 19
    (Autumn 1988): 259–76.

economic agreements, and shared environmental concerns? How much influence is exerted by international organizations or nonstate, transnational groups and movements?[9] How interdependent is the international system?[10]

Other questions guide, or should guide, analysis at the international level. How fast does information travel in international communications networks and how do governments communicate? How do new technologies, such as steam-powered ships or intercontinental ballistic missiles, influence international relations? Is the international system in a state of major transformation, as, for example, in the much swifter than anticipated process of decolonization after World War II? Which international troubles are man-made and which natural or ecological? If, as students of a systemic approach remind us, conflict is inherent in any setting, what are the international mechanisms or regimes for resolving disputes, addressing transnational questions, transmitting culture, or creating stability (such as the Pax Britannica, the League of Nations, or the Bretton Woods institutions)? Answers to such questions will establish the broad setting that has provided both opportunities and restraints for Americans and others. In other words, we need studies not only of state-to-state relations within the international system (which seem to be the most popular kind) but also of the very nature of that system itself.[11]

Second, the *regional* level of analysis assumes that geographical location or place in the international system matters. The terms are common enough; we talk about East, West, South, Third World, Western Hemisphere, Central America, Balkans, Eastern Europe, North Atlantic, South Asia, and the Northern Tier. What do we mean by such descriptions? The many area studies programs and institutes at colleges and universities press us to answer this question, as do the increasingly multipolar international setting and the many common markets and regional economic systems. Regional identity helps define any nation's security, vulnerability, freedom of choice, cultural, political, and economic ties, and the

9 On the eve of World War I, for example, 49 international intergovernmental organizations existed, as did more than 160 international nongovernmental organizations; by the 1970s the numbers had reached more than three hundred and twenty-four hundred, respectively. See Charles W. Kegley, Jr., and Eugene R. Wittkopf, *World Politics: Trend and Transformation* (New York, 1981), 104. They draw their data from Michael D. Wallace and J. David Singer, "Intergovernmental Organization in the Global System, 1915–1964: A Quantitative Description," *International Organization* 24 (Spring 1970): 239–87; and *Yearbook of International Organizations* (Brussels, 1978).

10 See Robert Keohane and Joseph S. Nye, Jr., *Power and Interdependence,* 2d ed. (Boston, 1989).

11 Political scientists, of course, have devoted a good deal of attention to the international system. For a summary of their findings see Ole R. Holsti's contribution to this volume, Chapter 5.

historical patterns that have shaped decisions and events. Thus we speak about long-standing U.S. hegemony in the Western Hemisphere, destabilizing religious tensions in the Middle East, and Russian/Soviet imperialism in Eastern Europe. To understand U.S. diplomacy, we study its particular regional relationships—for example, the nation's ties to the Atlantic community from the alliance with France in 1778 to the North Atlantic Treaty of 1949. We also explore how regional disputes such as those in South Asia between India and Pakistan and in the Middle East between Israel and the Arab states escalate into international conflicts.

Third, at the *national* level of analysis, foreign relations historians primarily explore domestic or internal characteristics. If we ask who holds power in the international and regional arenas, we also ask who has power in the nation itself. Why and how does a nation make the choices it does in the international and regional settings? These external settings have conditioned American foreign policy, but they have not controlled it. For that control, we look inward at a number of factors: economic, strategic, political, ideological, cultural, and social. We ask questions about the nation's economic needs, or perceived needs, and study strategic raw-material imports, the export trade, tariffs, and overseas investments. We also consider perceived security needs by examining calculations of threats, war planning, forward basing, interoceanic waterways, and budgets.

We also delve into American politics and government to determine how decisions are made and by whom—who has power? We study mass or public opinion (do leaders essentially hear what they have in fact already shaped?) and opinion elites (does a small group of educated, well-informed leaders dominate opinion?). The role of interest groups such as the "Jewish lobby" or "business," private-sector organizations like the American Banking Association and the National Foreign Trade Council, and political parties and bipartisanship command attention. Constitutional provisions, especially war powers and budgetary controls, also receive study. Bureaucratic competition and imperatives, the national security state, and the imperial presidency are other topics in this category. We wonder why Congress has so often abdicated its foreign policy powers, and we look at the impact of foreign policy crises on domestic politics and vice versa, as in McCarthyism.

We investigate the decision-making process and ask whether it is a hapless series of uncoordinated responses or a rational, systematic identification of tasks and weighing of alternatives—or perhaps an untidy mix of the two. We study it when it works, as when John Quincy Adams negotiated with European nations, and when it malfunctions, as in the Bay of Pigs operation. We look at the changing role of the American Foreign Service. We ask about the quality and quantity of information available to leaders when they made their decisions, such as during the Vietnam War. We study how policy is carried out once it is decided. What instruments—foreign aid, covert agencies, military forces—are available to implement decisions?

At the national level of analysis, we also probe social, ideological, and cultural categories. We explore the relationship between social and economic classes, political power, and decisions in the United States; the relationship between American elites and native elites who collaborate with them to dominate governments; lessons from the past such as the Munich syndrome; and tenacious beliefs like manifest destiny, republicanism, social Darwinism, and counterrevolution. We also study the difficult-to-define category of culture—those customs, ideas, images, and assumptions, including racism, ethnic ties, and sectionalism, that are distinctive to a people. This topic is important not only because the cultural milieu shapes thinking and policymaking but also because such cultural exports as movies and clothing designs have served to extend American influence abroad.

Finally, let us turn to the *individual* level of analysis. Resisting the "general depersonalization of history," many diplomatic historians study this level because individuals make decisions.[12] Individual leaders decide whether or not to negotiate and their styles of diplomacy help to shape results. In the national, regional, and international settings, moreover, some individuals have stood out as particularly influential, and therefore we must find out what made them tick. We study the personality traits, knowledge, ideology, political ties, ambitions, rivalries, prejudices, class, youth, and family background of American leaders and others. We study not only the idiosyncratic but also the shared, which is to say that we explore the cultural, political, social, and economic assumptions and environments that leaders have in common with their compatriots. We also study their illnesses and their handling of crisis-induced stress. Did their particular psychological and physical or medical conditions significantly influence decision making? Woodrow Wilson's and Franklin D. Roosevelt's neurological diseases and the deterioration of their intellectual function during and after the Paris Peace Conference and the Yalta Conference, respectively, have received a good deal of scholarly attention.[13] Historians of foreign relations, finally, reckon with style, with

12 Statement by Donald Cameron Watt, "Foreword: The New International History," *International History Review* 9 (November 1987): 518.
13 For examples of recent works on the relationship between health, stress, and leadership see Kenneth R. Crispell and Carlos F. Gomez, *Hidden Illness in the White House* (Durham, NC, 1989); Bert Edward Park, *The Impact of Illness on World Leaders* (Philadelphia, 1986); idem, "The Impact of Wilson's Neurologic Disease during the Paris Peace Conference," in *The Papers of Woodrow Wilson*, ed. Arthur S. Link (Princeton, 1988), 58:611–30; Edwin A. Weinstein, *Woodrow Wilson: A Medical*

how a diplomat goes about his or her work. In accounting for the origins of the Cold War, for example, how much of a difference did it make that a parochial, ill-informed, impatient man like Harry S. Truman replaced a cosmopolitan, compromising, knowledgeable Roosevelt just when the international system was undergoing tremendous change?

Working through these four levels of analysis, or writing in detail on a topic at one level but demonstrating its interconnectedness with the other three levels, affords us the opportunity to provide a comprehensive view of American foreign relations. Critics have complained that some American historians have focused too narrowly at the national and individual levels, dealing with their subjects in isolation. But let us not be snobbish or exclusionist. Should we not pursue what intellectually fascinates us? Who is to set the limits on intellectual curiosity? Who is to say that the study of how a certain member of Congress voted on a foreign aid bill is too narrow? We need the nitty-gritty, archive-based studies of this event or that person. Doing history, like doing any discipline, is knowledge building. It seems obvious that we need as many small pieces as possible to construct the whole. As somebody has put it, we need the bricklayers as well as the architects (and, of course, the critics of the architecture). Few of us, moreover, are blessed with substantial travel budgets, light teaching loads, large support staffs, and generous leaves to frequent international archives (many of which place major restrictions on access) or to crisscross the United States in search of documents. At the same time, it is incumbent upon historians to utilize all four levels of analysis, and that can be achieved, if not through multiarchival research, through wide reading in the vast and challenging literature in the field. We have to ask always where our discrete story fits into larger historical patterns.

Historians of American foreign relations, moreover, cannot meet their responsibilities alone. They must rely upon historians who have studied other nations—such as Louis A. Pérez, Jr., on Cuba, John K. Fairbank on China, Bruce Calder on the Dominican Republic, and Gerhard Weinberg on Nazi Germany, to name but a few.[14] One cannot imagine un-

and Psychological Biography (Princeton, 1981); Alexander L. George, "The Impact of Crisis-Induced Stress on Decision Making," in *The Medical Implications of Nuclear War,* ed. Frederic Solomon and Robert Q. Marston (Washington, 1986), 529–52; and idem, *Presidential Decisionmaking in Foreign Policy: The Effective Use of Information and Advice* (Boulder, 1980).

14 Pérez, *Cuba: Between Reform and Revolution* (New York, 1988); idem, *Cuba under the Platt Amendment, 1902–1934* (Pittsburgh, 1986); Fairbank, *The United States and China,* 4th enlarged ed. (Cambridge, MA, 1983); Calder, *The Impact of Intervention: The Dominican Republic during the U.S. Occupation of 1916–1924* (Austin, TX, 1984); Weinberg, *The Foreign Policy of Hitler's Germany: Diplomatic Revolution*

dertaking synthesis or overview without observing the many parts and diversity of the landscape. If historians of American foreign relations do research and write with alertness to all four levels of analysis, looking both outward and inward, if they immerse themselves in the histories of other countries, and if they are intellectually responsive to the contributions of other disciplines, they should be able to explain American foreign relations fully. In other words, they should be able to do the history of American foreign relations as international history, regional history, national history, and historical biography combined.

Many recent works have successfully integrated the four levels of analysis.[15] Many foreign relations historians conduct multinational archival research, know foreign languages, and read in the theoretical literature of other disciplines. Some among them have undertaken joint international projects.[16] Others have bravely reached for broad synthesis.[17] The

in Europe, 1933–36 (Chicago, 1970); idem, *The Foreign Policy of Hitler's Germany: Starting World War II, 1937–1939* (Chicago, 1980).

15 See, for example, Waldo Heinrichs, *Threshold of War: Franklin D. Roosevelt and American Entry into World War II* (New York, 1988); and Akira Iriye, *The Origins of the Second World War in Asia and the Pacific* (London, 1987). John Offner's articles (prelude to a book) on war in the late 1890s also reveal an appreciation for the several levels of analysis and for multinational research. See, for example, "The United States and France: Ending the Spanish-American War," *Diplomatic History* 7 (Winter 1983): 1–21, and "President McKinley's Final Attempt to Avoid War with Spain," *Ohio History* 94 (Summer–Autumn 1985): 125–38. In my own work I have tried to practice what I preach. See, for example, the chapter entitled "Threat to the Middle East? The Eisenhower Doctrine," in Thomas G. Paterson, *Meeting the Communist Threat: Truman to Reagan* (New York, 1988), 159–90; and idem, "Fixation with Cuba: The Bay of Pigs, Missile Crisis, and Covert War Against Fidel Castro," in *Kennedy's Quest for Victory: American Foreign Policy, 1961–1963*, ed. Paterson (New York, 1989), 123–55.

16 See, for example, Dorothy Borg and Shumpei Okamoto, eds., *Pearl Harbor as History: Japanese-American Relations, 1931–1941* (New York, 1973); Harry Harding and Yuan Ming, eds., *Sino-American Relations, 1945–1955: A Joint Reassessment of a Critical Decade* (Wilmington, DE, 1989); and Akira Iriye and Warren Cohen, eds., *The Great Powers in East Asia, 1953–1960* (New York, 1990).

17 The critics' complaints that we do not have syntheses does not quite hit the mark. Actually, we have a good number of them; but we find them contending or unsatisfying. Reaching for synthesis is, of course, a quest central to fertile intellectual engagement. But some critics seem to be suggesting that someday, somehow, we should come to agree on a synthesis. Given our intellectual pluralism and the happy departure of stultifying consensus, that moment of agreement seems quite remote. Few subfields of history have produced syntheses that have remained dominant. Diplomatic history is no different in this regard. Prominent among syntheses, of course, is William Appleman Williams, *The Tragedy of American Diplomacy* (1959; reprint New York, 1988). More recent attempts include Robert Dallek, *The American Style of Foreign Policy* (New York, 1983); Michael Hunt, *Ideology and U.S. Foreign Policy* (New Haven, 1987); and Thomas McCormick, " 'Every System Needs a Center Sometime': An Essay on Hegemony and Modern American Foreign Policy," in *Redefining the Past: Essays in Diplomatic History in Honor of William Appleman Williams*, ed. Lloyd C. Gardner (Corvallis, OR, 1986), 195–220.

vitality of the field of foreign relations history is also demonstrated in a growing number of "impact" studies in an international context—that is, the effect of American decisions and actions on the politics, society, and economy of other nations.[18] We are also favored by studies, too numerous to name here, of the Foreign Service and of the Central Intelligence Agency (CIA) as instruments of American policy, of such nonstate actors as missionaries, labor unions, and corporations, of military strategy, of the influence exerted on policymaking by domestic politics, the press, and public opinion, and of peace movements as viable intellectual if not political alternatives to the militarization of American foreign policy. Recent studies of missionaries have integrated foreign relations, cultural, and women's history.[19] Historians are starting to provide the historical background of a major international issue: the drug traffic and efforts to control it.[20] Theories of dependency and hegemony, constantly tested and revised by new empirical studies, continue to inform works on inter-American relations.[21] The question of how American foreign policy has measured up to international law has received careful scrutiny.[22] Some topics, like the origins of the Cold War, have been dissected to the extent that we have, at last, shifted the question from "whose fault was it?" to "who had power in the international system and how was it

18 Pérez and Calder, cited above, are Latin Americanists who have studied the impact of U.S. imperialism. For other examples see these studies of the U.S. impact on Greece: Lawrence S. Wittner, *American Intervention in Greece, 1943–1949* (New York, 1982); and John O. Iatrides, ed., *Greece in the 1940s: A Nation in Crisis* (Hanover, NH, 1981).

19 See, for example, Jane Hunter, *Gospel of Gentility: American Women Missionaries in Turn-of-the-Century China* (New Haven, 1984).

20 See especially the work of William O. Walker III: "Drug Control and the Issue of Culture in American Foreign Relations," *Diplomatic History* 12 (Fall 1988): 365–82, "Drug Control and National Security," ibid. (Spring 1988): 187–99, and *Drug Control in the Americas,* rev. ed. (Albuquerque, 1989).

21 Pérez in his several works, for example, has found them useful tools for interpreting Cuban-American relations, as his essay in this volume demonstrates. A major statement is Fernando Henrique Cardoso and Enzo Faletto, *Dependency and Development in Latin America,* trans. Marjory M. Urquidi (Berkeley, 1979). See also the discussion of modifications of the theory based upon a growing number of empirical case studies in Peter Evans, "After Dependency: Recent Studies of Class, State, and Industrialization," *Latin American Research Review* 20:2 (1985): 149–60. Robert A. Packenham is very critical of the *dependencia* approach in his "Capitalist Dependency and Socialist Dependency: The Case of Cuba," in *Dominant Powers and Subordinate States: The United States in Latin America and the Soviet Union in Eastern Europe,* ed. Jan F. Triska (Durham, 1986), 310–41. Hegemony is an organizing theme for Thomas J. McCormick, *America's Half-Century: United States Foreign Policy in the Cold War* (Baltimore, 1989).

22 For example John W. Coogan, *The End of Neutrality: The United States, Britain, and Maritime Rights, 1899–1915* (Ithaca, 1981).

used?"[23] Another challenging trend in the literature, <u>international wars</u> <u>as civil wars (Korea and Vietnam, for example)</u>, moves us between the <u>international and national levels</u>.[24] In short, the field of American foreign relations history is not floundering, but rather, flourishing.

Still, two large international topics, among others, deserve our greater attention: the environment and communications. We are teased into both subjects by contemporary worries and debates swirling around us. The Department of State applauds its new emphasis on environmental diplomacy.[25] Analysts have spoken of "The Global Commons" to emphasize the interdependence and precariousness of the world's environment.[26] They have identified an imposing list of issues: acid rain, drought-induced famine, despoliation of the oceans, diminishing clean water supplies, chemical and radioactive air, water and soil pollution, hazardous waste disposal, population explosion, depletion of the ozone layer, the "greenhouse effect," exploitation of rich resources in Antarctica, and the destruction of tropical forests. They have stressed that these numerous problems cannot be discussed within the context of the nation-state, because the issues respect no territorial boundaries and can be addressed only through international action. They have demonstrated that major political instability and conflict have arisen from these issues, bedeviling world politics and stimulating international conferences like that for the Law of the Sea—a conference that opened in 1973 and continued into the early 1980s.

These topics are rich in history. That diplomats themselves apparently did not begin seriously to discuss some of these questions until the 1960s and 1970s does not mean that the conditions and the careless, almost cavalier behavior that produced some of these problems have not been around for a long time.[27] Indeed, scientists have been sounding bells of

23 For a discussion of the changing interpretations on this subject see Thomas G. Paterson and Robert J. McMahon, eds., *The Origins of the Cold War*, 3d ed. (Lexington, MA, 1991).

24 For Korea see Bruce Cumings, *The Origins of the Korean War: Liberation and the Emergence of Separate Regimes, 1945–1947* (Princeton, 1981); idem, ed., *Child of Conflict: The Korean-American Relationship, 1943–1953* (Seattle, 1983); and Peter Lowe, *The Origins of the Korean War* (London, 1986). For citations to the vast literature on Vietnam see Robert J. McMahon, ed., *Major Problems in the History of the Vietnam War* (Lexington, MA, 1990).

25 U.S. Department of State, *Update from State*, July–August 1989, 1.

26 See, for example, Robert C. Johansen, *The National Interest and the Human Interest: An Analysis of U.S. Foreign Policy* (Princeton, 1980); Wesley T. Wooley, *Alternatives to Anarchy: American Supranationalism since World War II* (Bloomington, 1988); Robert L. Heilbroner, *An Inquiry into the Human Prospect* (New York, 1974); and *The Global 2000 Report to the President* (Washington, 1980).

27 Rachel Carson's popular alert and plea for the environment, *Silent Spring*, was first

alarm for decades. Perhaps the historical investigation of environmental issues must begin not with the history of diplomacy but with the histories of science and the scientific community, technology, the chemical and nuclear revolutions, weather, agriculture or agroecosystems, medical developments, public interest groups like the Worldwatch Institute, and more. Study might also begin with domestic history as prologue to international history: the rise of industrialization, the conservation movement, mechanized agriculture, the women's rights and birth control movements, mineral extraction, and the alliance between science and government, to cite a few examples related to global issues. Then inquiry might move on to policymaking—what individuals, nations, and regional and international organizations have done to meet environmental crises. Twentieth-century famines have generated major American relief expenditures and missions in Europe, Africa, and elsewhere. Studies of American foreign assistance programs, both public and private, help us to address the critical question of food production.[28] We can also provide historical treatment of meetings like the Global Conference on the Human Environment (held in Stockholm in 1972).[29]

The earth's remarkable environmental changes have created changes in the distribution of power in the international system and heightened world conflict. Abortion and birth control methods to stem population growth have become highly charged world issues. Weather conditions and pollution have rendered vast areas uninhabitable and stimulated refugee movements, creating pressures many governments have been unable to bear and making them dependent upon foreign assistance. Food riots have rocked nation after nation. Natural disasters like earthquakes—witness Nicaragua after the devastating tremor of 1972—have induced significant political transformation, which in turn has generated internal, regional, and global conflict. Shortages of commodities and raw

published in 1963. John Roberts, a Canadian official and scholar, has noted the influence of this book on his nation's environmental policies in his essay, "The Diplomacy of Acid Rain: The North American Experience in Global Perspective," in *Negotiating World Order: The Artisanship and Architecture of Global Diplomacy,* ed. Alan K. Henrikson (Wilmington, DE, 1986), 19–32. For a broad introduction to the subject of environmental history see Donald Worster, ed., *The Ends of the Earth: Perspectives on Modern Environmental History* (New York, 1988); and the several essays in "A Round Table: Environmental History," *Journal of American History* 76 (March 1990): 1087–1147.

28 See, for example, Randall E. Stross, *The Stubborn Earth: American Agriculturalists on Chinese Soil, 1898–1937* (Berkeley, 1986); and Dennis J. Merrill, *Bread and the Ballot: The United States and India's Economic Development, 1947–1963* (Chapel Hill, 1990).

29 For this conference and environmental issues since 1945 see John McCormick, *Reclaiming Paradise: The Global Environmental Movement* (Bloomington, 1989).

materials or fears that supplies are finite and irreplaceable have stimulated competition and conflict. At times nations that have produced food surpluses may have gained influence over those that must import food. A 1974 CIA study concluded that world grain shortages "could give the United States a measure of power it never had before—possibly an economic and political dominance greater than that of the immediate post–World War II years." Indeed, "in bad years . . . Washington would acquire virtual life-and-death power over the fate of the multitudes of the needy."[30] This was not just a momentary assessment; rather, it speaks to the longer history of the United States as an agricultural exporting nation.

Students of environmental questions have impressed on us the need to redefine the concept of national security, expanding it beyond consideration of military defense to an appreciation for environmental security. "The threats to security," Worldwatch's Lester R. Brown wrote more than a decade ago, "may now arise less from the relationship of nation to nation and more from the relationship of man to nature."[31] The questions surrounding the global ecosystem are not just contemporary concerns best left to scientific specialists. They are topics with a long past much in need of exploration by historians of American foreign relations.

Although some historians have spoken to a second subject deserving of major study—international communications as one of many U.S. interactions with the world—the topic begs for more, for it too is rich in history.[32] The subject of international communications and information

30   Quoted in Johansen, *National Interest and the Human Interest*, 13.
31   Brown, *Human Needs and the Security of Nations* (New York, Foreign Policy Association Headline Series 238, 1978), 6. Brown's other works include *World without Borders* (New York, 1972), *The Twenty-ninth Day* (New York, 1978), several *Worldwatch Papers*, and the annual books entitled *State of the World*, the first appearing in 1984.
32   See, for example, Michael J. Hogan, *Informal Entente: The Private Structure of Cooperation in Anglo-American Economic Diplomacy, 1918–1928* (Columbia, MO, 1977); Emily S. Rosenberg, *Spreading the American Dream: American Economic and Cultural Expansion, 1890–1945* (New York, 1982); Frank Costigliola, *Awkward Dominion: American Political, Economic, and Cultural Relations with Europe, 1919–1933* (Ithaca, 1984); Joseph S. Tulchin, *The Aftermath of War: World War I and U.S. Policy toward Latin America* (New York, 1971); John P. Rossi, "A 'Silent Partnership'? The U.S. Government, RCA, and Radio Communications with East Asia, 1919–1928," *Radical History Review* 33 (September 1985): 32–52; Gerald K. Haines, "Under the Eagle's Wing: The Franklin Roosevelt Administration Forges an American Hemisphere," *Diplomatic History* 1 (Fall 1977): 373–88; Susan J. Douglas, *Inventing American Broadcasting, 1899–1922* (Baltimore, 1987); Fred Fejes, *Imperialism, Media, and the Good Neighbor: New Deal Foreign Policy and United States Shortwave Broadcasting to Latin America* (Norwood, NJ, 1986); and James Schwoch, *The American Radio Industry and Its Latin-American Activities, 1900–1939* (Urbana, IL, 1990).

flow has a long history dating at least to the late nineteenth century when underwater cables and telegraph lines began to link the United States with Europe, Latin America, and Asia. The history extends into the twentieth century with the advent of film, radio, newspaper wire services, television, and satellites. Many reasons make international communications a compelling subject. We are curious, for example, about the movement of information and about communications delays. If there had been a transatlantic telegraph in 1812, would the United States have avoided war with Britain? During the late, highly charged stages of the Cuban missile crisis, Nikita Khrushchev's critical 26 October 1962 letter to Washington was delayed twelve hours because of communications snags. McGeorge Bundy, national security affairs adviser at the time, has concluded that the delay had a "damaging effect on the possibility of a more rapid resolution of the crisis."[33]

American diplomats have devoted considerable effort to communications issues in negotiations and in international bodies. Since 1947, for example, the United States has been a member of the International Telecommunications Union, a UN agency established to allocate radio frequencies, among other responsibilities (its forerunner was the International Telegraph Union, formed in 1865). The United States has also been active in the International Telecommunications Satellite Consortium (INTELSAT), founded in 1964 to coordinate the use of satellites. Through INTELSAT the United States has preserved control of the majority of the electromagnetic spectrum for itself and its European allies. U.S. domination of international communications has made it a target of criticism in world conferences, and such issues as the use of outer space for telecommunications satellites and the policy of some governments to restrict the transmission of computer-held data have been on the American agenda for some time.[34]

Communications can also be studied as an instrument of official U.S. policy. From the Voice of America (founded in 1942) to Radio Free Europe (established in 1950) to the United States Information Agency (founded in 1953), with its overseas libraries and its distribution of films abroad, the United States has used propaganda in "the battle for world

---

33 Bundy, *Danger and Survival: Choices About the Bomb in the First Fifty Years* (New York, 1989), 444.
34 See G. Russell Pipe, "Transborder Data Flow: New Frontiers — or None? National Policies, International Debates," *Journal of Communication* 29 (Summer 1979): 114–24; David E. Sanger, "Waging a Trade War over Data," *New York Times*, 13 March 1983; and Oswald H. Ganley and Gladys D. Ganley, *To Inform or to Control?: The New Communications Network* (New York, 1982).

opinion"—especially in waging the Cold War through a "strategy of truth."[35] In 1954 the CIA beamed false radio broadcasts to make Guatemalans—including officials of the Arbenz government the CIA successfully toppled—think that a massive invasion was underway against the Central American nation. In the 1930s, Rafael Trujillo consolidated dictatorial power in the Dominican Republic through control of an American-built national communications system. Two decades later the CIA helped Egypt's Gamal Abdel Nasser start a broadcasting station, Radio Cairo, which, in a classic example of unintended results, soon beamed pan-Arabist, anti-American propaganda to the Middle East. Washington's efforts to stir rebellion in Castro's Cuba through Radio Swan and Radio Martí, both of which Havana has denounced as assaults upon its sovereignty, also reveal the place of telecommunications in U.S. foreign relations.[36]

The growth of international communications has been closely intertwined with the growth of American power and economic expansion. In 1918, *Collier's* put it this way: the American "moving picture" is "familiarizing South America and Africa, Asia and Europe with American habits and customs. It is educating them up to the American standard of living. It is showing them American clothes and furniture, automobiles and homes. And it is subtly but surely creating a desire for these American-made articles."[37] The long-developing communications relationship between American television advertisements and Canadian consumers played no small part in preparing the case for the 1989 free trade agreement between Ottawa and Washington. As well, an important element in the expansion of American power has been the acquisition of intelligence "listening posts" around the world, a point driven home when revolutionary Iran in 1979 abruptly shut down such stations. The development in the 1950s of the U-2 reconnaissance plane and later of "imaging" satellites provided yet other links between international communications, information, and American foreign relations.

We can learn from this subject, too, because the depiction of foreign governments and peoples by American newspapers, cartoons, radio, television, and film has shaped American images of others. In the nineteenth century, sketches, cartoons, and writings helped popularize Anglo-Saxon

---

35 Wilson P. Dizard, *The Strategy of Truth: The Story of the U.S. Information Service* (Washington, 1961), 1. First-rate historical studies of the United States Information Agency are wanting.

36 Howard H. Frederick, *Cuban-American Radio Wars: Ideology in International Telecommunications* (Norwood, NJ, 1986).

37 This and similar statements can be found in Kristin Thompson, *Exporting Entertainment: America in the World Film Market, 1907–1934* (London, 1985), 121–22.

racism and notions of the inferiority of native Americans and Mexicans.[38] During the two world wars, government propaganda agencies and film makers mobilized public opinion around simple views of the enemy.[39] More recently, critics, especially from the Third World, have complained that the U.S.-dominated mass communications system prefers to report foreign events that are dramatic and often the aberrational or violent and to ignore deeply rooted traditions, long-term trends, or examples of achievement and progress. Thus, the ignorance of Americans and their government has been perpetuated through images of uncivilized foreigners who have lost their senses. Cultural stereotypes have been formed that becloud reality and obstruct sound policymaking.[40]

By studying international communications we can also explore the effect of mass media technology upon the political activities of dissidents, terrorists, and others, upon the governments they have opposed, upon international stability, and upon American foreign policy. For example, Ayatollah Ruhollah Khomeini, in exile in Paris in the 1970s, kept antishah revolutionary passions high in Iran by sending tape cassettes into the country. In the 1980s, videocassettes of American and Japanese newscasts of the assassination of Filipino critic Benigno Aquino were smuggled into the Philippines, where they were copied and distributed to home viewers. Videocassette recorders were thus used to help create the antigovernment sentiment that weakened and toppled the dictatorship of Ferdinand Marcos, an American ally. Terrorists, hijackers, and hostage takers in the Middle East have long attempted to propagandize their causes and make their demands known by playing to television cameras and by preparing videocassettes of captives.[41] Powerful governments have seemed powerless to silence critics and rebels who have easy access to inexpensive equipment for disseminating their messages.

International communications has also accentuated cultural diversity and hence world conflict. U.S. cultural exports have been and are controversial. In 1926, for example, C. J. North of the Department of Com-

38 Reginald Horsman, *Race and Manifest Destiny* (Cambridge, MA, 1981).
39 Stephen L. Vaughn, *Holding Fast the Inner Lines: Democracy, Nationalism, and the Committee on Public Information* (Chapel Hill, 1979); Allen M. Winkler, *The Politics of Propaganda: The Office of War Information, 1942–1945* (New Haven, 1978); Clayton R. Koppes and Gregory D. Black, *Hollywood Goes to War: How Politics, Profits and Propaganda Shaped World War II Movies* (New York, 1987).
40 A challenging study is Anthony Smith, *The Geopolitics of Information: How Western Culture Dominates the World* (New York, 1980).
41 Gladys D. Ganley and Oswald H. Ganley, *Global Political Fallout: The VCR's First Decade, 1976–1985* (Norwood, NJ, 1987), chap. 9. Also useful are James F. Larson, *Global Television and Foreign Policy* (New York, Foreign Policy Association Headline Series No. 283, 1988); and William C. Adams, ed., *Television Coverage of International Affairs* (Norwood, NJ, 1982).

merce explained that "the film is a silent salesman of great effectiveness.
. . . Moreover, through American motion pictures, the ideals, culture, customs, and tradition of the United States are gradually undermining those
of other countries" in a "subtle Americanization process."[42] French na-
tionalists have railed against the invasion of American films and Indians
have grown apprehensive about American influence in the Indian radio,
television, and motion picture industries and about the Associated Press's
dominance of foreign news coverage in Indian English-language newspapers.[43] Whether we interpret this expansion as "cultural imperialism"
or not, some statistics reveal why governments and individuals might
protest what seems to be an American cultural invasion: in 1969, 50
percent of all films shown in Chile and 70 percent of those shown in
Bolivia, Brazil, Ecuador, Paraguay, Peru, and Venezuela were American
imports; in 1974, 84 percent of the programs shown on television in
Guatemala and 34 percent in Colombia were of American origin; at
about the same time, 50 percent of world news published in South American newspapers came from two U.S. agencies, Associated Press and
United Press International.[44] Has the United States added cultural muscle
to its economic and military might in order to exert its will abroad, or
is this cultural expansion an example of "empire by invitation"?

International communications is a significant current topic, and knowledge of its history would help inform contemporary debate. Developing
nations have been calling since the 1970s for a "New International Information Order" in which the powerful developed nations would be
compelled to democratize access to information and to report news accurately and fairly. Like another appeal that originated in the nonaligned
movement, the "New International Economic Order," this one derived
from the assumption that control of information by the capitalist or
developed nations has created dependency in weaker states and has re-
tarded economic and political growth—in this case, that nations that lack
information facilities have become dependent upon those that do have
them. Within UNESCO, since the 1970s, nations have debated whether
governments should be able to restrict the flow of information from

---

42 Quoted in Thompson, *Exporting Entertainment*, 122.
43 See Frank Costigliola, *The Cold Alliance: Franco-American Relations since 1940*
    (Boston, in press); and Gary R. Hess, "Global Expansion and Regional Balances: The
    Emerging Scholarship on United States Relations with India and Pakistan," *Pacific
    Historical Review* 56 (May 1987): 259–95.
44 Anthony Smith has concluded that Latin American newspapers have been "deeply
    impregnated with an American attitude toward news." See *Geopolitics*, 71. The data
    are located on pp. 42, 70. For a classic statement of international communications
    domination as part of American imperialism see Herbert I. Schiller, *Mass Commu-
    nications and American Empire* (Boston, 1971).

newsreporting they consider biased in favor of Western views and from films they consider threatening to their cultures.[45] Third World critics have claimed that U.S. advocacy of "freedom of information" has actually meant the freedom for U.S. media industries to inform according to the transmitters' wishes.[46] If Third World nations have seen the issue as one of power and powersharing, Americans have complained about censorship.

Finally, the study of international communications will help us measure who has power in the international system. Some scholars have argued, for example, that in international negotiations over such questions as tariffs and the law of the sea, developed nations have held a decided advantage over developing nations because they can marshal greater information on weather, market conditions, natural resources, and the like. The ability of the United States since the early 1970s to use remote-sensing satellites to gather global information about mineral deposits and agricultural output provides one such advantage. The U.S. government's National Security Agency has developed high-tech devices that can home in on telephone conversations, fax messages, and bank transfers around the world.[47] In the last few decades, this differential access to information has become a major point of friction between the industrial North and the developing South.[48]

Besides tackling such international topics as communications and the environment, what can historians of American foreign relations do to improve their field, to combat the narrowness and provincialism that are sometimes evident, and to pay more attention to all four levels of analysis discussed earlier? Some changes can be instituted within their departments, colleges, and other institutions, and some steps necessarily require personal adjustments, including an openness to conceptual and methodological innovation. None demands a lot of money.

One task is to combat the danger of being "culture bound," to use John K. Fairbank's phrase.[49] For example, practitioners of the field can

---

45   The major UNESCO report is *Many Voices, One World: Communications and Society, Today and Tomorrow* (New York, 1980).

46   The international debate is outlined in Rita Cruise O'Brien, ed., *Information Economics and Power: The North-South Dimension* (Boulder, 1983); Anthony Smith, *Geopolitics;* and George Gerbner and Marsha Siebert, eds., *World Communications: A Handbook* (New York, 1984).

47   George Lardner, Jr., "No Such Agency: The National Security Agency Thrives on Obscurity," *Washington Post National Weekly Edition*, 26 March–1 April 1990.

48   The question of information power is discussed in Rita O'Brien and G. K. Helleiner, "The Political Economy of Information in a Changing International Economic Order," in O'Brien, ed., *Information*, 1–27; and Herbert I. Schiller, "Remote Sensing by Satellite: Global Hegemony or Social Utility," in Gerbner and Siefert, eds., *World Communications*, 236–45.

49   John K. Fairbank, *China Watch* (Cambridge, MA, 1987), 1. See also Paul M. Evans,

break out of their "self-imposed monolingual ghetto" by becoming fluent in a foreign language.[50] Too many of them simply nibble at the fringes, unable to use a foreign language effectively to understand another culture. It should go without saying that scholars of the history of foreign relations must fathom the history of the peoples and nations toward which American foreign policy is directed. As teachers and scholars, they can go abroad through the Fulbright and other programs. Through the National Endowment for the Humanities Summer Seminars for College Teachers many are afforded the opportunity to study foreign subjects. They can urge historical journals published in the United States to translate into English and then reprint articles first published abroad. Or they can read translated articles in such journals as *Chinese Studies in History.* They can also find ways to link their departments with campus or off-campus area studies centers and programs. They can bring in visiting scholars to offer colloquiums and courses on subjects where their own expertise is inadequate. They can organize conferences on international relations at their institutions, and seek whenever possible to invite speakers from abroad who are visiting in the United States. They can exploit local resources to stimulate discussion and broaden views, including former diplomats, Peace Corps Volunteers, Vietnam veterans, and American Catholics who have worked in Latin America (such as the Holy Cross Fathers). They must ask, as well, whether departments of history are offering an adequate array of courses beyond the traditional U.S. and European courses.

They can also require outside fields for graduate training so that their students contend with comparative government, international economics, environmental science, economic geography, and international relations, among others. They can try, as well, to attract to the field students with scientific literacy. We need historians who can profit from such journals as *Science, Scientific American, Technology Review, The Environmental Review,* and *Environment.* We need students who can master the language of science and technology to help us master not only nuclear but also environmental questions.

Historians have a responsibility to combat the American public's ignorance about U.S. foreign relations and to sensitize Americans to the diversity of humankind. Such ignorance was reflected in an extensive 1988 Gallup survey, which discovered that 14 percent of the American respondents could not pick out the United States on a world map and about 50 percent did not know that the Sandinistas and contras were

---

John Fairbank and the American Understanding of Modern China (New York, 1988), 293.

50 The quoted wording comes from University of Connecticut Associate Professor of German Barbara D. Wright.

battling in Nicaragua. A 1990 Gallup poll found that one third of the interviewees did not know whether the United States had fought on the side of the South Vietnamese or the North Vietnamese in the Vietnam War.[51] Historians can work to reduce this public ignorance or inattention by addressing the historical roots of contemporary problems. They can write stories on the background of current affairs and reviews for local newspapers and magazines; they can sponsor conferences for high school teachers and others; they can appear on local radio talk shows and television news programs; they can urge local school boards to introduce foreign languages in the early grades. They can also help Americans understand that events and decisions in far distant lands have had and will continue to have a direct impact upon their daily lives—that their jobs, supermarket and gasoline prices, taxes, interest rates, and more are and have been greatly determined by America's place in the global community.[52]

Historians of American foreign relations can also work to roll back restrictive rules at home and abroad that deny them access to historical documents. If governments can effectively hold documents back, as the United States has done in the last decade by impeding the declassification process, they can manage the questions historians ask and set the terms of historical inquiry. They can, in short, control the writing of history.[53] Historians can also do more collaborative work, bringing together scholars in one book, article, or journal issue to explore topics that might otherwise take a generation to complete, because of limited financial resources, widely dispersed documentary records, restricted access, language barriers, heavy teaching loads, and the like. In short, more diversified training, more languages, more international education, more foreign travel, more engagement with the general public, more access to information, and more collaboration, as well as greater use of all four levels of analysis, are some sensible steps historians of American foreign relations can take to make an already dynamic field even more so.

51 *Newsweek* 112 (8 August 1988): 31; *Washington Post National Weekly Edition*, 30 April – 6 May 1990.
52 A popular attempt is John Maxwell Hamilton, *Main Street America and the Third World* (Cabin John, MD, 1986).
53 My own discussion of this problem has appeared in Paterson, "The Present Danger of Thought Control," *Perspectives* 22 (April 1984): 14–16; and idem, "Thought Control and the Writing of History," in *Freedom at Risk: Secrecy, Censorship, and Repression in the 1980s*, ed. Richard O. Curry (Philadelphia, 1988), 60–68. See also Bruce R. Kuniholm, "Foreign Relations, Public Relations, Accountability, and Understanding," *Perspectives* 28 (May–June 1990): 1, 11–12.

Part Two

The History of American Foreign Relations: Explaining the Field

The chapters in this section illustrate many of the new or revitalized approaches to the history of American foreign relations. As many of the chapters demonstrate, specialists in the field are deriving fresh insights from the social sciences. Ole R. Holsti's contribution surveys the analytical models used by political scientists who specialize in international relations. Subsequent essays by Thomas J. McCormick, Louis A. Pérez, Jr., Stephen Pelz, J. Garry Clifford, and Richard H. Immerman suggest how historians might adapt some of these approaches to their own work. They explore the utility of world systems and dependency theory, balance-of-power paradigms, bureaucratic models, and cognitive psychology. The essays by Melvin Small, Alan K. Henrikson, Michael H. Hunt, and Melvyn P. Leffler also draw on insights from the social sciences. They show how historians are rethinking such traditional topics as public opinion, geography, and ideology, and such conventional categories of analysis as national security.

The current generation of historians of American foreign relations is also learning from specialists in other fields of history. This is true of Akira Iriye, whose contribution examines the cultural dimension of international history. It is also true of scholars who use a corporatist model, as Michael J. Hogan does in his essay here. These scholars have borrowed from economic, business, and public-policy historians, as well as from political scientists, in order to illuminate the linkages between the public and private sectors and the world order that American leaders sought to build.

5

International Relations Models

OLE R. HOLSTI

Universities and professional associations usually are organized in ways that tend to separate scholars in adjoining disciplines and perhaps even to promote stereotypes of each other and their scholarly endeavors. The seemingly natural areas of scholarly convergence between diplomatic historians and political scientists who focus on international relations have been underexploited, but there are also a few welcome signs that this may be changing. These include recent essays suggesting ways in which the two disciplines can contribute to each other; a number of prize-winning dissertations, later turned into books, by political scientists during the past decade that effectively combine political science theories and historical research and materials; collaborative efforts among scholars in the two disciplines; and the appearance of interdisciplinary journals such as *International Security* that provide an outlet for historians and political scientists with common interests.[1]

Another version of this essay originally appeared in the Winter 1989 issue of *Diplomatic History*, copyright 1989 by Scholarly Resources Inc. It is printed here by permission of Scholarly Resources Inc. The author has greatly benefited from helpful comments by Alexander L. George, Joseph Grieco, Michael J. Hogan, Timothy Lomperis, Roy Melbourne, James N. Rosenau, and Andrew M. Scott on earlier drafts of this essay, and also from reading K. J. Holsti, *The Dividing Discipline: Hegemony and Diversity in International Theory* (London, 1985).

1 See, for example, John Lewis Gaddis, "Expanding the Data Base: Historians, Political Scientists, and the Enrichment of Security Studies," *International Security* 12 (Summer 1987): 3–21; John English, "The Second Time Around: Political Scientists Writing History," *Canadian Historical Review* 57 (March 1986): 1–16; Jack S. Levy, "Domestic Politics and War," *Journal of Interdisciplinary History* 18 (Spring 1988): 653–73; Joseph S. Nye, Jr., "International Security Studies," in *American Defense Annual, 1988–1989*, ed. Joseph Kruzel (Lexington, MA, 1988), 231–43; Deborah Welch Larson, *Origins of Containment: A Psychological Explanation* (Princeton, 1985); Timothy Lomperis, *The War Everyone Lost—and Won: America's Intervention in Viet Nam's Twin Struggles* (Washington, 1987); Barry Posen, *The Sources of Military Doctrine: France, Britain, and Germany between the World Wars* (Ithaca, 1984); Paul Gordon Lauren, ed., *Diplomacy: New Approaches to History, Theory, and Policy* (New York, 1979); Richard R. Neustadt and Ernest R. May, *Thinking in Time: The Use of History for Decision-Makers* (New York, 1986); and Irving L. Janis, *Crucial Decisions: Leadership in Policymaking and Crisis Management* (New York, 1989). Many other examples could be cited.

This essay is an effort to contribute further to an exchange of ideas between the two disciplines by describing some of the theories, approaches, and "models" political scientists have used in their research on international relations during recent decades. A brief essay cannot do justice to the entire range of models that may be found in the current literature, if only because the period has witnessed a proliferation of approaches. But perhaps the models described here, when combined with citations of some representative works, will provide diplomatic historians with a useful, if sketchy, map showing some of the more prominent landmarks in a neighboring discipline.

Because "classical realism" is the most venerable and persisting model of international relations, it provides a good starting point and baseline for comparison with competing models. Robert Gilpin may have been engaging in hyperbole when he questioned whether our understanding of international relations has advanced significantly since Thucydides, but one must acknowledge that the latter's analysis of the Peloponnesian War includes concepts that are not foreign to contemporary students of balance-of-power politics.[2]

Following a discussion of classical realism, an examination of "modern realism" will identify the continuities and differences between the two approaches. The essay then turns to several models that challenge one or more core premises of both classical and modern realism. The first two challengers focus on the system level: Global-Society/Complex-Interdependence models and Marxist/World System/Dependency models. Subsequent sections discuss several "decision-making" models, all of which share a skepticism about the adequacy of theories that focus on the structure of the international system while neglecting political processes within units that comprise the system.

Three limitations should be stated at the outset. Each of the three systemic and three decision-making approaches described below is a composite of several models; limitations of space have made it necessary to focus on the common denominators rather than on subtle differences among them. This discussion will also avoid purely methodological issues and debates; for example, what Stanley Hoffmann calls "the battle of the literates versus the numerates."[3] Finally, efforts of some political scientists to develop "formal" or mathematical approaches to international relations are neglected here; such abstract, often ahistorical models are likely to be of limited interest to historians.[4] With these caveats, let

---

2 Robert Gilpin, *Change and War in World Politics* (Cambridge, England, 1981).
3 Stanley Hoffmann, "An American Social Science: International Relations," *Daedalus* 106 (Summer 1977): 54.
4 The British meteorologist Lewis Fry Richardson is generally regarded as the pioneer of

me turn now to classical realism, the first of the systemic models to be discussed in this essay.

There have always been Americans, such as Alexander Hamilton, who viewed international relations from a realist perspective, but its contemporary intellectual roots are largely European. Three important figures of the interwar period probably had the greatest impact on American scholarship: the historian E. H. Carr, the geographer Nicholas Spykman, and the political theorist Hans J. Morgenthau. Other Europeans who have contributed significantly to realist thought include John Herz, Raymond Aron, Hedley Bull, and Martin Wight, while notable Americans of this school include scholars Arnold Wolfers and Norman Graebner, as well as diplomat George F. Kennan, journalist Walter Lippmann, and theologian Reinhold Niebuhr.[5]

Although realists do not constitute a homogeneous school—any more than do any of the others discussed in this essay—most of them share at least five core premises about international relations. To begin with, they view as central questions the causes of war and the conditions of peace. They also regard the structure of the international system as a necessary if not always sufficient explanation for many aspects of international relations. According to classical realists, "structural anarchy," or the absence of a central authority to settle disputes, is the essential feature of the contemporary system, and it gives rise to the "security dilemma":

mathematical approaches to international relations. See his *Statistics of Deadly Quarrels* (Pittsburgh, 1960); and his *Arms and Insecurity* (Chicago, 1960). These are summarized for nonmathematicians in Anatol Rapport, "L. F. Richardson's Mathematical Theory of War," *Journal of Conflict Resolution* 1 (September 1957): 249–99. For a more recent effort see Bruce Bueno de Mesquita, *The War Trap* (New Haven, 1981); idem, "The War Trap Revisited: A Revised Expected Utility Model," *American Political Science Review* 79 (March 1985): 156–77; Bruce Bueno de Mesquita and David Lalman, "Reason and War," ibid. 80 (December 1986): 1113–30; and Seif M. Hussein, Bruce Bueno de Mesquita, and David Lalman, "Modelling War and Peace," ibid. 81 (March 1987): 223–30.

5 Among the works that best represent their realist perspectives are E. H. Carr, *Twenty Years' Crisis* (London, 1939); Nicholas Spykman, *America's Strategy in World Politics: The United States and the Balance of Power* (New York, 1942); Hans J. Morgenthau, *Politics among Nations: The Struggle for Power and Peace*, 5th ed. (New York, 1973); John Herz, *International Politics in the Atomic Age* (New York, 1959); Hedley Bull, *The Anarchical Society: A Study of Order in World Politics* (London, 1977); Raymond Aron, *Peace and War* (Garden City, 1966); Martin Wight, "The Balance of Power and International Order," in *The Bases of International Order: Essays in Honor of C. A. W. Manning*, ed. Alan James (London, 1973), 85–115; Arnold Wolfers, *Discord and Collaboration* (Baltimore, 1962); Norman A. Graebner, *America as a World Power: A Realist Appraisal from Wilson to Reagan* (Wilmington, DE, 1984); George F. Kennan, *American Diplomacy, 1900–1950* (Chicago, 1951); Walter Lippmann, *U.S. Foreign Policy: Shield of the Republic* (Boston, 1943); and Reinhold Niebuhr, *The Children of Light and the Children of Darkness* (New York, 1945).

Ole R. Holsti

in a self-help system one nation's search for security often leaves its current and potential adversaries insecure, any nation that strives for absolute security leaves all others in the system absolutely insecure, and it can provide a powerful incentive for arms races and other types of hostile interactions. Consequently, the question of *relative* capabilities is a crucial factor. Efforts to deal with this central element of the international system constitute the driving force behind the relations of units within the system; those that fail to cope will not survive. Thus, unlike "idealists" or "liberal internationalists," classical realists view conflict as a natural state of affairs rather than as a consequence that can be attributed to historical circumstances, evil leaders, flawed sociopolitical systems, or inadequate international understanding and education.[6]

A third premise that unites classical realists is their focus on geographically based groups as the central actors in the international system. During other periods the primary entities may have been city states or empires, but at least since the Treaties of Westphalia (1648), states have been the dominant units. Classical realists also agree that state behavior is rational. The assumption behind this fourth premise is that states are guided by the logic of the "national interest," usually defined in terms of survival, security, power, and relative capabilities. To Morgenthau, for example, "rational foreign policy minimizes risks and maximizes benefits." Although the national interest may vary according to specific circumstances, the similarity of motives among nations permits the analyst to reconstruct the logic of policymakers in their pursuit of national interests—what Morgenthau called the "rational hypothesis"—and to avoid the fallacies of "concern with motives and concern with ideological preferences."[7]

Finally, the nation-state can also be conceptualized as a *unitary* actor. Because the central problems for states are starkly defined by the nature of the international system, their actions are primarily a response to external rather than domestic political forces. At best, the latter provide very weak explanations for external policy. According to Stephen Krasner, for example, the state "can be treated as an autonomous actor pursuing goals associated with power and the general interest of the society."[8] Classical realists, however, sometimes use domestic politics as a residual category to explain deviations from rational policies.

6   For useful comparisons of realism and liberalism see Joseph Grieco, "Anarchy and the Limits of Cooperation: A Realist Critique of Neoliberal Institutionalism," *International Organization* 42 (Summer 1988): 485–507; and Joseph S. Nye, Jr., "Neorealism and Neoliberalism," *World Politics* 40 (January 1988): 235–51.
7   Morgenthau, *Politics*, 7, 5.
8   Stephen Krasner, *Defending the National Interest: Raw Materials Investment and U.S.*

Realism has been the dominant model of international relations during at least the past five decades, perhaps in part because it seemed to provide a useful framework for understanding World War II and the Cold War. Nevertheless, the classical versions articulated by Morgenthau and others have received a good deal of critical scrutiny. The critics have included scholars who accept the basic premises of realism but who found that in at least four important respects these theories lacked sufficient precision and rigor.

Classical realism has usually been grounded in a pessimistic theory of human nature, either a theological version (for example, Saint Augustine and Reinhold Niebuhr) or a secular one (for example, Machiavelli, Hobbes, and Morgenthau). Egoism and self-interested behavior are not limited to a few evil or misguided leaders, as the idealists would have it, but are basic to *homo politicus* and thus are at the core of a realist theory. But because human nature, if it means anything, is a constant rather than a variable, it is an unsatisfactory explanation for the full range of international relations. If human nature explains war and conflict, what accounts for peace and cooperation? In order to avoid this problem, most modern realists have turned their attention from human nature to the structure of the international system to explain state behavior.

In addition, critics have noted a lack of precision and even contradictions in the way classical realists use such concepts as "power," "national interest," and "balance of power."[9] They also see possible contradictions between the central descriptive and prescriptive elements of classical realism. On the one hand, nations and their leaders "think and act in terms of interests defined as power," but, on the other, statesmen are urged to exercise prudence and self-restraint, as well as to recognize the legitimate national interests of other nations.[10] Power plays a central role in classical realism, but the correlation between the relative power balance and political outcomes is often less than compelling, suggesting the need to enrich analyses with other variables. Moreover, the distinction between "power as capabilities" and "usable options" is especially important in the nuclear age.

Foreign Policy (Princeton, 1978), 33. Krasner's study compares realist, interest-group liberal, and Marxist theories.

9 Inis L. Claude, *Power and International Relations* (New York, 1962); James N. Rosenau, "National Interest," *International Encyclopedia of the Social Sciences* (New York, 1968), 11:34–40; Alexander L. George and Robert Keohane, "The Concept of National Interests: Uses and Limitations," in *Presidential Decision-Making in Foreign Policy: The Effective Use of Information and Advice*, ed. Alexander George (Boulder, 1980), 217–37; Ernst B. Haas, "The Balance of Power: Prescription, Concept or Propaganda," *World Politics* 5 (July 1953): 442–77; Dina A. Zinnes, "An Analytical Study of the Balance of Power," *Journal of Peace Research* 4:3 (1967): 270–88.

10 Morgenthau, *Politics*, 5.

Although classical realists have typically looked to history and political science for insights and evidence, the search for greater precision has led many modern realists to look elsewhere for appropriate models, analogies, metaphors, and insights. The discipline of choice is often economics, from which modern realists have borrowed a number of tools and concepts, including rational choice, expected utility, theories of firms and markets, bargaining theory, and game theory. Contrary to the assertion of some critics, however, modern realists *share* rather than reject the core premises of their classical predecessors.[11]

The quest for precision has yielded a rich harvest of theories and models, and a somewhat less bountiful crop of supporting empirical applications. Drawing in part on game theory, Morton Kaplan described several types of international systems—for example, balance-of-power, loose bipolar, tight bipolar, universal, hierarchical, and a unit-veto system in which any action requires the unanimous approval of all of its members. He then outlined the essential rules that constitute these systems. For example, the rules for a balance-of-power system are: "(1) increase capabilities, but negotiate rather than fight; (2) fight rather than fail to increase capabilities; (3) stop fighting rather than eliminate an essential actor; (4) oppose any coalition or single actor that tends to assume a position of predominance within the system; (5) constrain actors who subscribe to supranational organizational principles; and (6) permit defeated or constrained essential actors to re-enter the system."[12] Richard Rosecrance, J. David Singer, Karl Deutsch, Bruce Russett, and many others, although not necessarily realists, also have developed models that seek to understand international relations by virtue of system-level explanations. Andrew M. Scott's survey of the literature, which yielded a catalogue of propositions about the international system, also illustrates the quest for greater precision in systemic models.[13]

Kenneth Waltz's *Theory of International Politics,* the most prominent effort to develop a rigorous and parsimonious model of "modern" or "structural" realism, has tended to define the terms of a vigorous debate

11   Richard K. Ashley, "The Poverty of Neo-Realism," *International Organization* 38 (Spring 1984): 225–86.
12   Morton Kaplan, *System and Process in International Politics* (New York, 1957).
13   Richard Rosecrance, *Action and Reaction in International Politics* (Boston, 1963); idem, "Bipolarity, Multipolarity, and the Future," *Journal of Conflict Resolution* 10 (September 1966): 314–27; Kenneth Waltz, "The Stability of a Bipolar World," *Daedalus* 93 (Summer 1964): 881–909; J. David Singer, "Inter-Nation Influence: A Formal Model," *American Political Science Review* 57 (June 1963): 420–30; Bruce M. Russett, "Toward a Model of Competitive International Politics," *Journal of Politics* 25 (May 1963): 226–47; Karl Deutsch and J. David Singer, "Multipolar Power Systems and International Stability," *World Politics* 16 (April 1964): 390–406; Andrew Scott, *The Functioning of the International Political System* (New York, 1967).

during the past decade. It follows and builds upon another enormously influential book in which Waltz developed the Rousseauian position that a theory of war must include the system level (what he called the "third image") and not just first (theories of human nature) or second (state attributes) images. Why war? Because there is nothing in the system to prevent it.[14]

Theory of International Relations is grounded in analogies from microeconomics: international politics and foreign policy are analogous to markets and firms. Oligopoly theory is used to illuminate the dynamics of interdependent choice in a self-help anarchical system. Waltz explicitly limits his attention to a structural theory of international systems, eschewing the task of linking it to a theory of foreign policy. Indeed, he doubts that the two can be joined in a single theory and he is highly critical of many system-level analysts, including Morton Kaplan, Stanley Hoffmann, Richard Rosecrance, Karl Deutsch, J. David Singer, and others, charging them with various errors, including "reductionism," that is, defining the system in terms of the attributes or interactions of the units.

In order to avoid reductionism and to gain rigor and parsimony, Waltz erects his theory on the foundations of three core propositions that define the structure of the international system. The first concentrates on the principles by which the system is ordered. The contemporary system is anarchic and decentralized rather than hierarchical; although they differ in many respects, each unit (state) is formally equal.[15] A second defining proposition is the character of the units. An anarchic system is composed of similar sovereign units and therefore the functions that they perform are also similar rather than different; for example, all have the task of providing for their own security. In contrast, a hierarchical system would be characterized by some type of division of labor, as is the case in domestic politics. Finally, there is the distribution of capabilities among units in the system. Although capabilities are a unit-level attribute, the distribution of capabilities is a system-level concept.[16]

A change in any of these elements constitutes a change in system structure. The first element of structure as defined by Waltz is a quasi constant because the ordering principle rarely changes, and the second element drops out of the analysis because the functions of units are similar

14 Kenneth Waltz, *Theory of International Politics* (Reading, MA, 1979); idem, *Man, the State, and War* (New York, 1959).
15 Because Waltz strives for a universal theory that is not limited to any era, he uses the term "unit" to refer to the constituent members of the system. In the contemporary system, these are states, but in order to reflect Waltz's intent more faithfully, the term "unit" is used here.
16 Waltz, *Theory*, 82–101.

as long as the system remains anarchic. Thus, the last of the three attributes, the distribution of capabilities, plays the central role in Waltz's model.

Waltz uses his theory to deduce the central characteristics of international relations. These include some nonobvious propositions about the contemporary international system. For example, with respect to system stability (defined as maintenance of its anarchic character and no consequential variation in the number of major actors) he concludes that: because the present bipolar system reduces uncertainty, it is more stable than alternative structures; interdependence has declined rather than increased during the twentieth century, a tendency that has actually contributed to stability; and the proliferation of nuclear weapons may contribute to rather than erode system stability.[17]

Unlike some system-level models, Waltz's effort to bring rigor and parsimony to realism has stimulated a good deal of further research, but it has not escaped controversy and criticism.[18] Leaving aside highly charged polemics—for example, that Waltz and his supporters are guilty of engaging in a "totalitarian project of global proportions"—most of the vigorous debate has centered on four alleged deficiencies relating to interests and preferences, system change, misallocation of variables between the system and unit levels, and an inability to explain outcomes.[19]

Specifically, a spare structural approach suffers from an inability to identify completely the nature and sources of interests and preferences because these are unlikely to derive solely from the structure of the system. Ideology or domestic considerations may often be at least as important. Consequently, the model is also unable to specify adequately how interests and preferences may change. The three defining characteristics of system structure are too general, moreover, and thus they are not sufficiently sensitive to specify the sources and dynamics of system change. The critics buttress their claim that the model is too static by pointing to Waltz's assertion that there has only been a single structural change in the international system during the past three centuries.

Another drawback is the restrictive definition of system properties, which leads Waltz to misplace, and therefore neglect, elements of international relations that properly belong at the system level. Critics have

17 Waltz, "The Myth of National Interdependence," in *The International Corporation: A Symposium*, ed. Charles P. Kindleberger (Cambridge, MA, 1970), 205–23; idem, "The Spread of Nuclear Weapons: More May Be Better," *Adelphi Papers*, no. 171 (1981).
18 Joseph Grieco, *Cooperation among Nations* (Ithaca, 1990); Steven M. Walt, *The Origin of Alliances* (Ithaca, 1987). The best single source is Robert Keohane, ed., *Neorealism and Its Critics* (New York, 1986).
19 Ashley, "Poverty," 228.

focused on his treatment of the destructiveness of nuclear weapons and interdependence. Waltz labels these as unit-level properties, whereas some of his critics assert that they are in fact attributes of the system.

Finally, the distribution of capabilities explains outcomes in international affairs only in the most general way, falling short of answering the questions that are of central interest to many analysts. For example, the distribution of power at the end of World War II would have enabled one to predict the rivalry that emerged between the United States and the Soviet Union, but it would have been inadequate for explaining the pattern of relations between these two nations—the Cold War rather than withdrawal into isolationism by either or both, a division of the world into spheres of influence, or World War III.[20] In order to do so, it is necessary to explore political processes *within* states—at minimum within the United States and the Soviet Union—as well as *between* them.

Robert Gilpin shares with Waltz the core assumptions of modern realism, but his study of *War and Change in World Politics* also attempts to cope with some of the criticism leveled at Waltz's theory by focusing on the dynamics of system change. Drawing upon both economic and sociological theory, his model is based on five core propositions. The first is that the international system is stable—in a state of equilibrium—if no state believes that it is profitable to attempt to change it. Second, a state will attempt to change the status quo of the international system if the expected benefits outweigh the costs, that is, if there is an expected net gain for the revisionist state. Related to this is the proposition that a state will seek change through territorial, political, and economic expansion until the marginal costs of further change equal or exceed the marginal benefits. Moreover, when an equilibrium between the costs and benefits of further change and expansion is reached, the economic costs of maintaining the status quo (expenditures for military forces, support for allies, etc.) tend to rise faster than the resources needed to do so. An equilibrium exists when no powerful state believes that a change in the system would yield additional net benefits. Finally, if the resulting disequilibrium between the existing governance of the international system and the redistribution of power is not resolved, the system will be changed and a new equilibrium reflecting the distribution of relative capabilities will be established.[21]

Unlike Waltz, Gilpin includes state-level processes in order to explain change. Differential economic growth rates among nations—a structural-systemic level variable—play a vital role in his explanation for the rise

20   I am grateful to Alexander George for this example.
21   Gilpin, *War and Change*, 10–11.

and decline of great powers, but his model also includes propositions about the law of diminishing returns on investments, the impact of affluence on martial spirit and on the ratio of consumption to investment, and structural change in the economy.[22] Table 1 summarizes some key elements of realism. It also contrasts them to two other system-level models of international relations—the Global-Society/Complex-Interdependence and the Marxist/World System/Dependency models, to which we now turn our attention.

Just as there are variants of realism, there are several Global-Society/Complex-Independence (GS/CI) models, but this discussion focuses on two common denominators; they all challenge the first and third core propositions of realism identified earlier, asserting that inordinate attention to the war/peace issue and the nation-state renders it an increasingly anachronistic model of global relations.[23] The agenda of critical problems confronting states has been vastly expanded during the twentieth century. Attention to the issues of war and peace is by no means misdirected, according to proponents of a GS/CI perspective, but concerns for welfare, modernization, the environment, and the like are today no less potent sources of motivation and action. The diffusion of knowledge and technology, combined with the globalization of communications, has vastly increased popular expectations. The resulting demands have outstripped resources and the ability of existing institutions—notably the sovereign nation-state—to cope effectively with them. Interdependence arises from an inability of even the most powerful states to cope, or to do so unilaterally or at acceptable levels of cost and risk, with issues ranging from trade to AIDS, from immigration to environmental threats.

Paralleling the widening agenda of critical issues is the expansion of actors whose behavior can have a significant impact beyond national boundaries; indeed, the cumulative effects of their actions can have profound consequences for the international system. Thus, although nation-states continue to be important international actors, they possess a declining ability to control their own destinies. The aggregate effect of actions by multitudes of nonstate actors can have potent effects that

---

22 Ibid., chap. 4. Gilpin's thesis appears similar in a number of respects to Paul Kennedy, *The Rise and Fall of the Great Powers: Economic Change and Military Conflict from 1500 to 2000* (New York, 1987).

23 Robert Keohane and Joseph S. Nye, Jr., *Power and Interdependence* (Boston, 1977); Edward Morse, *Modernization and the Transformation of International Relations* (New York, 1976); James N. Rosenau, *The Study of Global Interdependence* (London, 1980); Richard Mansbach and John Vasquez, *In Search of Theory: A New Paradigm for Global Politics* (New York, 1981); Andrew M. Scott, *The Dynamics of Interdependence* (Chapel Hill, 1982); James N. Rosenau, *Turbulence in World Politics* (Princeton, 1990).

Table 1. *Three models of the international system*

	Realism	Global Society	Marxism
Type of model	Classical: descriptive and normative Modern: deductive	Descriptive and normative	Descriptive and normative
Central problems	Causes of war Conditions of peace	Broad agenda of social, economic, and environmental issues arising from gap between demands and resources	Inequality and exploitation Uneven development
Conception of current international system	Structural anarchy	Global society Complex interdependence (structure varies by issue-area)	World Capitalist system
Key actors	Geographically based units (tribes, city-states, nation-states, etc.)	Highly permeable nation-states *plus* a broad range of non-state actors, including IOs, IGOs, NGOs, and individuals	Classes and their agents
Central motivations	National interest Security Power	Human needs and wants	Class interests
Loyalties	To geographically based groups (from tribes to nation-states)	Loyalties to nation-state declining To emerging global values and institutions that transcend those of the nation-state and/or to sub-national groups	To class values and interests that transcend those of the nation-state
Central processes	Search for security and survival	Aggregate effects of decisions by national and non-national actors How units (not limited to nation-states) cope with a growing agenda of threats and opportunities arising from human wants	Modes of production and exchange International division of labor in a world capitalist system

Table 1 (*continued*)

	Realism	Global society	Marxism
Likelihood of system transforation	Low (basic structural elements of system have revealed an ability to persist despite many other kinds of changes)	High in the direction of the model (owing to the rapid pace of technological change, etc.)	High in the direction of the model (owing to inherent contradictions within the world capitalist system)
Sources of theory, insights, and evidence	Politics History Economics (especially "modern" realists)	Broad range of social sciences Natural and technological sciences	Marxist-Leninist theory (several variants)

transcend political boundaries. These may include such powerful or highly visible nonstate organizations as Exxon, the Organization of Petroleum Exporting Countries, or the Palestine Liberation Organization. On the other hand, the cumulative effects of decisions by less powerful or less visible actors may also have profound international consequences. For example, decisions by thousands of individuals, mutual funds, banks, pension funds, and other financial institutions to sell securities on 19 October 1987 not only resulted in an unprecedented "crash" on Wall Street but also within hours its consequences were felt throughout the entire global financial system. Governments might take such actions as loosening credit or even closing exchanges, but they were largely unable to contain the effects of the panic.

The widening agenda of critical issues, most of which lack a purely national solution, has also led to creation of new actors that transcend political boundaries; for example, international organizations, transnational organizations, nongovernment organizations, multinational corporations, and the like. Thus, not only does an exclusive focus on the war/peace issue fail to capture the complexities of contemporary international life but it also blinds the analyst to the institutions, processes, and norms that permit cooperation and significantly mitigate some features of an anarchic system. In short, according to GS/CI perspectives, an adequate understanding of the emergent global system must recognize that no single model is likely to be sufficient for all issues, and that if it restricts attention to the manner in which states deal with traditional security concerns, it is more likely to obfuscate than clarify the realities of contemporary world affairs.

The GS/CI models have several important virtues. They recognize that international behavior and outcomes arise from a multiplicity of motives, not merely security, at least if security is defined solely in military or strategic terms. They also alert us to the fact that important international processes and conditions originate not only in the actions of nation-states but also in the aggregated behavior of other actors. These models not only enable the analyst to deal with a broader agenda of critical issues but, more important, they force one to contemplate a much richer menu of demands, processes, and outcomes than would be derived from power-centered realist models. Stated differently, GS/CI models are more sensitive to the possibility that politics of trade, currency, immigration, health, the environment, and the like may significantly and systematically differ from those typically associated with security issues.

Some GS/CI analysts, however, underestimate the potency of nationalism and the durability of the nation-state. Two decades ago one of them wrote that "the nation is declining in its importance as a political unit to which allegiances are attached."[24] Objectively, nationalism may be an anachronism but, for better or worse, powerful loyalties are still attached to nation-states. The suggestion that, because even some well-established nations have experienced independence movements among ethnic, cultural, or religious minorities, the sovereign territorial state may be in decline is not wholly persuasive. Indeed, that evidence perhaps points to precisely the opposite conclusion: In virtually every region of the world there are groups that seek to create or restore geographically based entities in which its members may enjoy the status and privileges associated with sovereign territorial statehood. The dramatic events of 1989 in Eastern Europe and in several republics within the Soviet Union, as well as in Palestine, Sri Lanka, Eritrea, Afghanistan, and elsewhere, seem to indicate that obituaries for nationalism may be somewhat premature.

The notion that such powerful nonnational actors as major multinational corporations (MNCs) will soon transcend the nation-state seems equally premature. International drug rings do appear capable of challenging and perhaps even dominating national authorities in Colombia and Panama. But the pattern of outcomes in confrontations between

---

24 Rosenau, "National Interest," 39. A more recent statement of this view may be found in Richard Rosecrance, *The Rise of the Trading State* (New York, 1986). See also John H. Herz, "The Rise and Demise of the Territorial State," *World Politics* 9 (July 1957): 473–93; and his reconsideration in "The Territorial State Revisited: Reflections on the Future of the Nation-State," *Polity* 1 (Fall 1968): 12–34.

MNCs and states, including cases involving major expropriations of corporate properties, indicate that even relatively weak nations are not always the hapless pawns of the MNCs. Case studies by Joseph Grieco and Gary Gereffi, among others, indicate that MNC-state relations yield a wide variety of outcomes.[25]

Underlying the GS/CI critique of realist models is the view that the latter are too wedded to the past and are thus incapable of dealing adequately with change. At least for the present, however, even if global dynamics arise from multiple sources (including nonstate actors), the actions of nation-states and their agents would appear to remain the major sources of change in the international system. The last group of systemic models to be considered in this essay, the Marxist/World System/Dependency (M/WS/D) models, downplays the role of the nation-state even further.

As in other parts of this essay, many of the distinctions among M/WS/D models are lost by treating them together and by focusing on their common features, but in the brief description possible here only common denominators will be presented. These models challenge both the war/peace and state-centered features of realism, but they do so in ways that differ sharply from challenges of GS/CI models.[26] Rather than focusing on war and peace, these models direct attention to quite different issues, including uneven development, poverty, and exploitation within and between nations. These conditions, arising from the dynamics of the modes of production and exchange, are basic and they must be incorporated into any analysis of intra- and inter-nation conflict.

At a superficial level, according to adherents of these models, what exists today may be described as an international system—a system of nation-states. More fundamentally, however, the key groups within and between nations are classes and their agents: As Immanuel Wallerstein

25 Joseph Grieco, *Between Dependence and Autonomy: India's Experience with the International Computer Industry* (Berkeley, 1984); Gary Gereffi, *The Pharmaceutical Industry and Dependency in the Third World* (Princeton, 1983).

26 Johan Galtung, "A Structural Theory of Imperialism," *Journal of Peace Research* 8:2 (1971): 81–117; James Cockroft, André Gunder Frank, and Dale L. Johnson, *Dependence and Under-development* (New York, 1972); Immanuel Wallerstein, *The Modern World-System* (New York, 1974); idem, "The Rise and Future Demise of the World Capitalist System: Concepts for Comparative Analysis," *Comparative Studies in Society and History* 16 (September 1974): 387–415; Christopher Chase-Dunn, "Comparative Research on World System Characteristics," *International Studies Quarterly* 23 (December 1979): 601–23; idem, "Interstate System and Capitalist World-Economy: One Logic or Two," ibid. 25 (March 1981): 19–42; J. Kubalkova and A. A. Cruickshank, *Marxism and International Relations* (Oxford, 1985). Debates among advocates of these models are illustrated in Robert A. Denemark and Kenneth O. Thomas, "The Brenner-Wallerstein Debates," *International Studies Quarterly* 32 (March 1988): 47–66.

put it, "in the nineteenth and twentieth centuries there has been only one world system in existence, the world capitalist world-economy."[27] The "world capitalist system" is characterized by a highly unequal division of labor between the periphery and core. Those at the periphery are essentially the drawers of water and the hewers of wood whereas the latter appropriate the surplus of the entire world economy. This critical feature of the world system not only gives rise to and perpetuates a widening rather than narrowing gap between the wealthy core and poor periphery but also to a dependency relationship from which the latter are unable to break loose. Moreover, the class structure within the core, characterized by a growing gap between capital and labor, is faithfully reproduced in the periphery so that elites there share with their counterparts in the core an interest in perpetuating the system. Thus, in contrast to realist theories, M/WS/D models encompass and integrate theories of both the global and domestic arenas.

M/WS/D models have been subjected to trenchant critiques.[28] The state, nationalism, security dilemmas, and related concerns essentially drop out of these analyses; they are at the theoretical periphery rather than at the core: "Capitalism was from the beginning an affair of the world-economy," Wallerstein asserts, "not of nation-states."[29] A virtue of many M/WS/D models is that they take a long historical perspective on world affairs rather than merely focusing on contemporary issues. Yet, by neglecting nation-states and the dynamics arising from their efforts to deal with security in an anarchical system—or at best relegating these actors and motivations to a minor role—M/WS/D models lose much of their appeal. Models of world affairs during the past few centuries that fail to give the nation-state a central role seem as deficient as analyses of *Hamlet* that neglect the central character and his motivations.

Second, the concept of "world capitalist system" is central to these models, but its relevance for the late twentieth century can be questioned. Whether this term accurately describes the world of the 1880s could be debated, but its declining analytical utility or even descriptive accuracy for international affairs of the 1980s seems clear. Thus, one can question Wallerstein's assertion that "there are today no socialist systems in the world economy any more than there are feudal systems because there is only *one world system*. It is a world-economy and it is *by definition*

---

27 Wallerstein, "Rise and Future Demise," 390.

28 Tony Smith, "The Underdevelopment of Development Literature: The Case of Dependency Theory," *World Politics* 31 (January 1979): 247–88; Aristide Zolberg, "Origins of the Modern World System: A Missing Link," ibid. 33 (January 1981): 253–81.

29 Wallerstein, "Rise and Future Demise," 401.

capitalist in form."[30] Where within a system so defined do we locate the Soviet Union or Eastern Europe? This area includes enough "rich" industrial nations that it hardly seems to belong in the periphery. Yet to place these states in the core of a "world capitalist system" would require terminological and conceptual gymnastics of a high order. Does it increase our analytical capabilities to describe the Soviet Union and East European countries as "state capitalists"? Where do we locate China in this conception of the system? How do we explain dynamics within the "periphery," or the differences between rapid-growth Asian nations such as South Korea, Taiwan, or Singapore, and their slow-growth neighbors in Bangladesh, North Korea, and the Philippines? The inclusion of a third structural position—the "semi-periphery"—does not wholly answer these questions.

Third, M/WS/D models have considerable difficulty in explaining relations between noncapitalist nations—for example, between the Soviet Union and its East European neighbors or China—much less outright conflict between them. Indeed, advocates of these models have usually restricted their attention to West-South relations, eschewing analyses of East-East or East-South relations. Does one gain greater and more general analytical power by using the lenses and language of Marxism or of realism to describe relations between dominant and lesser nations; for example, the Soviet Union and Eastern Europe (at least until the collapse of Communist regimes throughout much of Eastern Europe in 1989), the Soviet Union and India or other Third World nations, China and Vietnam, India and Sri Lanka, or Vietnam and Kampuchea? Are these relationships better described and understood in terms of such M/WS/D categories as "class" or such realist ones as "relative capabilities"?

Finally, the earlier observations about the persistence of nationalism as an element of international relations seem equally appropriate here. Perhaps national loyalties can be dismissed as prime examples of "false consciousness," but even in areas that have experienced almost two generations of one-party Communist rule, as in Poland, evidence that feelings of solidarity with workers in the Soviet Union or other nations have replaced nationalist sentiments among Polish workers is in short supply. Indeed, the collapse of Marxist-Leninist regimes in Eastern Europe, combined with the possibility of receding Soviet influence in the area, gives rise to fears that the region may be wracked by conflicts originating in historic national rivalries and hatreds.

Many advocates of realism recognize that it cannot offer fine-grained analyses of foreign policy behavior and, as noted earlier, Waltz denies

30   Ibid., 412 (emphasis added).

that it is desirable or even possible to combine theories of international relations and foreign policy. Decision-making models challenge the premises that it is fruitful to conceptualize the nation as a unitary rational actor whose behavior can adequately be explained by reference to the system structure—the second, fourth, and fifth realist propositions identified earlier—because individuals, groups, and organizations acting in the name of the state are also sensitive to pressures and constraints other than international ones, including elite maintenance, electoral politics, public opinion, pressure group activities, ideological preferences, and bureaucratic politics. Such core concepts as "the national interest" are not defined solely by the international system, much less by its structure alone, but they are also likely to reflect elements within the domestic political arena. Thus, rather than assuming with the realists that the state can be conceptualized as a "black box"—that the domestic political processes are both hard to comprehend and quite unnecessary for explaining its external behavior—decision-making analysts believe one must indeed take these internal processes into account, with special attention directed at decision makers and their "definitions of the situation."[31] To reconstruct how nations deal with each other, it is necessary to view the situation through the eyes of those who act in the name of the nation-state: decision makers and the group and bureaucratic-organizational contexts within which they act. Table 2 provides an overview of three major types of decision-making models that form the subject of the remainder of this essay, beginning with the bureaucratic-organizational models.[32]

Traditional models of complex organizations and bureaucracy emphasized the positive contributions to be expected from a division of labor, hierarchy, and centralization, coupled with expertise, rationality, and obedience. Such models assumed that clear boundaries should be maintained between politics and decision making, on the one hand, and administration and implementation on the other. Following pioneering works by Chester I. Barnard, Herbert Simon, James G. March and Simon,

---

31   Richard C. Snyder, H. W. Bruck, and Burton Sapin, eds., *Foreign Policy Decision-Making* (New York, 1962).
32   There are also models that link types of politics with foreign policy. Two of the more prominent twentieth-century versions—the Leninist and Wilsonian—have been effectively criticized by Waltz in *Man, the State, and War.* Although space limitations preclude a discussion here, for some recent and interesting research along these lines see, among others, Rudolph J. Rummel, "Libertarianism and Violence," *Journal of Conflict Resolution* 27 (March 1983): 27–71; Michael Doyle, "Liberalism and World Politics," *American Political Science Review* 80 (December 1986): 1151–70; idem, "Kant, Liberal Legacies, and Foreign Affairs," *Philosophy and Public Affairs* 12 (Winter 1983): 205–35; and Thomas R. Dye and Harmon Ziegler, "Socialism and Militarism," *PS: Political Science and Politics* 22 (December 1989): 800–13.

Table 2. *Three models of decision making*

	Bureaucratic politics	Group dynamics	Individual decision making
Conceptualization of decision making	Decision making as the result of bargaining within bureaucratic organizations	Decision making as the product of group interaction	Decision making as the result of individual choice
Premises	Central organizational values are imperfectly internalized Organizational behavior is political behavior Structure and SOPs affect substance and quality of decisions	Most decisions are made by small elite groups Group is different than the sum of its members Group dynamics affect substance and quality of decisions	Importance of subjective appraisal (definition of the situation) and cognitive processes (information processing, etc.)
Constraints on rational decision making	Imperfect information, resulting from: centralization, hierarchy, and specialization Organizational inertia Conflict between individual and organizational utilities Bureaucratic politics and bargaining dominate decision making and implementation of decisions	Groups may be more effective for some tasks, less for others Pressures for conformity Risk-taking propensity of groups (controversial) Quality of leadership "Groupthink"	Cognitive limits on rationality Information processing distorted by cognitive consistency dynamics (unmotivated biases) Systematic and motivated biases in causal analysis Individual differences in abilities related to decision making (e.g., problem-solving ability tolerance of ambiguity, defensiveness and anxiety, information seeking, etc.) Cognitive dissonance
Sources of theory, insights, and evidence	Organization theory Sociology of bureaucracies Bureaucratic politics	Social psychology Sociology of small groups	Cognitive psychology Dynamic psychology

and others, more recent theories depict organizations quite differently.[33] The central premise is that decision making in bureaucratic organizations is not constrained only by the legal and formal norms that are intended to enhance the rational and eliminate the capricious aspects of bureaucratic behavior. Rather, all (or most) complex organizations are seen as generating serious "information pathologies."[34] There is an *emphasis* upon rather than a denial of the political character of bureaucracies, as well as on other "informal" aspects of organizational behavior. Complex organizations are composed of individuals and units with conflicting perceptions, values, and interests that may arise from parochial self-interest ("what is best for my bureau is also best for my career"), and also from different perceptions of issues arising ineluctably from a division of labor ("where you stand depends on where you sit"). Organizational norms and memories, prior policy commitments, normal organizational inertia, routines, and standard operating procedures may shape and perhaps distort the structuring of problems, channeling of information, use of expertise, and implementation of executive decisions. The consequences of bureaucratic politics within the executive branch or within the government as a whole may significantly constrain the manner in which issues are defined, the range of options that may be considered, and the manner in which executive decisions are implemented by subordinates. Consequently, organizational decision making is essentially political in character, dominated by bargaining for resources, roles and missions, and by compromise rather than analysis.[35]

Perhaps owing to the dominant position of the realist perspective, most students of foreign policy have only recently incorporated bureaucratic-organizational models and insights into their analyses. An ample literature of case studies on budgeting, weapons acquisitions, military doctrine, and similar situations confirms that foreign and defense policy bureaucracies rarely conform to the Weberian "ideal type" of rational organization.[36] Some analysts assert that crises may provide the motivation and

---

33 Chester Barnard, *Functions of the Executive* (Cambridge, MA, 1938); Herbert Simon, *Administrative Behavior: A Study of Decision-Making Processes in Administrative Organization* (New York, 1957); James G. March and Herbert Simon, *Organizations* (New York, 1958).

34 Harold Wilensky, *Organizational Intelligence: Knowledge and Policy in Government and Industry* (New York, 1967).

35 Henry A. Kissinger, "Conditions of World Order," *Daedalus* 95 (Spring 1960): 503–29; Graham T. Allison, *Essence of Decision: Explaining the Cuban Missile Crisis* (Boston, 1971); Graham T. Allison and Morton Halperin, "Bureaucratic Politics: A Paradigm and Some Policy Implications," *World Politics* 24 (Supplement 1972): 40–79; Morton Halperin, *Bureaucratic Politics and Foreign Policy* (Washington, 1974).

36 The literature is huge. See, for example, Samuel R. Williamson, Jr., *The Politics of Grand Strategy: Britain and France Prepare for War, 1904–1914* (Cambridge, MA,

means for reducing some of the nonrational aspects of bureaucratic behavior: crises are likely to push decisions to the top of the organization
where a higher quality of intelligence is available; information is more
likely to enter the top of the hierarchy directly, reducing the distorting
effects of information processing through several levels of the organization; and broader, less parochial values may be invoked. Short decision
time in crises reduces the opportunities for decision making by bargaining,
log rolling, incrementalism, lowest-common-denominator values, "mud-
dling through," and the like.[37]

Even studies of international crises from a bureaucratic-organizational
perspective, however, are not uniformly sanguine about decision making
in such circumstances. Graham T. Allison's analysis of the Cuban missile
crisis identified several critical bureaucratic malfunctions concerning dis-
persal of American aircraft in Florida, the location of the naval blockade,
and grounding of weather-reconnaissance flights from Alaska that might
stray over the Soviet Union. Richard Neustadt's study of two crises
involving the United States and Great Britain revealed significant misperceptions of each other's interests and policy processes. And an examination of three American nuclear alerts found substantial gaps in
understanding and communication between policymakers and the military leaders who were responsible for implementing the alerts.[38]

Critics of some organizational-bureaucratic models and the studies
employing them have directed their attention to several points.[39] They
point out, for instance, that the emphasis on bureaucratic bargaining fails
to differentiate adequately between the positions of the participants. In
the American system, the president is not just another player in a complex

1969); Paul Gordon Lauren, *Diplomats and Bureaucrats: The First International Responses to Twentieth-Century Diplomacy in France and Germany* (Stanford, 1975); and Posen, *Sources of Military Doctrine.*

37 Wilensky, *Organizational Intelligence;* Theodore Lowi, *The End of Liberalism: Ideology, Policy and the Crisis of Public Authority* (New York, 1969); Sidney Verba, "Assumptions of Rationality and Non-Rationality in Models of the International System," *World Politics* 14 (October 1961): 93–117.

38 Charles F. Hermann, "Some Consequences of Crises Which Limit the Viability of Organizations," *Administrative Science Quarterly* 8 (June 1963): 61–82; Allison, *Essence;* Richard Neustadt, *Alliance Politics* (New York, 1970); Scott Sagan, "Nuclear Alerts and Crisis Management," *International Security* 9 (Spring 1985): 99–139.

39 Robert Rothstein, *Planning, Prediction, and Policy-Making in Foreign Affairs: Theory and Practice* (Boston, 1972); Stephen D. Krasner, "Are Bureaucracies Important? (Or Allison Wonderland)" *Foreign Policy* 7 (Summer 1972): 159–70; Robert J. Art, "Bureaucratic Politics and American Foreign Policy: A Critique," *Policy Sciences* 4 (December 1973): 467–90; Desmond J. Ball, "The Blind Men and the Elephant: A Critique of Bureaucratic Politics Theory," *Australian Outlook* 28 (April 1974): 71–92; Amos Perlmutter, "Presidential Political Center and Foreign Policy," *World Politics* 27 (October 1974): 87–106.

bureaucratic game. Not only must he ultimately decide but he also selects who the other players will be, a process that may be crucial in shaping the ultimate decisions. If General Matthew Ridgway and Attorney General Robert Kennedy played key roles in the American decisions not to intervene in Indochina in 1954 or not to bomb Cuba in 1962, it was because Presidents Eisenhower and Kennedy chose to accept their advice rather than that of other officials. Also, the conception of bureaucratic bargaining tends to emphasize its nonrational elements to the exclusion of genuine intellectual differences that may be rooted in broader concerns—including disagreements on what national interests, if any, are at stake in a situation—rather than narrow parochial interests. Indeed, properly managed, decision processes that promote and legitimize "multiple advocacy" among officials may facilitate high-quality decisions.[40]

These models may be especially useful for understanding the slippage between executive decisions and foreign policy actions that may arise during implementation, but they may be less valuable for explaining the decisions themselves. Allison's study of the Cuban missile crisis does not indicate an especially strong correlation between bureaucratic roles and evaluations of the situation or policy recommendations, as predicted by his "Model III" (bureaucratic politics), and recently published transcripts of deliberations during the crisis do not offer more supporting evidence for that model.[41] Yet Allison does present some compelling evidence concerning policy implementation that casts considerable doubt on the adequacy of "Model I" (the traditional realist conception of the unitary rational actor).

Another decision-making model used by some political scientists supplements bureaucratic-organizational models by narrowing the field of view to top policymakers. This approach lends itself well to investigations of foreign policy decisions, which are usually made in a small-group context. Some analysts have drawn upon sociology and social psychology to assess the impact of various types of group dynamics on decision making.[42] Underlying these models are the premises that the group is not

---

40 Alexander L. George, "The Case for Multiple Advocacy in Making Foreign Policy," *American Political Science Review* 66 (September 1972): 751–85, 791–95.
41 David A. Welch and James G. Blight, "The Eleventh Hour of the Cuban Missile Crisis: An Introduction to the ExComm Transcripts," *International Security* 12 (Winter 1987/88): 5–29; McGeorge Bundy and James G. Blight, "October 27, 1962: Transcripts of the Meetings of the ExComm," ibid., 30–92. See also James G. Blight and David A. Welch, *On the Brink: Americans and Soviets Reexamine the Cuban Missile Crisis* (New York, 1989).
42 Joseph de Rivera, *The Psychological Dimension of Foreign Policy* (Columbus, OH, 1968); Glenn D. Paige, *The Korean Decision, June 24–30* (New York, 1968); Irving L. Janis, *Victims of Groupthink: A Psychological Study of Foreign Policy Decisions and Fiascos* (Boston, 1972); idem, *Groupthink: Psychological Studies of Policy De-*

merely the sum of its members (thus decisions emerging from the group are likely to be different from what a simple aggregation of individual preferences and abilities might suggest), and that group dynamics, the interactions among its members, can have a significant impact on the substance and quality of decisions.

Groups often perform better than individuals in coping with complex tasks owing to diverse perspectives and talents, an effective division of labor, and high-quality debates centering on evaluations of the situation and policy recommendations for dealing with it. Groups may also provide decision makers with emotional and other types of support that may facilitate coping with complex problems. Conversely, they may exert pressures for conformity to group norms, thereby inhibiting the search for information and policy options or cutting it off prematurely, ruling out the legitimacy of some options, curtailing independent evaluation, and suppressing some forms of intragroup conflict that might serve to clarify goals, values, and options. Classic experiments by the psychologist Solomon Asch revealed the extent to which group members will suppress their beliefs and judgments when faced with a majority adhering to the contrary view, even a counterfactual one.[43]

Drawing on a series of historical case studies, social psychologist Irving L. Janis has identified a different variant of group dynamics, which he labels "groupthink" to distinguish it from the more familiar type of conformity pressure on "deviant" members of the group.[44] Janis challenges the conventional wisdom that strong cohesion among the members of a group invariably enhances performance. Under certain conditions, strong cohesion can markedly degrade the group's performance in de-

cisions and Fiascos (Boston, 1982); Margaret G. Hermann, Charles F. Hermann, and Joe D. Hagan, "How Decision Units Shape Foreign Policy Behavior," in *New Directions in the Study of Foreign Policy,* ed. Charles F. Hermann, Charles W. Kegley, and James N. Rosenau (London, 1987), 309–36; Charles F. Hermann and Margaret G. Hermann, "Who Makes Foreign Policy Decisions and How: An Empirical Inquiry," *International Studies Quarterly* 33 (December 1989): 361–88; Philip D. Stewart, Margaret G. Hermann, and Charles F. Hermann, "The Politburo and Foreign Policy: Toward a Model of Soviet Decision Making" (Paper presented at the annual meeting of International Society for Political Psychology, Amsterdam, 1986).

43 Leon Festinger, "A Theory of Social Comparison Processes," in *Small Groups: Studies in Social Interaction,* ed. A. Paul Hare, Edgar F. Borgatta, and Robert F. Bales (New York, 1965), 163–87; Asch, "Effects of Group Pressures upon Modification and Distortion of Judgment," in *Group Dynamics: Research and Theory,* ed. Dorwin Cartwright and Alvin Zander (Evanston, IL, 1953), 151–62.

44 Janis, *Victims;* idem, *Groupthink.* See also Philip Tetlock, "Identifying Victims of Groupthink from Public Statements of Decision Makers," *Journal of Personality and Social Psychology* 37 (August 1979): 1314–24; and the critique in Lloyd Etheredge, *Can Governments Learn? American Foreign Policy and Central American Revolutions* (New York, 1985), 112–14.

cision making. Thus, the members of a cohesive group may, as a means of dealing with the stresses of having to cope with consequential problems and in order to bolster self-esteem, increase the frequency and intensity of face-to-face interaction. This results in a greater identification with the group and less competition within it. The group dynamics of what Janis calls "concurrence seeking" may displace or erode reality-testing and sound information processing and judgment. As a consequence, groups may be afflicted by unwarranted feelings of optimism and invulnerability, stereotyped images of adversaries, and inattention to warnings. Janis's analyses of both "successful" (the Marshall Plan, the Cuban missile crisis) and "unsuccessful" (Munich Conference of 1938, Pearl Harbor, the Bay of Pigs invasion) cases indicate that "groupthink" or other decision-making pathologies are not inevitable, and he develops some guidelines for avoiding them.[45]

Still other decision-making analysts focus on the individual. Many approaches to the policymaker emphasize the gap between the demands of the classical model of rational decision making and the substantial body of theory and evidence about various constraints that come into play in even relatively simple choice situations.[46] The more recent perspectives, drawing upon cognitive psychology, go well beyond some of the earlier formulations that drew upon psychodynamic theories to identify various types of psychopathologies among political leaders: paranoia, authoritarianism, the displacement of private motives on public objects, etc.[47] These more recent efforts to include information-processing behavior of the individual decision maker in foreign policy analyses have been directed at the cognitive and motivational constraints that, in varying degrees, affect the decision-making performance of "normal" rather than pathological subjects. Thus, attention is directed to all leaders, not merely those, such as Hitler or Stalin, who display evidence of clinical abnormalities.

The major challenges to the classical model have focused in various ways on limited human capabilities for performing the tasks required by objectively rational decision making. The cognitive constraints on ra-

45 Janis, *Groupthink*, 260–76; idem, *Crucial Decisions*, 231–64.
46 For a review of the vast literature see Robert Abelson and A. Levi, "Decision Making and Decision Theory," in *Handbook of Social Psychology*, 3d ed., vol. 1, ed. Gardner Lindzey and Elliot Aronson (New York, 1985). The relevance of psychological models and evidence for international relations are most fully discussed in Robert Jervis, *Perception and Misperception in International Politics* (Princeton, 1976); John Steinbruner, *The Cybernetic Theory of Decision: New Dimensions of Political Analysis* (Princeton, 1974); and Robert Axelrod, *The Structure of Decision: The Cognitive Maps of Political Elites* (Princeton, 1976).
47 See, for example, Harold Lasswell, *Psychopathology and Politics* (Chicago, 1931).

tionality include limits on the individual's capacity to receive, process, and assimilate information about the situation; an inability to identify the entire set of policy alternatives; fragmentary knowledge about the consequences of each option; and an inability to order preferences on a single utility scale.[48] These have given rise to several competing conceptions of the decision maker and his or her strategies for dealing with complexity, uncertainty, incomplete or contradictory information and, paradoxically, information overload. They variously characterize the decision maker as a problem solver, naive or intuitive scientist, cognitive balancer, dissonance avoider, information seeker, cybernetic information processor, and reluctant decision maker.

Three of these conceptions seem especially relevant for foreign policy analysis. The first views the decision maker as a "bounded rationalist" who seeks satisfactory rather than optimal solutions. As Herbert Simon has put it, "the capacity of the human mind for formulating and solving complex problems is very small compared with the size of the problem whose solution is required for objectively rational behavior in the real world—or even a reasonable approximation of such objective rationality."[49] Moreover, it is not practical for the decision maker to seek optimal choices; for example, because of the costs of searching for information. Related to this is the more recent concept of the individual as a "cognitive miser," one who seeks to simplify complex problems and to find short cuts to problem solving and decision making.

Another approach is to look at the decision maker as an "error prone intuitive scientist" who is likely to commit a broad range of inferential mistakes. Thus, rather than emphasizing the limits on search, information processing, and the like, this conception views the decision maker as the victim of flawed heuristics or decision rules who uses data poorly. There are tendencies to underuse rate data in making judgments, believe in the "law of small numbers," underuse diagnostic information, overweight low probabilities and underweight high ones, and violate other requirements of consistency and coherence. These deviations from classical decision theory are traced to the psychological principles that govern perceptions of problems and evaluations of options.[50]

The final perspective I will mention emphasizes the forces that dominate the policymaker, forces that will not or cannot be controlled.[51] Decision

48   March and Simon, *Organizations*, 113.
49   Simon, *Administrative Behavior*, 198.
50   Amos Tversky and Daniel Kahneman, "The Framing of Decisions and the Psychology of Choice," *Science* 211 (30 January 1981): 453–58; idem, "On the Psychology of Prediction," *Psychological Review* 80 (July 1973): 251–73; Daniel Kahneman, Paul Slovic, and Amos Tversky, *Judgment under Uncertainty: Heuristics and Biases* (Cambridge, England, 1982).
51   Irving L. Janis and Leon Mann, *Decision Making: A Psychological Analysis of Conflict,*

makers are not merely rational calculators; important decisions generate conflict, and a reluctance to make irrevocable choices often results in behavior that reduces the quality of decisions. These models direct the analyst's attention to policymakers' belief systems, images of relevant actors, perceptions, information-processing strategies, heuristics, certain personality traits (ability to tolerate ambiguity, cognitive complexity, etc.), and their impact on decision-making performance.

Despite this diversity of perspectives and the difficulty of choosing between cognitive and motivational models, there has been some convergence on several types of constraints that may affect decision processes.[52] One involves the consequences of efforts to achieve cognitive consistency on perceptions and information processing. Several kinds of systematic bias have been identified in both experimental and historical studies. Policymakers have a propensity to assimilate and interpret information in ways that conform to rather than challenge existing beliefs, preferences, hopes, and expectations. Frequently they deny the need to confront tradeoffs between values by persuading themselves that an option will satisfy all of them. And finally, they indulge in rationalizations to bolster the selected option while denigrating those that were not selected.

An extensive literature on styles of attribution has revealed several types of systematic bias in causal analysis. Perhaps the most important for foreign policy analysis is the basic attribution error—a tendency to explain the adversary's behavior in terms of his characteristics (for example, inherent aggressiveness or hostility) rather then in terms of the context or situation, while attributing one's own behavior to the latter (for example, legitimate security needs arising from a dangerous and uncertain environment) rather than to the former. A somewhat related type of double standard has been noted by George Kennan: "Now is it our view that we should take account only of their [Soviet] capabilities, disregarding their intentions, but we should expect them to take account only of our supposed intentions, disregarding our capabilities?"[53]

Analysts also have illustrated the effect on decisions of policymakers' assumptions about order and predictability in the environment. Whereas

Choice, and Commitment (New York, 1977); Miriam Steiner, "The Search for Order in a Disorderly World: Worldviews and Prescriptive Decision Paradigms," *International Organization* 37 (Summer 1983): 373–414; Richard Ned Lebow, *Between Peace and War* (Baltimore, 1981).

52 Donald Kinder and J. R. Weiss, "In Lieu of Rationality: Psychological Perspectives on Foreign Policy," *Journal of Conflict Resolution* 22 (December 1978): 707–35; Ole R. Holsti, "Foreign Policy Formation Viewed Cognitively," in Axelrod, ed., *Structure of Decision.*

53 George F. Kennan, *The Cloud of Danger: Current Realities of American Foreign Policy* (Boston, 1978), 87–88.

a policymaker may have an acute appreciation of the disorderly environment in which he or she operates (arising, for example, from domestic political processes), there is a tendency to assume that others, especially adversaries, are free of such constraints. Graham T. Allison, Robert Jervis, and others have demonstrated that decision makers tend to believe that the realist "unitary rational actor" is the appropriate representation of the opponent's decision processes and, thus, whatever happens is the direct result of deliberate choices. For example, the hypothesis that the Soviet destruction of KAL flight 007 may have resulted from intelligence failures or bureaucratic foulups, rather than from a calculated decision to murder civilian passengers, was either not given serious consideration or it was suppressed for strategic reasons.[54]

Drawing upon a very substantial experimental literature, several models linking crisis-induced stress to decision processes have been developed and used in foreign policy studies.[55] Irving L. Janis and Leon Mann have developed a more general conflict-theory model that conceives of man as a "reluctant decision maker" and focuses upon "when, how and why psychological stress generated by decisional conflict imposes limitations on the rationality of a person's decisions."[56] One may employ five strategies for coping with a situation requiring a decision: unconflicted adherence to existing policy, unconflicted change, defensive avoidance, hypervigilance, and vigilant decision making. The first four strategies are likely to yield low-quality decisions owing to an incomplete search for information, appraisal of the situation and options, and contingency planning, whereas vigilant decision making, characterized by a more adequate performance of vital tasks, is more likely to result in a high quality choice. The factors that will affect the employment of decision styles are information about risks, expectations of finding a better option, and time for adequate search and deliberation.

A final approach we should consider attempts to show the impact of personal traits on decision making. There is no shortage of typologies

---

54 Allison, *Essence;* Jervis, *Perception;* Seymour M. Hersh, *The Target Is Destroyed: What Really Happened to Flight 007 and What America Knew about It* (New York, 1986).

55 Charles F. Hermann, *International Crises: Insights from Behavioral Research* (New York, 1972); Margaret G. Hermann and Charles F. Hermann, "Maintaining the Quality of Decision-Making in Foreign Policy Crises," in *Report of the Commission on the Organization of the Government for the Conduct of Foreign Policy,* vol. 2 (Washington, 1975); Margaret G. Hermann, "Indicators of Stress in Policy-Makers during Foreign Policy Crises," *Political Psychology* 1 (March 1979): 27–46; Ole R. Holsti, *Crisis, Escalation, War* (Montreal, 1972); Ole R. Holsti and Alexander L. George, "The Effects of Stress on the Performance of Foreign Policy-Makers," *Political Science Annual,* vol. 6 (Indianapolis, 1975); Lebow, *Between Peace and War.*

56 Janis and Mann, *Decision Making,* 3.

that are intended to link leadership traits to decision-making behavior, but systematic research demonstrating such links is in much shorter supply. Still, some efforts have borne fruit. Margaret G. Hermann has developed a scheme for analyzing leaders' public statements of unquestioned authorship for eight variables: nationalism, belief in one's ability to control the environment, need for power, need for affiliation, ability to differentiate environments, distrust of others, self-confidence, and task emphasis. The scheme has been tested with impressive results on a broad range of contemporary leaders.[57] Alexander L. George has reformulated Nathan Leites's concept of "operational code" into five philosophical and five instrumental beliefs that are intended to describe politically relevant core beliefs, stimulating a number of empirical studies and, more recently, further significant conceptual revisions.[58] Finally, several psychologists have developed and tested the concept of "integrative complexity," defined as the ability to make subtle distinction along multiple dimensions, flexibility, and the integration of large amounts of diverse information to make coherent judgments.[59] A standard content analysis technique has been used for research on documentary materials generated by top decision makers in a wide range of international crises, including World War I, Cuba (1962), Morocco (1911), Berlin (1948–49 and 1961), Korea, and the Middle East wars of 1948, 1956, 1967, and 1973.[60]

Decision-making approaches clearly permit the analyst to overcome

---

57 Margaret G. Hermann, "Explaining Foreign Policy Behavior Using Personal Characteristics of Political Leaders," *International Studies Quarterly* 24 (March 1980): 7–46; idem, "Personality and Foreign Policy Decision Making: A Study of 53 Heads of Government," in *Foreign Policy Decision Making: Perception, Cognition, and Artificial Intelligence,* ed. Donald Sylvan and Steve Chan (New York, 1984), 53–80.

58 Nathan Leites, *The Operational Code of the Politburo* (New York, 1951); Alexander L. George, "The 'Operational Code': A Neglected Approach to the Study of Political Leaders and Decision Making," *International Studies Quarterly* 13 (June 1969): 190–222; Stephen G. Walker, "The Interface between Beliefs and Behavior: Henry Kissinger's Operational Code and the Vietnam War," *Journal of Conflict Resolution* 21 (March 1977): 129–68; idem, "The Motivational Foundations of Political Belief Systems: A Re-Analysis of the Operational Code Construct," *International Studies Quarterly* 27 (June 1983): 179–202; idem, "Parts and Wholes: American Foreign Policy Makers as 'Structured' Individuals" (paper presented at the annual meeting of the International Society of Political Psychology, Secaucus, New Jersey, 1988).

59 Integrative simplicity, on the other hand, is characterized by simple responses, gross distinctions, rigidity, and restricted information usage.

60 Peter Suedfeld and Philip Tetlock, "Integrative Complexity of Communications in International Crises," *Journal of Conflict Resolution* 21 (March 1977): 169–86; Peter Suedfeld, Philip Tetlock, and C. Romirez, "War, Peace and Integrative Complexity," ibid. (September 1977): 427–42; Theodore D. Raphael, "Integrative Complexity Theory and Forecasting International Crises: Berlin 1946–1962," ibid. 26 (September 1982): 423–50; Philip Tetlock, "Integrative Complexity of American and Soviet Foreign Policy Rhetoric: A Time Series Analysis," *Journal of Personality and Social Psychology* 49 (December 1985): 1565–85.

many limitations of the systemic models described earlier, but not without costs. The three decision-making models described here impose increasingly heavy data burdens on the analyst. Moreover, there is a danger that adding levels of analysis may result in an undisciplined proliferation of categories and variables with at least two adverse consequences: it may become increasingly difficult to determine which are more or less important, and ad hoc explanations for individual cases erode the possibilities for broader generalizations across cases. Several well-designed, multicase, decision-making studies, however, indicate that these and other traps are not unavoidable.[61]

The study of international relations and foreign policy has always been a somewhat eclectic undertaking, with extensive borrowing from disciplines other than political science and history.[62] At the most general level, the primary differences today tend to be between two broad approaches. Analysts of the first school focus on the structure of the international system, often borrowing from economics for models, analogies, insights, and metaphors, with an emphasis on *rational preferences and strategy* and how these tend to be shaped and constrained by the structure of the international system. Decision-making analysts, meanwhile, display a concern for domestic political processes and tend to borrow from psychology and social psychology in order to understand better the *limits and barriers* to information processing and rational choice.

At the risk of ending on a platitude, it seems clear that for many purposes both approaches are necessary and neither is sufficient. Neglect of the system structure and its constraints may result in analyses that depict policymakers as relatively free agents with an almost unrestricted menu of choices, limited only by the scope of their ambitions and the resources at their disposal. At worst, this type of analysis can degenerate into Manichean explanations that depict foreign policies of the "bad guys" as the external manifestation of inherently flawed leaders or domestic structures, whereas the "good guys" only react from necessity.

---

61 Alexander L. George and Richard Smoke, *Deterrence in American Foreign Policy: Theory and Practice* (New York, 1974); Richard Smoke, *Escalation* (Cambridge, MA, 1977); Glenn H. Snyder and Paul Diesing, *Conflict among Nations: Bargaining, Decision Making, and System Structure in International Crises* (Princeton, 1977); Michael Brecher and Barbara Geist, *Decisions in Crisis: Israel, 1967 and 1973* (Berkeley, 1980); Lebow, *Between Peace and War*. Useful discussions on conducting theoretically relevant case studies may be found in Harry Eckstein, "Case Study and Theory in Political Science," in *Handbook of Political Science*, 9 vols., ed. Fred I. Greenstein and Nelson W. Polsby (Reading, MA, 1975), 7:79–138; and Alexander L. George, "Case Studies and Theory Development: The Method of Structured, Focused Comparison," in Lauren, ed., *Diplomacy*, 43–68.

62 The classic overview of the field and the disciplines that have contributed to it is Quincy Wright, *The Study of International Relations* (New York, 1955).

Radical right explanations of the Cold War usually depict Soviet foreign policies as driven by inherently aggressive totalitarian communism and the United States as its blameless victim; radical left explanations tend to be structurally similar, with the roles of aggressor and victim reversed.[63]

Conversely, neglect of foreign policy decision making not only leaves one unable to explain the dynamics of international relations, but many important aspects of a nation's external behavior will be inexplicable. Advocates of the realist model have often argued its superiority for understanding the "high" politics of deterrence, containment, alliances, crises, and wars, if not necessarily for "low" politics. But there are several rejoinders to this line of reasoning. First, the low politics of trade, currencies, and other issues that are almost always highly sensitive to domestic pressures are becoming an increasingly important element of international relations. Second, the growing literature on the putative domain par excellence of realism, including deterrence, crises, and wars, raises substantial doubts about the universal validity of the realist model even for these issues.[64] Finally, exclusive reliance on realist models and their assumptions of rationality may lead to unwarranted complacency about dangers in the international system. Nuclear weapons and other features of the system have no doubt contributed to the "long peace" between major powers.[65] At the same time, however, a narrow focus on power balances, "correlations of forces," and other features of the international system will result in neglect of dangers—for example, the command, communication, control, intelligence problem or inadequate information processing—that can only be identified and analyzed by a decision-making perspective.[66]

At a very general level, this conclusion parallels that drawn three de-

63 Ole R. Holsti, "The Study of International Politics Makes Strange Bedfellows," *American Political Science Review* 68 (March 1974): 217–42.
64 In addition to the literature on war, crises, and deterrence already cited see Richard Betts, *Nuclear Blackmail and Nuclear Balance* (Washington, 1987); Robert Jervis, Richard Ned Lebow, and Janice G. Stein, *Psychology and Deterrence* (Baltimore, 1985); Richard Ned Lebow, *Nuclear Crisis Management: A Dangerous Illusion* (Ithaca, 1987); and Ole R. Holsti, "Crisis Decision Making," and Jack S. Levy, "The Causes of War: A Review of Theories and Evidence," in *Behavior, Society, and Nuclear War*, vol. 1, ed. Philip E. Tetlock et al. (New York, 1989), 8–84, 209–333.
65 John Lewis Gaddis, "The Long Peace: Elements of Stability in the Postwar International System," *International Security* 10 (Spring 1986): 99–142.
66 Paul Bracken, *Command and Control of Nuclear Forces* (New Haven, 1983); Bruce Blair, *Strategic Command and Control: Redefining the Nuclear Threat* (Washington, 1985); John Steinbruner, "Nuclear Decapitation," *Foreign Policy* 45 (Winter 1981–82): 16–28; Sagan, "Nuclear Alerts"; Alexander L. George, *Presidential Decision Making in Foreign Policy: The Effective Use of Information and Advice* (Boulder, 1980).

cades ago by the foremost contemporary proponent of modern realism: The third image (system structure) is necessary for understanding the context of international behavior, whereas the first and second images (decision makers and domestic political processes) are needed to understand dynamics within the system.[67] But to acknowledge the existence of various levels of analysis is not enough. *What* the investigator wants to explain and the *level of specificity and comprehensiveness* to be sought should determine which level(s) of analysis are relevant and necessary. In this connection, it is essential to distinguish between two different dependent variables: foreign policy decisions by states, on the one hand, and the outcomes of policy and interactions between two or more states, on the other. If the goal is to understand the former—foreign policy decisions—Harold and Margaret Sprout's notion of "psychological milieu" is relevant and sufficient; that is, the objective structural variables influence the decisions via the decision maker's perception and evaluation of those "outside" variables.[68] If the goal is to explain outcomes, however, the "psychological milieu" is quite inadequate; the objective factors, if misperceived or misjudged by the decision maker, will influence the outcome. Political scientists studying international relations are increasingly disciplining their use of multiple levels of analysis in studying outcomes that cannot be adequately explained via only a single level of analysis.[69]

Which of these models and approaches are likely to be of interest and utility to the diplomatic historian? Clearly there is no one answer: political scientists are unable to agree on a single multilevel approach to international relations and foreign policy; thus they are hardly in a position to offer a single recommendation to historians. In the absence of the often-sought but always-elusive unified theory of human behavior that could provide a model for all seasons and all reasons, one must ask at least one further question: a model for what purpose? For example, in some circumstances, such as research on major international crises, it may be important to obtain systematic evidence on the beliefs and other intellectual baggage that key policymakers bring to their deliberations. Some of the approaches described above should prove very helpful in

---

67 Waltz, *Man, the State, and War,* 238.
68 Harold and Margaret Sprout, "Environmental Factors in the Study of International Politics," *Journal of Conflict Resolution* 1 (December 1957): 309–28.
69 See, for example, David B. Yoffie, *Power and Protectionism: Strategies of the Newly Industrializing Countries* (New York, 1983); John Odell, *U.S. International Monetary Policy: Markets, Power, and Ideas as Sources of Change* (Princeton, 1982); Jack Snyder, *The Ideology of the Offensive: Military Decision Making and the Disaster of 1914* (Ithaca, 1984); Vinod K. Aggarwal, *Liberal Protectionism: The International Politics of Organized Textile Trade* (Berkeley, 1985); Larson, *Origins of Containment;* Posen, *Sources of Military Doctrine;* and Walt, *Alliances.*

this respect. Conversely, there are many other research problems for which the historian would quite properly decide that this type of analysis requires far more effort than could possibly be justified by the benefits to be gained.

Of the systemic approaches described here, little needs to be said about classical realism because its main features, as well as its strengths and weaknesses, are familiar to most diplomatic historians. Those who focus on security issues can hardly neglect its central premises and concepts. Modern or structural realism of the Waltz variety, though, is likely to have rather limited appeal to historians, especially if they take seriously his doubts about being able to incorporate foreign policy into it. It may perhaps serve to raise consciousness about the importance of the systemic context within which international relations take place, but that may not be a major gain—after all, such concepts as "balance of power" have long been a standard part of the diplomatic historian's vocabulary. Gilpin's richer approach, which employs both system- and state-level variables to explain international dynamics, may well have greater appeal. It has already been noted that there are some interesting parallels between Gilpin's *War and Change in World Politics* and Paul Kennedy's recent *The Rise and Fall of the Great Powers*.

The Global-Society/Complex-Interdependence models will be helpful to historians with an interest in the evolution of the international system and with the growing disjuncture between demands on states and their ability to meet them, the "sovereignty gap." One need not be very venturesome to predict that this gap will grow rather than narrow in the future. Historians of all kinds of international and transnational organizations are also likely to find useful concepts and insights in these models.

It is much less clear that the Marxist/World System/Dependency models will provide useful new insights to historians. They will no doubt continue to be employed, but for reasons other than demonstrated empirical utility. If one has difficulty in accepting certain assumptions as *true by definition*—for example, that there has been and is today a single "world capitalist system"—then the kinds of analyses that follow are likely to seem seriously flawed. Most diplomatic historians also would have difficulty in accepting models that relegate the state to a secondary role. Until proponents of these models demonstrate a greater willingness to test them against a broader range of cases, including East-South and East-East relations, their applicability would appear to be limited at best. Finally, whereas proponents of GS/CI models can point with considerable justification to current events and trends that would appear to make them more rather than less relevant in the future, supporters of the M/WS/D models have a much more difficult task in this respect. The declining legitimacy of Marxism-Leninism as the basis for government does not, of course, necessarily invalidate social science models that draw upon Marx, Lenin, and their intellectual heirs. It might, however, at least be the occasion for second thoughts, especially because Marx and his followers have always placed a heavy emphasis on an intimate connection between theory and practice.

Although the three decision-making models sometimes include jargon that may be jarring to the historian, many of the underlying concepts are familiar. Much of diplomatic history has traditionally focused on the decisions, actions, and interactions of national leaders who operate in group contexts, such as cabinets or ad hoc advisory groups, and who draw upon the resources of such bureaucracies as foreign and defense ministries or the armed forces. The three types of models described above typically draw heavily upon psychology, social psychology, organizational theory, and other social sciences; thus for the historian they open some important windows to highly relevant developments in these fields. For example, theories and concepts of "information processing" by individuals, groups, and organizations should prove very useful to diplomatic historians.

Decision-making models may also appeal to diplomatic historians for another important reason. Political scientists who are accustomed to working with fairly accessible information such as figures on gross national products, defense budgets, battle casualties, alliance commitments, UN votes, trade and investments, and the like, often feel that the data requirements of decision-making models are excessive. This is precisely the area in which the historian has a decided comparative advantage, for the relevant data are usually to be found in the paper trails—more recently, also in the electronic trails—left by policymakers, and they are most likely to be unearthed by archival research. Thus, perhaps the appropriate point on which to conclude this essay is to reverse the question posed earlier: Ask not only what can the political scientist contribute to the diplomatic historian but ask also what can the diplomatic historian contribute to the political scientist. At the very least political scientists could learn a great deal about the validity of their own models if historians would use them and offer critical assessments of their strengths and limitations.

6

World Systems

THOMAS J. McCORMICK

Ideally, studies of international relations should explore the relations between a given society's domestic changes and concurrent changes in the international system. Contemporary historians of American foreign relations, however, have generally invested more energy in debating the relative primacy of the internal and the external than in articulating their connectedness.[1] Was the Cold War, for example, the outgrowth of internal American economic need, domestic political constraints, exceptionalist ideology, or race thinking; or was it a response to the external realities of Soviet expansionism, global insecurity, or postwar economic chaos? Was the United States to blame itself for the Cold War or to lay that guilt at the feet of some other? In that sometimes either/or context, the internal dynamic has received the greater and more imaginative attention. The external context has often been intuited and assumed rather than specified and analyzed. Many historians have seemed more concerned with American perceptions of the international system than with the system as such. Did American leaders and the American people properly understand that system, its imperatives, and the place of the United States in it? If they did, they were approvingly deemed "realists"; if they did not, they were denigrated as "idealists."

Fifteen years ago, however, Immanuel Wallerstein's *The Modern World-System* exploded a conceptual bombshell whose shock waves have belatedly reached the study of American foreign relations. The result has been renewed scholarly interest in the international system, but in a system much different from the traditional interstate system of national actors, geopolitical imperatives, and balance of power. Much influenced by Fernand Braudel's monumental works on early capitalism, Wallerstein posited the existence since 1500 of a world system or capitalist world economy. Its chief actors have been transnational business organizations and operations, driven by the premise that capitalism functioned most

Another version of this essay originally appeared in the June 1990 issue of the *Journal of American History*. It is printed here by permission of the *Journal of American History*.

1 See Christopher Thorne, *Border Crossings: Studies in International History* (Oxford, 1988), 37.

efficiently and thus most profitably when its universe of options was sufficiently large and fluid for capital, goods, services, and people to move from one place to another to secure greater returns, even if that place was both distant and foreign. Its chief process was the spatial expansion of European capitalism at the expense of autarkic empires in Russia, China, and the Near East, as well as the subsistence, village minisystems of eastern Europe, Ireland, the Americas, Africa, and Asia. Its chief consequence was a system of three successive zones, each performing a specialized function in a complex, hierarchical, international division of labor. *Core* countries (the First World) monopolize high-tech, high-profit enterprises. The *periphery* (the Third World) specializes in primary production of agricultural commodities and raw materials: "hewers of wood and carriers of water." In between, the *semiperiphery* (the Second World) performs intermediate functions of transport, local capital mobilization, and less complex, less profitable forms of manufacturing.[2]

World systems theory, also called systemic theory, was an interesting hybrid of two competing developmental theories—dependency and modernization (a mix that generated ideological displeasure on both the right and the left). It shared with the former most of its basic premises and its emphasis on the uneven and exploitative nature of capitalist development. Popularized by revolutionary Third World nationalism and anti-imperialism in the 1960s and early 1970s, dependency theory had argued that the development of "rich lands" and the underdevelopment of "poor lands" were symbiotic, that the latter was a structural outgrowth of the needs of the former. Systemic theory largely accepted and built on that perspective. Even when dependency theory came under increasing attack in the late 1970s and 1980s, proponents of world systems analysis continued to argue its applicability for the Less Developed Countries (LDCs) in the Caribbean basin, most of Africa, and much of Southeast Asia.[3] It also suggested that the Newly Industrializing Countries of the semiperiphery (NICs) had achieved only "dependent development," based on borrowed money, whose consequence was the international debt trap, and borrowed technology, whose time lag limited development to less profitable product lines being discarded by core countries as they moved to more profitable high-tech sectors.

On the other hand, systemic theorists parted company with *dependencia* in some fundamental ways. In echoes of modernization theory,

---

2 Wallerstein, *The Modern World-System: Capitalist Agriculture and the Origins of the European World-Economy in the Sixteenth Century* (New York, 1974).
3 See Steve J. Stern, "Feudalism, Capitalism, and the World-System in the Perspective of Latin America and the Caribbean," *American Historical Review* 93 (October 1988): 829–72.

they expressed skepticism about the ability of revolutionary regimes in the periphery to plan and implement programs of autonomous, autarkic industrialization. Undersized production runs for undersized local markets were inherently inefficient and likely to fail. Similarly, its treatment of the industrializing semiperiphery suggested that specialized production for the world market, like that of market economies in the Pacific rim, was more successful than diversified production for the internal market, like that of import-substitution economies in South America or planned economies in Eastern Europe. Moreover, its concession that mobility from semiperiphery to core had been historically possible for a select few, like the United States and Japan, inferred that similar mobility might be possible for a few countries now on the semiperiphery, such as China and Brazil.

The treatment of internecine relations between great powers in world systems theory has been stimulating and unsettling. Its emphasis renders political-military power merely a subordinate extension of economic power, and its use of a global unit of analysis—the capitalist world economy—relegates national, state actors to a backup role. Never fond of cosmic theories that obscure the discrete and specific, historians have been especially unhappy with what appears to be the static and reductionist quality of this approach. World systems theory seems to endow its subject with an anthropomorphic quality, so that systemic imperatives of capital accumulation and profit making—expressions more of process than of tangible structures—acquire a kind of logic and quasi consciousness. Systemic theory also seems to endow its subject with a certain omniscience and near omnipotence. Individual nation-states, like Napoleonic France or Nazi Germany, might attempt to divide the world into fragmented power blocs; and revolutionary regimes, such as the Soviet Union or the People's Republic of China, might attempt either to remake the system or to opt out of it altogether; but the economic logic of the world system requires that the market economy become global and integrated: a free world, one world. All such deviant ventures by individual nation-states, while hardly irrelevant, are nonetheless doomed to failure in the long run. In humankind's historical saga of winners and losers, the system always wins. Only when capitalism reaches its spatial limits and class conflict becomes globalized will the losers have their temporal moment.[4]

The criticisms of world systems theory pinpoint real or potential weak-

---

4 For a more extended treatment of hegemony see Thomas J. McCormick, " 'Every System Needs a Center Sometimes': An Essay on Hegemony and Modern American Foreign Policy," in *Redefining the Past: Essays in Diplomatic History in Honor of William Appleman Williams*, ed. Lloyd C. Gardner (Corvallis, OR, 1986), 195–220.

nesses in making the model relevant to historians. The weaknesses, however, are far from fatal. In the first place they do not obviate the central truth of world systems analysis. There *is* an extant economic system driven by the aggregate actions of private economic actors engaged in the process of capital accumulation and labor exploitation; it possesses a logic that is inherently internationalist; and it coexists in uneasy tension with the political power of individual nation-states and their nationalist biases. Historians who treat the interstate system must also analyze how it interacts with that world economy, and how the two constrain or reinforce each other. For example, Eastern Europe's recent shift toward democratic capitalism dramatically illustrates not merely the strength of domestic dissent but also the interconnected attraction of global market forces and consumer culture on the one hand and the facilitating power of Soviet-American détente and greater European autonomy on the other.

In the second place, the alleged weaknesses of world systems analysis are not inherent in the model itself. One might choose to concede that world systems analysis, as often practiced, tends to understate and diminish the capacity of classes, races, peoples, and nations to resist core dominance, and that their resistance forces significant modifications in the system. For example, pressure by NICs for a more equitable division of labor in the international economy may have speeded the transfer of manufacturing operations from the core to the semiperiphery. But nothing in the model prevents the portrayal of such facts. The spread of market forces may indeed be ineluctable in the long term, but in the short and intermediate term in which most historians rightfully dwell, such forces may be markedly slowed or altered. For example, the impact of British capital in the nineteenth century and American capital in the twentieth may have preordained Mexico's eventual integration into a global economy, but the power of the Mexican Revolution in the 1910s profoundly influenced the pace and form of that integration. Wielded in a dynamic, dialectical way, the world systems model seems fully capable of absorbing such complexities.

There is ample evidence that world systems theory is not incompatible with interstate theory. Both systems do exist. They are, however, asymmetrical. One is political, the other is economic; one's unit of analysis is particularized (the nation-state), the other's is holistic (the world economy); one's spatial boundaries encompass the part of the world organized into nation-states; the other embraces only the part of the world organized according to a capitalist mode of production. Yet their recurring cycles and secular trends do intersect. Those intersections offer scholars the chance to combine insights suggested by world systems theory and interstate theory.[5] Perhaps the best example is the contemporary schol-arship on hegemony.

For historians of American foreign relations, the greatest contribution of world systems analysis is its understanding of hegemony's rise and fall. Building on Braudel's central premise that "each time decentering occurs, a recentering begins," Wallerstein and other like-minded social scientists have attempted both to identify and to explain the cycles of "concentration" and "diffusion" that Brooks Adams described almost a century ago in his book *The Law of Civilization and Decay*: that is, the international system's oscillation between unicentric hegemony and poly-centric balance of power.[6]

The systemic school of thought defines hegemony as a single power's possession of "simultaneous superior economic efficiency in production, trade and finance." That "superior economic position vis-à-vis competing core states" is the consequence of such historical variables as technolog-ical innovation, resources, flexible and supportive state structures, su-perior geography (especially that of sea powers over land powers), entrepreneurially oriented religions, and national ideology.[7] The conse-quent economic suzerainty provides the productive base for generating military power, and the invocation of economic and military muscle ensures that one's ideology will command attention and respect from the rest of the world. Many systemic theorists have stressed the role of long-wave economic cycles, especially the downside, in eliminating marginal competitors and elevating the more efficient: for example, the long depres-sion of the late nineteenth century that initiated British decline and Amer-ican ascendancy and the Great Depression of the 1930s that solidified the process. More recently, some have emphasized the role of lengthy, global wars, whose radical redistribution of systemic power made he-

5   See Ole R. Holsti's contribution to this volume, Chapter 5. Holsti also describes a third model, the global society, but it remains more a series of related secular trends and tendencies than an extant system or structure.
6   For Braudel's statement see Thomas J. McCormick, *America's Half-Century: United States Foreign Policy in the Cold War* (Baltimore, 1989), 1. Many of the systemic theorists, among them Nicole Bousquet, Christopher Chase-Dunn, and Terrence Hop-kins, are to be found in Wallerstein's many edited anthologies. The most useful for American historians are Wallerstein, ed., *World Inequality* (Montreal, 1975); Wall-erstein, ed., *The Capitalist World-Economy* (New York, 1979); Wallerstein and Ter-rence K. Hopkins, eds., *World-Systems Analysis, Theory, and Methodology* (Beverly Hills, 1982); and Wallerstein, ed., *Politics of the World Economy* (New York, 1984).
7   Terry Boswell and Mike Sweat, "Hegemony, Long Waves, and Major Wars: A Time Series Analysis of Systemic Dynamics, 1496–1967" (paper presented at the joint Con-vention of the International Studies Association and the British International Studies Association, London, 1989).

gemony possible: for example, the Napoleonic Wars that ushered in the era of Pax Britannica and the two world wars that commenced "America's Half-Century" as hegemon.

A single hegemonic power has a built-in incentive to force other nations to abandon their economic nationalism and protectionist controls and to accept a world of free trade, free capital flows, and free currency convertibility. As the world's dominant economic power, a hegemonic nation has the most to gain from such a free world, and the most to lose from nationalist efforts to limit the free movement of capital, goods, and currencies. So the preponderant world power has an unequivocal self-interest in using its economic power as workshop and banker of the free world to create institutions and ground rules that foster the internationalization of capital. It finds it inherently advantageous to use its political power as ideologue of the world system to preach the universal virtues of freedom of the seas, free trade, Open Door policies, comparative advantage, and a specialized division of labor. It finds it necessary to use its military power as global policeman to protect the international system against external antagonists, internal rebellions, and internecine differences. Great Britain and the United States did so in the nineteenth and twentieth centuries, respectively.

The chief consequence of hegemony is to soften the contradiction between the internationalist imperatives of the economic world system and the nationalist rivalries and autarkic instincts of the geopolitical interstate system. Witness most recently the ability of the hegemonic United States to create the Bretton Woods multilateral monetary system, to move Europe and a reintegrated Germany toward an economically more viable common market, to use force in the Korean and Vietnam wars to salvage the Pacific rim and facilitate Japanese reindustrialization, to nudge the Third World away from neomercantilism and import substitution to specialized production for the world market, and in general to make the world economy more unitary and interdependent. The result was a golden age of capitalism between 1950 and 1973 that perhaps witnessed the highest sustained, global rate of aggregate profit in capitalism's half-millennium history: an era so prosperous that its chief beneficiaries, the great core states, saw no need to use war as a means to redistribute global resources and wealth.[8]

Hegemony carries with it the seeds of its own economic destruction. Great Britain discovered that fact, and so now does the United States. The twin functions of the hegemon as global banker and global policeman

---

8 See John Lewis Gaddis, *The Long Peace: Inquiries into the History of the Cold War* (New York, 1987).

lead it to overinvest in multinational ventures abroad and in military production at home. It becomes easier and more profitable to live off one's overseas dividends and rents (to become a rentier economy) and off state-subsidized military contracts (to become a warfare economy) than to sustain high investment levels in the civilian industrial sector, and the consequent deindustrialization initiates a relative economic decline. That helps slow the global economy, and the hegemon's competitors—less burdened by military demands—use the slowdown to wrest additional market shares from their less efficient patron. In the end, the dominant core power faces a catch–22 situation. If it sustains the high-level military spending necessary to carry out its global policing, it neglects civilian research and development, distorts its economy, and reduces its capacity to compete in world markets. On the other hand, if it cuts military spending to restore civilian productivity and trade competitiveness, it diminishes its role as global protector of a capitalist free world. It becomes less efficient in containing or confronting the system's enemies or in forcing its friends to depend on its protection and therefore to defer to its rules of the game. Hegemony necessarily rests upon both military and economic power, and the dilemma facing a maturing hegemon is that it cannot sustain both. Such is the nature of world system dynamics, and both the British experience after 1870 and the American experience after 1970 provide ample evidence to support its plausibility.[9]

Such systemic theories of hegemony both contest with and complement so-called realist theories that have emerged in the 1980s. Though it avoids the use of the term hegemony and its theories are largely implicit, Paul Kennedy's *The Rise and Fall of the Great Powers* is the most visible of such realist studies. More explicit are the works of Robert Gilpin and David P. Calleo.[10] These realist interpretations approach the dynamics of hegemony—of the waves of stability and instability, of centralization and decentralization—from the vantage point of the interstate system. Their chief actors are nation-states and nation-state coalitions, and their main imperative is the maximization of geopolitical power in a global zero-sum game. This will to power knows only those limits imposed by the extent of one's internal resources and the ability of other nations or

9 See Nigel Harris, *Of Bread and Guns: The World Economy in Crisis* (Middlesex, England, 1983).
10 Kennedy, *The Rise and Fall of the Great Powers: Economic Change and Military Conflict from 1500 to 2000* (New York, 1987); Calleo, *The Imperious Economy* (Cambridge, MA, 1982); idem, *Beyond American Hegemony: The Future of the Western Alliance* (New York, 1987); Gilpin, *War and Change in World Politics* (New York, 1981); idem, *The Political Economy of International Relations* (Princeton, 1987).

coalitions to resist that will. Gilpin, for example, hypothesizes that any nation will continue to expand its power until it reaches a point where the liabilities of continued expansion overweigh its gains. Periodically, a single nation develops such total power—defined in military and political as well as economic terms—that it has the near omnipotence to impose much of its will on the whole interstate system. The hegemon does so to sustain a status quo from which it benefits. Over time, the mounting costs of maintaining that status quo, compounded by the competition of ascending states expanding toward their outer limits (their pain-gain equilibrium), force the paramount power to diminish its military role or experience economic decline.

The realist approach to hegemony and the international system differs from systemic approaches in several key respects. Perhaps the most salutary has been the realists' definition of hegemonic power as total rather than exclusively economic. In particular, the realist emphasis on military power as intrinsic to hegemony has encouraged systemic theorists to see large-scale war, and its redistribution of global power, as a key catalyst for hegemony's ascent. The more substantive disagreements between realist and systemic schools about the importance of economic forces are more difficult to resolve. Systemic theories, for all their flaws, do treat those forces in a dynamic, historical way. Their treatments of economic forces have concrete historical actors—Braudel's "long-distance" entrepreneurs and today's multinational corporations. They have process—the accumulation of capital and the maximization of profits. And they have systemic consequences—a world economy whose medium-term existence ebbs and flows cyclically but whose long-term, secular tendency is to expand and encompass the globe. Realist treatments of economic power are more static. Economic power is merely a tool of expanding national influence; it is not a dynamic cause. Economic gain is merely part of a general aggrandizement pursued by all nations if they can get away with it, but it has no specific relation to business cycles, contesting economic theories, or the rate of profit. Economic force is the determined by-product of the available resource base and the given level of technology, rather than the contested consequence of competing ideologies and interest groups making concrete choices about economic strategies (for example, income redistribution for a protected domestic market versus expanded production for an open world market).[11] In realist hands, economics is a factor, but never a system. Capitalism, for example, is

---

11 See Fred L. Block, *The Origins of International Economic Disorder* (Berkeley, 1977); and Charles S. Maier, *Recasting Bourgeois Europe: Stabilization in France, Germany, and Italy in the Decade after World War I* (Princeton, 1975).

essentially a nonword and a nonconcept in Kennedy's *The Rise and Fall of the Great Powers.*

"You may be right in African terms," said Henry A. Kissinger to a corporate critic of his Angolan policy in 1976, "but I am thinking globally."[12] So too must scholars of America's foreign relations. From its colonial beginnings, America served as a political-military battleground for the European interstate system and as an integrated, spatial extension of European capitalism. The Republic itself was born in an unstable, war-ridden international system, poised on the brink of global war and of Britain's ascent to global hegemony, and at a time when a stagnating world economy was primed to expand so explosively that the United States's share of its export and reexport profits would bring within its grasp economic independence as well as political autonomy. From that moment to this, America's transformation from colony to colossus—from periphery to semiperiphery to core to hegemon—was not simply the linear product of domestic dynamics but the dialectical consequence of external constraints and demands from the international system. Never isolated, always integrated, the spatial expansion, economic development, and political nation-building of the United States would be powerfully influenced and partly determined by the long waves of economic expansion and contraction and the global division of economic labor; and by the long swings of political centralization and decentralization and the global rhythms of stability and instability.

Recognizing the conjunctures and disjunctures of the interstate and world systems enormously facilitates our analysis of American foreign affairs. Witness, for example, the period of American hegemony that coincides with the Cold War epoch since the end of World War II. The global unit of analysis helps overcome our often myopic preoccupation with Soviet-American relations and locates them inside a larger framework. The stress on long-term time and long-term process helps divest the Cold War of its mystique of uniqueness, so we can view it as part of the historical cycle of centering, decentering, and recentering that has been a patterned feature of the global system. The appreciation of hegemony as a rare yet recurring phenomenon of the system helps us understand, for example, the historical imperatives that led to the fight by the United States, as hegemon, to keep Southeast Asia inside the global market economy, less to serve America's own marginal interests than to serve the major interests of Japan and the larger systemic interests of world capitalism. Conversely, the awareness of hegemony's structurally derived impermanence makes it easier to view the contemporary decline

12 *New York Times,* 14 March 1976.

of the United States in a comparative framework (for example, by comparing the United States of today with the Britain of a century ago), and to understand more keenly the essential paradox of hegemony: Decades of playing global policeman weaken the economic underpinnings of hegemony itself. "Peace requires hegemony or balance of power," said the ever quotable Dr. Kissinger in 1988. "We have neither the resources nor the stomach for the former. The only question is how much we have to suffer before we realize this."[13]

13   McCormick, *America's Half-Century,* 216.

7

Dependency

LOUIS A. PÉREZ, JR.

Donald Duck is a ubiquitous presence in Latin America. He speaks Spanish and Portuguese, and he appears serialized in the comic strips of scores of newspapers and magazines. He is featured in at least four different Spanish-language editions of the Disney comic book. And in thousands of movie houses and on hundreds of thousands of television screens, the accumulated inventory of decades of Disney animated films has been played and replayed to the squealing delight of successive generations of unsuspecting Latin American children.

Who is this Latin American incarnation of Donald Duck ("el Pato Donald")? He is North American, and he transmits cultural values and diffuses ideological imperatives. In dialogue with his nephews, he talks politics; in conversation with his uncle, he discusses economics. The moral may not be obvious, but it is never disguised: the virtues of capitalism, the vices of communism. Donald Duck is an agent of imperialism.[1]

Donald Duck does not typically pass under the scrutiny of diplomatic historians in the United States. In fact, some North American historians of U.S.–Latin American relations experience discomfort with the very constructs of "empire" and "imperialism." This uneasiness is due in part to vague normative devotions: a characteristic inability to examine the purpose and consequences of U.S.–Latin American relations in terms other than the objectives and achievements proclaimed in Washington. This disposition is just as often accompanied by explicit ideological assumptions, including a belief that the means and ends of U.S. policy are proper and righteous and that, in any case, whatever happens in the Western Hemisphere is entirely a matter between the U.S. government and its electorate.

The terms "empire" and "imperialism" do, to be sure, periodically enter mainstream historiography, at irregular intervals and often with

Another version of this essay originally appeared in the June 1990 issue of the *Journal of American History*. It is printed here by permission of the *Journal of American History*.

1 This theme is examined in Ariel Dorfman and Armand Mattelhart, *How to Read Donald Duck: Imperialist Ideology in the Disney Comic*, trans. David Kunzle (New York, 1975).

salutary effect. For many historians there can be no denying the signs. The dismemberment of Mexico, the seizure of Puerto Rico, mischief in Panama, the acquisition of the Virgin Islands, and countless armed interventions, military occupations, and seized customhouses make for a powerful prima facie case for something like imperialism.

For the most part, however, scholars of U.S.–Latin American relations have deemed the concept of imperialism to be of limited analytical value and of even less methodological utility. Not a few have assumed that the "misdeeds" of the United States have been confined largely to the Caribbean region. As a result, relations with Mexico, Central America, and the Caribbean are often treated differently from those with South America. If the proposition of "empire" has any value at all, it is restricted to the circum-Caribbean region.

Reservations about the utility of theories of imperialism are not entirely unfounded. Mainstream theoretical approaches have long tended to identify imperialism with territorial expansion and to emphasize the political and military over the economic and social. From that perspective, U.S. imperialism is understood as isolated "events," acts attributed to the idiosyncratic behavior of well-intended if often misguided administrations but neither inherent in nor intrinsic to the character of U.S. relations with Latin America. Imperialism was the exception, not the rule, a deed or two that could somehow be undone by a more enlightened government in Washington: Wilson's new diplomacy was an antidote to Theodore Roosevelt's gunboat diplomacy; the Good Neighbor policy made amends for previous decades of armed interventions; the Alliance for Progress repudiated past support of Latin American dictatorships.

Concern with these issues has long preoccupied Latin Americans also, and in recent decades it has found expression in dependency theory. The formulation of dependency theory emerged from Latin America in the 1960s, during years of deepening political crisis, social unrest, and economic uncertainty. The Cuban revolution (1959) had signaled a momentous break with the hegemonic consensus through which the United States had presided over the Western Hemisphere, and it offered Latin Americans new and alternative strategies for change. At the same time, existing developmental theories had fallen into disfavor and disrepute. The notion that national development could be attained through import-substitution industrialization had proven false and had failed to fulfill the promise of autonomous and balanced economic growth. On the contrary, underdevelopment persisted and dependence increased; disparities of income distribution widened and vast sectors of the population remained marginalized—and all signs pointed to more of the same, only worse. Ill-conceived industrialization strategies, moreover, had further served to open Latin American economies to multinational corporations, and industrialization that had occurred was undertaken principally by foreign capital for the benefit of foreign capital. Modernization schemes and reform projects had failed, and the much-heralded Alliance for Progress had expired ingloriously and unmourned. Military regimes were in power throughout the region, and repression was on the rise.

New questions about old and persisting problems absorbed Latin American attention. Not perhaps since the Great Depression had a sense of crisis cast a shadow so dark or so long over the region. The inquiry into the sources of inequality, both within the nation and among nations, assumed a deepening urgency as revolutionary movements sought to develop both new explanations for conditions past and present and new strategies for changing conditions in the future. Dependency developed early into an important theoretical concern within the larger context of expanding revolutionary movements across Latin America; it was a way to understand class conflict and to aid in the formulation of strategies to restructure Latin American societies. Implied in most—but not all—*dependentista* formulations was the need to replace capitalism with socialism, peacefully if possible but by arms if necessary.

Dependency theory also served to place imperialism in a different and broader context: within the social reality of the underdeveloped nation. Its arguments were derived from a number of central assumptions, loosely similar if not always equally weighted, all of which shared with Marxism the central proposition that economic relationships are the principal determinants of political, social, and cultural forms.[2]

The dependency paradigm emerged principally as an explanation of development and underdevelopment, expressed in a number of interlocking formulations. Underdevelopment is seen as a function of the expansion of capitalism, not as a natural state through which all economic systems evolve. Conditions of underdevelopment, hence, cannot be examined solely in a national context, for development and underdevelopment represent two aspects of a single and simultaneous international process that are linked together structurally and organically.[3] "By de-

2 A somewhat dated but still useful bibliographical guide to the dependency literature is found in Roberto Jiménez, *América Latina y el mundo desarrollado: Bibliografía comentada sobre relaciones de dependencia* (Bogota, 1977).
3 These themes are most clearly developed in André Gunder Frank, *Capitalism and Underdevelopment in Latin America: Historical Studies of Chile and Brazil* (New York, 1967); Theotonio dos Santos, *El nuevo caràcter de la dependencia* (Santiago, 1986); Susanne Bodenheimer Jonas, "Dependency and Imperialism: The Roots of Latin American Underdevelopment," *NACLA* [North American Congress on Latin America]

pendence," posited Theotonio dos Santos in 1970, "we mean a situation in which the economy of certain countries is conditioned by the development and expansion of another economy to which the former is subjected."[4]

Not all subsets of dependency theory are directly relevant or equally usable for historians of U.S.–Latin American relations. Dependency propositions on imperialism, however, and specifically those formulations that address the internal workings of foreign domination, provide a generally coherent conceptual framework in which to examine the dynamic of inter-American relations.

In its most usable form, dependency theory establishes the relationship between development and underdevelopment as the context in which to examine relations between the United States and Latin America. The United States (the center or metropolis) flourishes at the expense of Latin America (the periphery), and the impoverishment of the latter is a function of the prosperity of the former. Imperialism as the expansion of monopoly capital abhors competition and seeks to create structures to guarantee that whatever development occurs in Latin America is dependent upon and complementary to U.S. needs. That is, the United States structurally influences economic growth in Latin America as a function of its own national economic interests, and toward this end it obtains the service of a broad range of internal institutions to assure the primacy of North American needs over Latin American ones.

The subordination of Latin America results from internal structures that operate in behalf of U.S. interests. Imperialism functions as domination institutionalized from within, and it shapes the internal dynamics of Latin American societies through structures whose intrinsic properties in a national setting are defined by their roles in the international system. That the system "works" is due less to external constraints than internal ones, is related less to political and military relationships than to economic and social ones. An inexorable reciprocity binds internal structures of the periphery to the development needs of the center and results in the emergence in Latin America of an institutional order that functions to underwrite the primacy and propriety of U.S. hegemony.

The literature is rich with explanations of the means and mechanisms by which dependent relationships are initially established and subsequently maintained. Dependency penetrates all levels of national insti-

Newsletter 4 (May–June 1979): 18–27; and Fernando Henrique Cardoso and Enzo Faletto, *Dependency and Development in Latin America,* trans. Majorie Mettingly Urquidi (Berkeley, 1979).

4 Theotonio dos Santos, "The Structure of Dependence," *American Economic Review* 60 (May 1970): 231.

tutions and assumes a variety of forms. The structure of foreign trade—historically, exports of raw materials and imports of manufactured products—arrests economic growth, skews income distribution, and fosters stagnation. These conditions in turn are maintained through foreign aid, private investments, trade negotiations, and credit transactions—instruments of U.S. policy that act to preserve the internal balance of social forces favoring U.S. interests.

The dependency paradigm also implies dependent social classes and dependent military organizations. Latin American elites enjoy privileged status and obtain political ascendancy as a function of their role in the defense of U.S. interests. Shared ideological assumptions and similar political interests serve to link together the dominant classes of the center and periphery and to create in the process a common stake in containing the forces of revolution and nationalism.[5] In like fashion, Latin American army officers educated in the United States, trained by U.S. military personnel, and equipped by (and dependent on) U.S. arms suppliers are unlikely to interpret reality in ways too dissimilar from their benefactors.

Dependent relationships define the function of other national structures, particularly economic institutions and social classes. Dependency limits the options available for political change as well as the means available for change. Supporting ideological formulations and cultural forms provide the normative bases to validate dependent relationships. They also summon a moral vision that invokes values as a way to define and defend the place of various groups within a social hierarchy. It thus becomes possible to isolate specific elements within this institutional order: technological dependency, cultural dependency, capital dependency, ideological dependency, and industrial dependency.[6] In sum, dependency

5 Discussion of dependent classes is most clearly developed in André Gunder Frank, *Lumpenbourgeoisie: Lumpendevelopment. Dependence, Class, and Politics in Latin America*, trans. Marion Davis Berdecio (New York, 1972).
6 See, for example, Robert Girling, "Mechanism of Imperialism: Technology and the Dependent State: Reflections on the Jamaican Case," *Latin American Perspectives* 3 (Fall 1976): 54–64; Armand Mattelhart, Carmen Castillo, and Leonardo Castillo, *La ideologia de la dominaciòn en una sociedad dependiente: La respuesta ideològica de la clase dominante chilena al reformismo* (Santiago, 1970); Pedro F. Paz, "Dependencia financiera y desnacionalizaciòn de la industria interna," *Trimestre Econòmico* 37 (April–June 1970): 297–329; Martin Carnoy, "Financial Institutions and Dependency," in *Structures of Dependency*, ed. Frank Bonilla and Robert Girling (Stanford, 1973), 34–45; Juan Eugenio Corradi, "Cultural Dependence and the Sociology of Knowledge: The Latin American Case," *International Journal of Contemporary Sociology* 8 (January 1971): 35–55; Evelina Dagnino, "Cultural and Ideological Dependence: Building a Theoretical Framework," in Bonilla and Girling, eds., *Structures of Dependency*, 129–48; Fernando Carmona, "Profundizaciòn de la dependencia tecnològica," *Problemas del Desarrollo* 3 (August–October 1972): 19–22; Dario Abad Arango, "Tecnologica y dependencia," *Trimestre Econòmico* 40 (April–June 1973): 371–92; and

arguments suggest that, directly or indirectly, elements that obstruct or otherwise limit the possibility for change and autonomous development in the periphery are in some way associated with the center.

Not all who subscribe to dependency theory share similar concerns or assign similar weight to the concerns they do share. Dependency theory examines the internal dynamics of Latin American society as determined by conditions of underdevelopment, which are in turn shaped by the region's place in the international system. It provides a framework for examining a broad range of elements and for understanding how they interact and form part of a total system. The importance ascribed to these variables or combinations of variables has been the subject of debate and dispute. Indeed, *dependentistas* have shown themselves to be a mixed lot, and over time dependency theory has evolved in sufficiently different directions to create distinctions not dissimilar to schools of thought.

Dependency theory has appeared in three principal formulations. The first formulation assigns more or less equal emphasis to internal (national) and external (international) factors as sources of dependency. Emphasis falls more on such formal and institutional relationships as foreign aid, foreign investment, and trade relations than on class relations and class conflict, which are given attention but not prominence.[7]

The second current treats dependency theory as a subfield of the Marxist analysis of capitalism and a refinement of the Leninist theory of imperialism. The center and the periphery stand in antagonistic relationship to one another, and the influence of the former on the latter is all-encompassing and at all times pernicious and exploitative. Emphasis falls on the formation of classes and on class conflict and on the interplay between classes and economic change.[8]

The third formulation represents variations of those two schools and a mixture of both. Underdevelopment as an externally induced condition is not the sole consideration; its effects on relations among different social

Simon Teitel, "Tecnologia, industrializaciòn y dependencia," ibid. 38 (January–March 1973): 601–25.

7   Representative works include Celso Furtado, "Development and Stagnation in Latin America: A Structural Approach," *Studies in Comparative Economic Development* 1 (1965): 159–75; Osvaldo Sunkel and Pedro Paz, *El subdesarrollo latinoamericano y la teoria del desarrollo* (Mexico, 1970); dos Santos, "Structure of Dependence," 231–36; and Joseph Kahl, *Modernization, Exploitation, and Dependency in Latin America* (New Brunswick, 1976).

8   See Joel Edelstein, "Dependency: A Special Theory within Marxist Analysis," *Latin American Perspectives* 8 (Summer–Fall 1981): 103–7; André Gunder Frank, *Latin America: Underdevelopment or Revolution* (New York, 1969); Timothy F. Harding, "Dependency, Nationalism, and the State in Latin America," *Latin American Perspectives* 3 (Fall 1976): 3–11; and James Petras, *Politics and Social Structure in Latin America* (New York, 1970).

classes operating within the same dependent structures is of even greater prominence. The possibility is acknowledged that capitalism, including foreign capital, can play an economically useful role in development; its considerable social and economic costs, however, bring it within the realm of discussion and debate in political arenas.[9]

Critics of dependency theory challenge *dependentistas* at a variety of points and on a number of issues. They range across the full ideological spectrum and include *dependentistas* themselves, who have quarrels with specific formulations of one school or another. The debate among *dependentistas* turns principally on theoretical issues and originates from a radical perspective; the challenge from the critics of dependency centers on methodological concerns and emanates largely from liberal traditions.

Dependency theorists clash at any number of points. Some bemoan too much theory; others decry the ambiguity of theory. Some warn against the perils of emphasizing the dominance of the political over the economic; others insist upon it. Some *dependentistas* emphasize market and trade relations; others examine relations of production. Some are critical of paradigms that stress competition and conflict among nations rather than among classes. Some reject the emphasis on distribution over production. These differences in emphasis have led to differences of other kinds. Some suggest that capitalism retains the potential to contribute to development and assign a leadership role to the national bourgeoisie, the owners of the means of production; others see no alternative to socialism and no place for the national bourgeoisie. Some writers contend that the emphasis on imperialism as the principal source of dependency overlooks the importance of internal social and cultural factors as sources of underdevelopment, specifically, that dependency formulations tending to ignore questions of culture, race, gender, and ethnicity risk overlooking noneconomic dimensions of dependency and underdevelopment.[10]

The liberal critique of dependency theory turns on a number of inter-related methodological issues. Not that theoretical concerns are unim-

9 These writers include Fernando Henrique Cardoso and Enzo Faletto, *Dependencia y desarrollo in América Latina* (Mexico, 1969); Fernando Henrique Cardoso, "Imperialism and Dependency in Latin America," in Bonilla and Girling, eds., *Structures of Dependency*, 7–16; and Anibal Quijano, *Redefinizaciòn de la dependencia y marginalizaciòn en América Latina* (Santiago, 1970).

10 The debate among *dependentistas* has produced a vast literature. A summary of the *dependentista* critiques of dependency theory is found in Ronald H. Chilcote, "Dependency: A Critical Synthesis of the Literature," *Latin American Perspectives* 1 (Spring 1974): 4–29; idem, "Issues of Theory in Dependency and Marxism," ibid. 8 (Summer–Fall 1981): 3–16; Ronaldo Munck, "Imperialism and Dependency: Recent Debates and Old Dead-Ends," ibid., 162–79; and Fernando Henrique Cardoso, "The Consumption of Dependency Theory in the United States," *Latin American Research Review* 12:3 (1977): 7–24.

portant; on the contrary, in a larger sense, theory is a central issue. Most liberal critics are essentially attacking Marxist analysis and charging that dependency is more ideological than empirical. They argue that *dependentistas* have been long on theory and short on data, that dependency formulations have not been subject to sufficiently rigorous examination. The lack of empirical data and the absence of concrete case studies, critics charge, mean further that the central premises of dependency remain speculative and untested. The absence of empirical data thus appears to reduce the dependency paradigm to a circular argument: Dependent countries are those without the capacity to sustain independent development, and they lack this capacity because economic structures are dependent ones.[11]

The critiques of dependency theory both from within its ranks and from without have generally had a salutary effect. Theoretical disputation continues unabated, to be sure, and given the variety of ideological stances, there is no reason to believe it will end anytime soon. At the same time, however, the reworking of theoretical formulations has been accompanied by a comparable narrowing of research focus, and claims have been scaled down to more modest and manageable levels. Greater attention has been given to methodological rigor and to the collection of empirical data. This in turn has encouraged *dependentistas* to respond to critics precisely where dependency had been most vulnerable: case studies.

Research on dependent industrialization, for example, has provided empirical case studies to corroborate key elements of *dependentista* arguments. The links between dependent industrialization in Argentina, Brazil, and Chile on one hand and U.S. penetration on the other have been examined in detail. Multinational corporations raise capital from local sources and thereby integrate local capitalists into the dominant economies. By this means, multinational corporations act to repatriate capital in the form of profits, royalties, licensing charges, franchise fees, interest payments, and commissions. This outflow of capital, in conjunction with other forms through which Latin Americans send capital abroad, contributes to a chronic balance-of-payments crisis in Latin America, which is then offset by foreign loans. Receipt of foreign loans results in still greater diminution of national decision-making autonomy, for borrowers are obliged to concede to lenders, as a condition of the

11   See C. Richard Bath and Dilmus D. James, "Dependency Analysis of Latin America: Some Criticisms, Some Suggestions," *Latin American Research Review* 11:3 (1976): 3–54; and David Ray, "The Dependency Model of Latin American Underdevelopment: Three Basic Fallacies," *Journal of Inter-American Studies and World Affairs* 15 (February 1973): 4–20.

loan, greater participation in national policy formulation. Policies must be explained to and approved by lenders, and invariably these circumstances open the local economy to foreign capital. Loans must be repaid with interest; the subsequent necessity of obtaining new loans to finance the interest on old loans serves further to facilitate economic penetration, expand foreign political control, and sustain subservient relationships.[12]

Prerevolutionary Cuba provides a representative case study, albeit in somewhat exaggerated form. But precisely because the Cuban case stands in such sharp relief, it offers insight into the sources and consequences of dependent relationships and the means by which internal structures served U.S. interests. Through the first half of the twentieth century, U.S. capital all but overwhelmed the Cuban economy. Successively, sugar, tobacco, banking, transportation, mining, utilities, ranching, and commerce passed under U.S. control. The Cuban economy was dominated by U.S. capital, operated by U.S. technicians and managers, and organized around U.S. needs. Almost all elements of public life, including government organization, the armed forces, and public administration, were in varying degrees shaped by U.S. interests. The line that properly divided Cuban interests from U.S. needs grew ever so blurred, and the blurring almost always favored the latter. A vast middle class came into existence, dependent upon and identified with U.S. interests. Cubans were integrated directly into U.S. consumption patterns, and in the process developed familiarity with and fondness for things North American, not only consumer goods but also normative structures, which influenced vast areas of the public and private lives of middle-class Cubans. In almost everything but name, Cuba had become a part of the United States.[13]

12 Some representative case studies include Theotonio dos Santos, "Foreign Investment and Large Enterprise in Latin America: The Brazilian Case," in *Latin America: Reform or Revolution?* ed. James Petras and Maurice Zeitlin (Greenwich, 1968), 431–53; James Petras, *Latin America: From Dependence to Revolution* (New York, 1973); Dale L. Johnson, "The National and Progressive Bourgeoisie in Chile," in *Dependence and Underdevelopment*, ed. James D. Cockcroft, André Gunder Frank, and Dale L. Johnson (New York, 1972), 165–217; William G. Tyler and J. Peter Wogart, "Economic Dependence and Marginalization: Some Empirical Evidence," *Journal of Inter-American Studies and World Affairs* 15 (February 1973): 36–45; Frederick Stirton Weaver, *Class, State, and Industrial Structures: The Historical Process of South American Growth* (Westport, 1980); George L. Beckford, *Caribbean Economy: Dependence and Backwardness* (Mona, Jamaica, 1975); idem, *Persistent Poverty. Underdevelopment in Plantation Economies of the Third World* (New York, 1972); Clive Y. Thomas, *Monetary and Financial Arrangements in a Dependent Monetary Economy. A Study of British Guiana, 1945–1962* (Mona, Jamaica, 1965); and idem, *Dependence and Transformation: The Economics of the Transition to Socialism* (New York, 1974).
13 See Donald W. Bray and Timothy F. Harding, "Cuba," in *Latin America: The Struggle with Dependency and Beyond*, ed. Ronald H. Chilcote and Joel C. Edelstein (New York, 1974), 583–739; Francisco Lòpez Segrera, *Cuba: capitalismo dependiente y*

The Cuban revolution served to expose the nature of dependency; the pursuit of independent development provoked the wrath of the United States. In order to overcome conditions of dependency, Cubans found it necessary to transform existing internal structures. That is, it became necessary to control natural, industrial, and technical resources and, most important, to redefine the terms of Cuba's relations with the United States, the central player in the island economy. The historic integration of Cuba's economy into the U.S. system had advanced to the point where the changing of internal structures in Cuba all but guaranteed confrontation with international structures, over which the United States had enjoyed virtually unchallenged control. Collision was inevitable.

In the years since its initial formulation, the dependency paradigm has been reworked, revised, and refined. It has evolved in different directions, and in the process dependency arguments have found wider application, most notably in relation to underdevelopment in Africa.[14]

Dependency propositions also raise important historiographical issues, including the continued efficacy of the very craft of diplomatic history. An alternative model of U.S.–Latin American relations serves to underscore the need for alternative methodological and theoretical frameworks. Nowhere perhaps is this more apparent than in the need to redress the normative imbalance so long a dominant feature of the historiography of U.S.–Latin American relations. An understanding of inter-American relations cannot be derived from research conducted principally in Washington and based largely on the use of presidential papers and a reading of the State Department cable traffic. The research scope must expand to include the use of Latin American archival sources and public records as well as Latin American newspapers, periodicals, and other published and unpublished materials—all as a means of obtaining some understanding of relations within the Latin American context: that is, at least as much from within up as from outside down.

Nor can relations with Latin America be subsumed into or replaced

subdesarrollo (1510–1959) (Havana, 1981); and Louis A. Pérez, Jr., *Cuba under the Platt Amendment, 1902–1934* (Pittsburgh, 1986).

14 See Juan Corradi, "Dependency and Foreign Domination in the Third World," *Review of Radical Economics* 4 (Spring 1972): 1–125; Walter Rodney, *How Europe Underdeveloped Africa* (London, 1972); Samir Amen, *Neo-Colonialism in West Africa* (New York, 1973); Tony Barnett, "The Gezira Scheme: Production of Cotton and the Reproduction of Underdevelopment," in *Beyond the Sociology of Development: Economy and Society in Latin America and Africa,* ed. Ivar Oxaal, Tony Barnett, and David Booth (London, 1975), 183–207; J. Esseks, "Economic Dependency and Political Development in New States of Africa," *Journal of Politics* 33 (November 1971): 1052–75; and Barbara Stallings, "Economic Dependence in Africa and Latin America," *Comparative Political Series* 3 (1972): 5–60.

by the study of policy formulation or the conduct of political relations between governments. U.S.–Latin American relations suggest a reality of another kind, one that requires an alternative conceptual framework within which to analyze the points of contact and the consequences of those contacts. The dependency paradigm frames the structural relationships of imperialist domination within which all other inter-American contacts must be located and understood. To state this in slightly different terms: The central issue is that the inter-American interaction, at almost all levels and all the time, is between states vastly unequal in power and resources. Dependency constructs seek to address the question of internal development in Latin America as a function of unequal relations. Internal developments in the United States are themselves increasingly subject to the consequences of a political economy of domination, and nowhere perhaps more dramatically than in the growing legal and illegal immigration from Latin America.

The focus thus shifts to the context and consequences of this inequality, specifically to the means and mechanisms of domination by the United States. It has not been the same everywhere in Latin America, of course; nor has it been the same in any one place over time. Imperialism itself is often required to confront the contradictions generated by domination. Imperialism creates over time, and often at one and the same time, conditions that subvert as well as sustain continued domination. The system is not perfect and breaks down, often. But as dependency theorists have argued forcefully, a system there is, and by focusing on the power of the United States, in its multiple forms as well as in its maintenance and extension, the meaning of "relations" changes significantly.

Acknowledgment must be made, moreover, of the means by which people in the periphery create space and thus autonomy within the interstices of these contradictions. Through wile and cunning, with resourcefulness and ingenuity, dependent societies learn to exploit vulnerabilities of the metropolis, wherever and whenever exposed, and up to a point they can limit the reach and effect of imperial systems.

Dependency formulations offer historians of U.S.–Latin American relations an alternative perspective from which to examine the workings of the inter-American system, specifically the form and function of the presence of the United States in Latin America and the manner in which it contributes internally to shaping economic growth, delineating political options, forming ideological values, and influencing cultural patterns, and finally how the sum of all the foregoing serves to give context and content to inter-American relations. It expands the notion of "relations" between the United States and Latin America into a totality of things political, social, economic, military, cultural, and ideological. It is within this all-encompassing environment that the presence of Donald Duck looms large, for he discharges an important social function—at once product and proponent of the universality of dependent relationships.

8

Balance of Power

STEPHEN PELZ

American diplomatic historians use a variety of analytical approaches in their work. Many of these approaches—nationalist, realist, corporatist, and eclectic—focus on different analytical levels, from domestic economic and political structures or international systems to individual and governmental decisions. I have argued elsewhere that diplomatic historians should consider all of these levels of activity and all of these structures when they analyze diplomatic decisions, in order to be sure that they do not neglect any important causal factor.[1] The realist school stresses the importance of one international level—the structure of the international balance of power—and realism has recently enjoyed something of a resurgence in the United States. In spite of this renewed interest, however, American diplomatic historians have yet to develop a full body of theory to support the realist approach.[2] Fortunately, international relations spe-

Another version of this essay originally appeared in the Winter 1991 issue of *Diplomatic History*, copyright 1991 by Scholarly Resources Inc. It is printed here by permission of Scholarly Resources Inc. The author is grateful for the aid provided by the National Fellows Program, Hoover Institution, Stanford, CA; the International Security Studies Program of the Woodrow Wilson International Center for Scholars, Washington, DC; and the East Asian Institute, Columbia University, New York. He also wishes to thank Ole Holsti and Richard Immerman for their helpful comments on an earlier draft. He is solely responsible for the contents of the essay.

1 For an overview of historiography see Jerald A. Combs, *American Diplomatic History: Two Centuries of Changing Interpretations* (Berkeley, 1983). For analytical eclecticism see Gerald K. Haines and J. Samuel Walker, eds., *American Foreign Relations: A Historiographical Review* (Westport, 1981), xii, 76, 83, 92, 146, 160, 198, 215, 226, 335; for levels of analysis in diplomatic history see Stephen E. Pelz, "A Taxonomy for American Diplomatic History," *Journal of Interdisciplinary History* 19 (Autumn 1988): 259–76. For levels of analysis in international relations theory see J. David Singer, "The Level-of-Analysis Problem in International Relations," in *The International System: Theoretical Essays*, ed. Klaus Knorr and Sidney Verba (Princeton, 1961), 77–92.

2 The basic realist texts are Hans J. Morgenthau, *Politics among Nations: The Struggle for Power and Peace* (New York, 1949); George F. Kennan, *American Diplomacy, 1900–1950* (Chicago, 1951); Samuel Flagg Bemis, *A Diplomatic History of the United States* (New York, 1965); Robert Osgood, *Ideals and Self-Interest in America's Foreign Relations: The Great Transformation* (Chicago, 1953); Norman A. Graebner, *Foundations of American Foreign Policy: A Realist Appraisal from Franklin to McKinley* (Wilmington, DE, 1985); idem, *America as a World Power: A Realist Appraisal from Wilson to Reagan* (Wilmington, DE, 1984); idem, *Ideas and Diplomacy: Readings in*

cialists have been developing realist theories.[3] I propose to use the best of these political science theories to describe the operations of international systems since 1750 and to sketch very briefly the effects those systems had, or should have had, on U.S. policymakers.

Realists assume that a high degree of anarchy reigns among nation-states and that each state tries to expand its power relative to the others. Each state has vital territorial, economic, and industrial regions that are particularly vulnerable to other powers, and each state seeks to make these areas more secure by expanding its power until it has a comfortable margin of superiority over its rivals.[4] Each state can augment its security by building up its own military forces; hence realists include in their analyses those national characteristics that affect the size and use of each nation's armed forces.[5]

Realist diplomatic historians also assume that the need for security transcends all other needs. The struggle for power is dangerous and if a state does not put its security needs first, it may fall prey to other nations.[6] Consequently, realists believe that they can explain many of America's diplomatic decisions by using the changing balances and imbalances of the international system. They portray U.S. decision makers as responding to threats to the vital assets of the United States or as taking advantage of the opportunities that the international system gives U.S. leaders to increase the security of the nation by expanding its military strength or by making alliances. Realists would argue that only when such international incentives and disincentives fail to explain policymakers' actions should the diplomatic historian consider other causal factors. On the other hand, if the structure of the international system does not change, but diplomatic and military policies do change, then of course the his-

the *Intellectual Tradition of American Foreign Policy* (New York, 1964); and Jerald A. Combs, "Norman Graebner and the Realist View of American Diplomatic History," *Diplomatic History* 11 (Summer 1987): 251–64.

3   K. J. Holsti, *The Dividing Discipline: Hegemony and Diversity in International Theory* (Boston, 1985), 1, 5–6, 11–12, 44–54, 82, 133, 137–40; Michael Banks, "The Inter-Paradigm Debate," in *International Relations: A Handbook of Current Theory*, ed. Margot Light and A. J. R. Groom (Boulder, 1985), 7–26.

4   Robert Gilpin, *War and Change in World Politics* (Cambridge, England, 1981), 25; Nicholas Spykman, *America's Strategy in World Politics: The United States and the Balance of Power* (New York, 1942), 21–22.

5   Kenneth N. Waltz, "Reflections on *Theory of International Relations*: A Response to My Critics," in *Neorealism and Its Critics*, ed. Robert O. Keohane (New York, 1986), 329.

6   Benjamin A. Most and Randolph M. Siverson, "Substituting Arms and Alliances, 1870–1914: An Exploration in Comparative Foreign Policy," in *New Directions in the Study of Foreign Policy*, ed. Charles F. Hermann, Charles W. Kegley, Jr., and James N. Rosenau (Boston, 1987), 134.

torian has to look to other levels of analysis for the causes of those changes.

Balance-of-power systems are stable to the extent that they satisfy three conditions. First, they must have an alliance structure and a distribution of benefits that reflects the balance of power among the members of the system. Second, there must be substantial ideological agreement among the principal powers on what the system exists to protect. And third, there must be commonly accepted procedures for managing changes within the system.[7] When one state grows in power and achieves more security, it often threatens other states proportionally. If the threat grows large enough, the decision makers in the threatened states have a strong incentive to unite and oppose the rising power. The threatened states can restore the balance by expanding their alliances, by negotiating economic or territorial concessions in order to compensate for the power of the rising state, or by engaging in a limited war that curbs the rising nation without destroying it. Thus, the structure of the balance of power and the rules of the international system shape the options that are open to decision makers, occasionally in decisive ways.[8] If the decision makers follow the rules of such a balance-of-power system by making adjustments for the changing strengths of the members, then the system can persist for decades.[9]

The structure of each international system provides a different set of incentives and disincentives for policymakers, and in turn those incentives and disincentives provide tacit rules that decision makers should follow. These rules take two forms: first, there are behavioral rules that describe how policymakers can respond rationally to the structure of incentives and disincentives; second, there are internalized social norms that describe what actors should do to maintain the system.[10] We can term these

7 Gordon A. Craig and Alexander L. George, *Force and Statecraft: Diplomatic Problems of Our Time* (New York, 1983), x; James K. Oliver, "The Balance of Power Heritage of 'Interdependence' and 'Traditionalism,' " *International Studies Quarterly* 26 (September 1982): 305; C. Fred Bergsten, Robert O. Keohane, and Joseph S. Nye, "International Economies and International Politics: A Framework for Analysis," in *World Politics and International Economics*, ed. C. Fred Bergsten and Lawrence B. Krause (Washington, 1975), 4–6.

8 See Ole R. Holsti's Chapter 5 in this volume; and Pelz, "Taxonomy," 261–71.

9 James E. Dougherty and Robert L. Pfaltzgraff, Jr., *Contending Theories of International Relations: A Comprehensive Survey* (New York, 1981), 23–28. This essay owes much to Richard N. Rosecrance, *Action and Reaction in World Politics: International Systems in Perspective* (Boston, 1963), 17–20, 23–25. See also Ole R. Holsti, P. Terrence Hopmann, and John D. Sullivan, *Unity and Disintegration in International Alliances: Comparative Studies* (New York, 1973), 4–6.

10 Stephen D. Krasner, "Structural Causes and Regime Consequences: Regimes as Intervening Variables," in *International Regimes*, ed. Stephen D. Krasner (Ithaca, 1983),

the economic and social rules of the various systems. Because international systems are anarchical, they usually encourage the policymakers of each power to maximize their gains, a fact that creates constant tension between the economic rules and social norms of each system.

Changes of power and status can occur frequently within one historical system, but the structure of the system and its rules can also be transformed entirely. There are three main causes of such fundamental transformations. Political and social revolution within one or more of the key players in a system can release vast new political and ideological strength within the revolutionary states and simultaneously threaten the stability of the other powers' spheres of influence and even their domestic stability, military security, and continued existence.[11] Examples of such upheavals are the French Revolution and the spread of Maoist peasant revolts. The rise of powerful new military methods or technologies can also transform systems. Some examples of such new methods are Napoleon's use of the nationalistic levée en masse to smash the professional armies of his enemies, the rise of industrialized warfare, and the advent of complex and numerous nuclear weapons systems in the twentieth century.[12]

Changes in systems can also result from uneven economic and technological development among the great powers that cause permanent shifts of leadership.[13] This type of leadership change is more common than the more fundamental military or political revolutions. It does not disrupt traditional balance-of-power systems, because it merely replaces one leader with another, while the rules of the system remain the same.

For most of its early years, the United States existed in a multipolar balance-of-power system. This type of balance of power can be called System I. It existed from 1776 to 1793 and again from 1815 to 1892. During these years there were five or more great powers\that were fairly equal in national strength. Most of these states had fairly similar polities

3. For a purely structural analysis see Kenneth Waltz, *Theory of International Relations* (Reading, MA, 1979). For both structural and social rules see Morton Kaplan's important works, *System and Process in International Politics* (New York, 1957), and *Towards Professionalism in International Theory: Macrosystem Analysis* (New York, 1979). Kaplan's rules are models for those in this essay, especially for Systems I and IV.

11 Rosecrance, *Action and Reaction*, 31–35, 44–47, 236–39; Henry A. Kissinger, *A World Restored: The Politics of Conservatism in a Revolutionary Age* (New York, 1964), 1–3.

12 William H. McNeill, *The Pursuit of Power: Technology, Armed Force, and Society since A.D. 1000* (Chicago, 1982), 158–77, 190–215, 307–87.

13 Gilpin, *War and Change*, 11, 13–15, 22, 48, 54–59, 69–85, 124–27, 148–68, 177–82, 186–87, 198–202; Ole R. Holsti, Randolph M. Siverson, and Alexander L. George, *Change in the International System* (Boulder, 1980), xvii–xxiii, xxv–xxvi; Paul Kennedy, *The Rise and Fall of the Great Powers: Economic Change and Military Conflict from 1500 to 2000* (New York, 1987), xxii–xxiii, 439–40, 539–40.

(the governments of England and France were partial exceptions to the monarchical rule prevalent in the first half of the nineteenth century).

Most of these states also employed a diplomatic corps that tried to make the balance of power work by opposing hegemony and by redistributing territory (mostly outside western Europe) to compensate for shifting national strengths. The members of this cosmopolitan aristocracy believed in the legitimacy of the monarchical states in the system, as well as in the overall justice and efficacy of the last major territorial settlement their predecessors had achieved. Consequently, they rarely tried to appeal to disaffected regional or religious groups or to alienate classes among the populations of their rivals, nor did they try to overthrow the system by impinging on the members' vital interests or by destroying some of its members.[14] For the most part, the citizens of these states took little notice of foreign policies, which in fact affected the great majority of people very little (except, once again, in England and France). As a result, diplomats and generals were free to make alliances, wars, and peace treaties in ways that would support the balance of power. Any nation could ally with any other, and alliances were often brief and flexible.[15]

The aims of these alliance partners were usually very limited and constrained by military weakness. In most of the states, the government's powers of taxation were slight and armies were expensive. The monarchs would not conscript peasants and merchants, because these groups comprised the so-called productive classes. Therefore, the sovereigns hired mercenaries of various nationalities to fill the ranks of their standing armies. The commanders of these professional units were often unwilling to risk their highly trained and expensively armed men in frontal assaults, and the mercenary generals were likely to defect if offered a bribe by a desperate opponent.[16] In addition, the incentives for taking the offensive were low, and the advantages of the defense were many. Until 1793, defensive fortifications were difficult to overcome, because of the deadening effects of *tracé italien* walls on shot and shell. Overland logistics also proved difficult for aggressors. Professional soldiers would not make forced marches or live off the land for any considerable period; therefore, generals had to erect large supply depots filled with fodder, food, and munitions before being able to move their armies any great distance. Topographical maps, all-weather roads, and rail lines were scarce or did

---

14 Craig and George, *Force and Statecraft*, 7–8, 22–24, 30–31, 44–47; Graebner, *Foundations of American Foreign Policy*, xiv–xvii; Andrew M. Scott, *The Functioning of the International Political System* (New York, 1967), 11–16.
15 R. R. Palmer and Joel Colton, *A History of the Modern World* (New York, 1971), 165–66, 281–82.
16 Rosecrance, *Action and Reaction*, 17–25.

not exist at all. As a result, a nation that was challenged had time to construct defensive alliances. There was little possibility of surprise attack.[17] Wars consisted primarily of maneuver and siege along the borders and in the buffer zones and colonies of the great powers.

There was a similar structure of incentives at sea. Until 1850, sea transport was much cheaper than land transport, and that gave Britain a military and industrial advantage.[18] Nevertheless, in an era of wooden sailing ships armed with cannon, achieving command of the sea could prove difficult, because many powers were able to build up fleets of capital ships and privateers quickly after war was declared. England's control of the sea was often tenuous, and its large merchant fleets and supplies of imported food were often at risk.

In the end, no power could put its faith in a knockout blow, whether on land or at sea. Each nation preferred to gain its ends by peaceful negotiation, and when a power did fight, it limited its war aims. War was still cheap enough, however, to be justified on occasion when decision makers disagreed about the distribution of power, territory, and trade.[19]

According to international relations theorists, System I multipolar balance-of-power structures operated according to a number of assumptions, rules, and requirements. Such systems required at least five actors of fairly equal power. All actors tried to improve their security by choosing policies that provided a high probability of survival, rather than take risks that might yield either hegemony or annihilation. Thus the goal of the realist diplomat was always to be on the side of the more powerful alliance. Policymakers were especially wary of war between 1815 and 1850, because the earlier challenges of the French Revolution and Napoleon led them to fear that a systemwide war would produce a revolutionary hegemon.[20]

In System I, each actor feared a rise in productivity in another state and, therefore, each sought an extra margin of safety beyond that which its existing capabilities would justify—through new alliances, more colonies, economic concessions, or the acquisition of buffer zones. A gain for any one state, however, had to entail comparable economic or territorial compensation for all other states, in order to maintain the balance of power. Each power was thus free to pursue its national interests amorally as long as it did not try to overthrow the system.[21] Unlike their

17   McNeill, *Pursuit of Power*, 90–93, 158–75, 177–84; Scott, *Functioning of the International System*, 16.
18   Paul Kennedy, *The Rise and Fall of British Naval Mastery* (London, 1976), 195–96.
19   Scott, *Functioning of the International System*, 16.
20   Robert Jervis, "Security Regimes," in Krasner, ed., *International Regimes*, 178–84.
21   Scott, *Functioning of the International System*, 11–15.

counterparts in other systems, though, decision makers tended to take the social norms of System I fairly seriously.

In the classical multipolar balance-of-power system, policymakers tended to follow certain rules, which are outlined here:

System I: 1776–93, 1815–92
  A. Great power relations with other great powers
     1. Each power maintains or increases capabilities relative to those of its opponents
     2. Each power opposes any single actor or coalition that tries to dominate the system
  B. Great power relations with smaller powers
     1. Major powers try to dominate or heavily influence smaller powers, particularly those that occupy strategic positions or possess important resources
     2. In times of change in the balance of power, the weaker coalition of great powers bids for the support of the smaller powers
  C. Conduct of small powers
     1. In peacetime, small powers try to play great powers against other great powers in order to maintain independence or gain concessions
     2. In times of tension or war, small powers try to extort disproportionate concessions for their neutrality or their participation in wars that are threatened or are in progress
  D. Diplomacy
     1. Each great power tries to join or construct the preponderant coalition
     2. Frequent and businesslike diplomatic conferences adjust the balance of power by distributing monetary and territorial compensation, but usually without resort to war
  E. Military action
     1. The powers use limited amounts of force to adjust the balance of power or to oppose potential hegemons
     2. Each power goes to war rather than pass up a chance to increase its capabilities
  F. Constraints on the use of force
     1. Each power has to rationalize the war as necessary for maintaining or adjusting the balance[22]
     2. Each power permits defeated actors to reenter the system as acceptable alliance partners on terms that do not greatly alienate them

22 Bruce Russett and Harvey Starr, *World Politics: The Menu for Choice* (New York, 1985), 102–4, 106, 112–13, 117–21; Spykman, *America's Strategy in World Politics*, 21–22; William Riker, *The Theory of Political Coalitions* (New Haven, 1962), 32–33. For a philosophical discussion of what constitutes a just war under balance-of-power theory see Michael Walzer, *Just and Unjust Wars: A Moral Argument with Historical Illustrations* (New York, 1977), 74–85.

G. Military assets, technologies, and doctrines
   1. Economic: Most belligerents rely on limited national taxes, merchant ship prizes, and forage and loot
   2. Troops: Most belligerents use professional standing armies and some conscripts
   3. Technology: Most belligerents use muskets, light field artillery, and sailing ships of the line
   4. Strategy: Most belligerents use incremental encirclement, attrition, and limited campaigns
H. Ideology: Each power opposes any actor or coalition that engages in supranational activities, such as subversive appeals, religious or revolutionary campaigns, or collective security operations
I. Risk taking
   1. Major powers risk wars of adjustment fairly frequently
   2. Major powers attempt hegemonic wars very rarely
J. Domestic politics: Elites are able to make foreign policy decisions with little interference[23]

System I motivated the decision makers to follow these rules, for it was in the long-term interest of each ruling group to do so. Consequently, the system policed itself, ensuring the security of its members.

The classic form of the multipolar balance of power is:

$$A + B \text{ vs. } C + D$$
$$< - E - >.$$

In this case, E is the holder of the balance and joins the weaker side to redress the balance. A nation in this position often exacted rewards far beyond its contribution to the coalition, because its participation was vital to each side.[24] The balance of power in Europe frequently took this form or followed rule (A)(2), under which the lesser powers united against a potential hegemon. Realists among U.S. diplomatic historians look back at these System I rules and the decision makers who succeeded under them for models of how the international system works and how policymakers should act.

The rules of System I shaped decision makers' behavior between 1715 and 1793. During this period, England and France struggled for global power and the British were able to play the role of holder of the balance in Europe by allying first with the Austrians and then with the Prussians to defeat the French on land. At the same time, the Royal Navy was able to defeat France and Spain in the Americas. The result was a massive

---

23 I have adapted these rules from Kaplan's theory sketch of the balance of power. See *Towards Professionalism*, 134–41.
24 Dougherty and Pfaltzgraff, *Contending Theories*, 156–58; Morgenthau, *Politics among Nations*, 194–97.

victory for Britain in 1763 that threatened French and Spanish positions across the globe. Consequently, the British found themselves in a singularly unsplendid isolation during the American Revolution.[25] The French came to believe that the ultimate winner in the contest for colonies might also be the winner in a future European struggle, and they decided to aid the Americans after 1776.[26] The American revolutionaries established their credibility as a worthy alliance partner by declaring independence, building a standing army, and inflicting an occasional defeat on the British.[27]

Britain had also made the mistake of neglecting the Royal Navy, whose strength had declined below that of the combined fleets of France and Spain.[28] Consequently, in 1779, the admiralty concentrated its ships of the line near the channel, allowing the French to achieve intervals of superiority in North America.[29] The British army could find no vital zone to conquer in the largely agricultural American colonies and controlled only the ground its troops occupied; nationalistic American militias controlled the countryside and denied supplies to British foraging parties.[30] As a result, the British had to transport food and munitions across thousands of miles of ocean and up hundreds of miles of cart paths to supply their troops. The effects of distance on the British—formally known as the loss of strength gradient—helped to protect the Americans.[31]

The Spanish and French also threatened to cut Britain's links with India, and French fleets were able to land soldiers in Rhode Island and Virginia to aid the American revolutionaries. In the end the French, Spanish, Dutch, and Americans were able to force the British to abandon many of their positions in America in 1783 by threatening them at home and bleeding them abroad. The American diplomats recognized the limits of the coalition victory, however, and settled for a peace of moderation.[32]

The rise of the new American nation left the Americans and the British as the principal rivals in North America; thus, there was an asymmetrical

25 Kennedy, *British Naval Mastery*, 98, 104; Marvin R. Zahniser, *Uncertain Friendship: American-French Diplomatic Relations through the Cold War* (New York, 1975), 38; Palmer and Colton, *The Modern World*, 196–202, 280–93, 366–72.
26 Max Savelle, "The American Balance of Power and European Diplomacy, 1713–78," in *The Era of the American Revolution: Studies Inscribed to Evarts Boutell Greene*, ed. Richard B. Morris (New York, 1939), 157–68.
27 Graebner, *Foundations of American Foreign Policy*, xxv.
28 Kennedy, *British Naval Mastery*, 99–116; Zahniser, *Uncertain Friendship*, 38.
29 Kennedy, *British Naval Mastery*, 96–100, 109–16, 137.
30 Russell F. Weigley, *The American Way of War: A History of United States Military Strategy and Policy* (Bloomington, 1973), 3–39.
31 Kennedy, *Rise and Fall*, 116–19: Kenneth E. Boulding, *Conflict and Defense: A General Theory* (New York, 1962), 244–47, 260–62, 268–69.
32 Graebner, *Foundations of American Foreign Policy*, xxix–xxxiii.

bipolarity in the North American subsystem. Britain still had many advantages and might well have strangled the new nation by using its position as holder of the balance in Europe to exact concessions from France and Spain in the Americas. But before Britain could put such strategies into effect, the British found themselves transfixed by the complete breakdown of the System I multipolar balance and the rise of a revolutionary France bent on hegemony. Consequently, the United States had time to grow in strength, while the British and the continental powers exhausted themselves in the Napoleonic struggles. (See System II below.)

Between 1815 and 1892 there was a return to System I. The British were still the major threat to the United States, but their attention necessarily remained fixed on the multipolar balance of power in Europe and the Middle East. After the demise of Napoleon, the European powers watched France carefully for a revival of its hegemonic ambitions, and after 1849 the far-reaching schemes of Napoleon III gave some substance to their fears. The British remained vulnerable in the Low Countries, where Napoleon III was still seeking railway concessions as late as 1869, and in the Mediterranean, where the French schemed against the British and Austrians in Spain, Italy, North Africa, and Egypt.[33] After the 1830s the rise of Russia further distracted the British in the Ottoman Empire and Afghanistan. For the most part the British had to try to exclude other European powers from the Americas or restrict their influence there.[34]

While England remained the Americans' main rival in North America, Britain's deployable military strength was severely limited in the Western Hemisphere. Great Britain had a small professional army, whose units were stationed in garrisons at home to police working class mobs and abroad to shore up the native armies of its global empire.[35] Although individual units of the British army were more than a match for the Americans on any battlefield, the British found it impossible to control the American hinterlands or maintain supply lines deep in American territory, because of the Americans' militia system. In time of war American armies could also easily threaten the Canadian heartland, while American ships could join the French fleet to harass the British West Indies, which were a major source of Britain's foreign investment in-

---

33 Rosecrance, *Action and Reaction*, 55–101, 232–36, 239–57. Rosecrance divides the period 1740–1960 into nine separate systems. Because I am interested in the relations of the United States to the central balance, I have found it convenient to reduce the number of systems to four.

34 Kenneth Bourne, *Britain and the Balance of Power in North America, 1815–1908* (London, 1967), 409.

35 Kennedy, *British Naval Mastery*, 159; idem, *Rise and Fall*, 152–54.

come.[36] Until the 1850s the British could still use their naval bases at Halifax, Bermuda, or Kingston to land expeditionary forces, burn the Americans' coastal cities, and decimate the U.S. merchant marine, but they could not credibly threaten the American interior.[37] When the French built a new battlefleet at midcentury, even those operations became more risky to contemplate.[38]

There was also a potentially unstable balance of power in western Europe from 1776 to 1793 and from 1815 through 1892—a balance that caused periods of great tension or war. The British were vulnerable in the Low Countries, the channel, and the homeland. Although France had a much larger population and army than Britain, Paris was also very vulnerable to attack by Britain, Prussia, and Russia. In addition, the French had to cover long borders, which were open to overland invasion and seaborne landings.[39]

In spite of Britain's apparent advantages, therefore, it was the United States that had the advantage in the North American subsystem, and it was the United States that benefited from a free ride in security matters. With Britain pinned in Europe by France and distracted by rivals across the globe, the Americans did not need alliances, permanent or otherwise. Nor did the United States have to sustain most of the burdens of a great power to deter the British during these years of the industrial revolution. Consequently, its people had greater funds to invest in the latest technologies with which to exploit the advantages of backwardness. By 1830 the United States was the sixth largest industrial power in the world.[40]

America's early diplomats exploited Anglo-French, Anglo-Spanish, and Anglo-Russian rivalries to enlarge American territory, thereby playing the game by rule (C)(2) of System I. In 1782, when France considered compensating the Spanish for their failure to take Gibraltar by giving them American territory, astute American diplomats made a separate peace with Britain and were able to secure the territory from the Appalachians to the Mississippi River as a reward for overthrowing the French alliance and making peace. Federalist diplomats like John Adams recognized that the United States should remain neutral and do what it could to maintain a balance between England and France. George Washington also followed that policy during the early stages of the French revolutionary wars.

36 Kennedy, *British Naval Mastery*, 128–29; Graebner, *Foundations of American Foreign Policy*, 70–73, 103–8.
37 Bourne, *Britain and the Balance of Power*, 46, 247.
38 Kennedy, *British Naval Mastery*, 156–57.
39 Kennedy, *Rise and Fall*, 88–89.
40 Ibid., 93–94.

When Spain's Latin American colonies revolted in the early nineteenth century, the British used the Royal Navy to prevent the French from intervening, thereby opening Mexico to American pressure.[41] By playing the British and French against each other and against Spain, the Americans were able to take Spanish Florida and secure the southwest from Mexico, where a power vacuum existed.[42] During the Mexican War, a new French fleet of steam warships threatened to bridge the channel. The French ships created such a panic in England that they distracted attention from Polk's war of expansion against Mexico.[43] The British and French would not ally with each other to support independence for Texas; nor would they agree to aid Mexico or the Confederate revolt; nor would the British encourage the establishment of a French puppet state in Mexico during the American Civil War. Realists among U.S. diplomatic historians give American policymakers high marks for pursuing an ambitious, but rational policy of expansion during the Mexican War.[44] The continued Anglo-French competition prevented joint action against the United States from abroad.[45]

Between 1854 and 1871, System I collapsed temporarily, as Prussia and France struggled for leadership of the system. Napoleon III renewed the French naval threat to Britain during the American Civil War by building a considerable number of sea-going ironclads.[46] In 1865 the United States had an army of a million men, a navy of 671 warships, and a population of 31.4 million.[47] With the end of the American Civil War, the United States could send this great military strength against the French in Mexico, who in any case were increasingly distracted by the aggressive expansion of Bismarck's Prussia. Prussia's acquisition of Silesia in 1866 turned Prussia into a threat to France's rear and dampened any French desire to continue their intervention in Mexico.[48] The rising Prussian threat also ended for all time France's attempts to recreate a balance of power in North America. Realists applaud the American diplomats for their steady pressure on France during the American Civil War, which

---

41 Graebner, *Ideas and Diplomacy*, 11–12, 16–17, 77–79, 90, 214–18.
42 Norman A. Graebner, ed., *Manifest Destiny* (New York, 1968), xv–xxvii, xlvi–lx, 178–79.
43 Kennedy, *British Naval Mastery*, 171–72.
44 Graebner, *Ideas and Diplomacy*, 162–63, 214–16; idem, *Foundations of American Foreign Policy*, 186–205, 257.
45 René Albrecht-Carrié, *A Diplomatic History of Europe since the Congress of Vienna* (New York, 1958), 116–21.
46 Kennedy, *British Naval Mastery*, 172–74.
47 Kennedy, *Rise and Fall*, 178–80.
48 Bemis, *Diplomatic History*, 393–94; Zahniser, *Uncertain Friendship*, 164.

secured a peaceful French withdrawal from Mexico.[49] And, in fact, U.S. diplomats were following rule (D)(2).

In the years after 1870 the French longed to revenge the loss of Alsace-Lorraine, creating a nationalistic Franco-German rivalry on the Continent.[50] Consequently, the legitimacy of the multipolar balance-of-power system declined. Bismarck was able to maintain the system, however, by isolating France. He appealed to the monarchical ideologies of the Austrian and Prussian emperors while mediating their rivalries. And he was able to pacify England by supporting that nation in its colonial rivalries with France.[51]

British interest in North America waned as American power grew. The successful Canadian drive for autonomy also made colonial pickings seem much richer elsewhere. The British recognized that they could not support a naval force on the Great Lakes large enough to defend western Canada, and therefore they planned to assume the defensive in time of war by holding fortresses at Montreal, Quebec, and Halifax. But the proximity of so many potential American volunteers armed with modern artillery made their prospects seem quite unpromising. Worse still, after 1871 the small British army could supply only 1,000 men to help the 773 Canadian regulars defend the fortresses. The Americans were able to put 25,000 regulars and 216,000 volunteers in the field within four months in 1898, while the most the Anglo-Canadian forces could hope to muster in that year was 33,000, most of whom were militia.[52] Britain and Canada thus refused to follow the continental states in adopting conscription and raising a large army, and those decisions spared the Americans much of the financial drain of the military revolution. Toward the end of the century, Britain's naval position also deteriorated again, and by 1884 the British faced a French fleet in the channel that had as many battleships as their own.[53]

Thus the multipolar balance of power that existed in Europe between 1815 and 1892 did not extend to North America, except for brief interludes. North America was a subsystem in which there was a bipolar balance between Britain and the United States. The two countries found it useful to negotiate a series of agreements adjusting their spheres of

49 Graebner, *Ideas and Diplomacy*, 220.
50 Kaplan, *Towards Professionalism*, 154.
51 Rosecrance, *Action and Reaction*, 250–57; William L. Langer, *European Alliances and Alignments, 1871–1890* (New York, 1950).
52 Bourne, *Britain and the Balance of Power*, 3–5, 18, 32, 43, 45–46, 118–19, 173–75, 206–11, 224, 295–304, 318–20, 336–53, 359–401; Kennedy, *British Naval Mastery*, 197.
53 Kennedy, *British Naval Mastery*, 178–79, 214–29.

influence. As the century waned and Britain's relative power fell, purely realistic American diplomats would have pressed the British as hard as they did the Spanish and Mexicans earlier, and they might have succeeded in clearing the British out of the Western Hemisphere by diplomatic pressure alone. A threat to ally with France might have proven compelling. But the United States was an atypical System I power, because its people were able to shape policy through such movements as manifest destiny, Young America, and the public reaction against the bloodshed of the U.S. Civil War, which curbed American aggressiveness between 1865 and 1885. In any case, astute English diplomacy led to a détente with the United States.[54]

The Americans benefited even more greatly from the rise of a tight bipolar revolutionary–counterrevolutionary system in Europe in the years between 1789 and 1815 (System II). One of the reasons for the collapse of the multipolar balance of power (System I) was the American Revolution itself, for it created a new model for arming the people and conducting a war of liberation. The success of the Americans encouraged French revolutionaries, who quickly became the leaders of a new bloc that aimed at hegemony. What made this challenge different from earlier French hegemonic challenges was its reliance on a nationalistic army of citizens supported by a national taxation system and by a national mobilization of the economy. Citizen soldiers were cheap to pay and replace, and they were willing to live off the land, make forced marches, and drive home mass attacks. With such forces Napoleon could aim at complete conquest.

Because national armies were easy to mobilize and deploy, tension increased within the system and standing alliances became more important. The French armies drove deep into other nations' heartlands, where the French would depose the old rulers, extend the Napoleonic code, and install their own government. During the early years of the revolution, the French could also appeal to sympathizers among their enemies' populations. For the leaders of the other great powers, war also had to become total in its aims, and they hastened to create armies large enough to destroy Napoleon's regime. The only way to end the French menace was to invade France and create a counterrevolution, which they finally did in 1815.[55]

Between 1918 and 1939, an even greater menace arose in Eurasia.

54 Samuel F. Wells, Jr., "British Strategic Withdrawal from the Western Hemisphere, 1904–1906," *Canadian Historical Review* 49 (December 1968): 335–56.
55 Rosecrance, *Action and Reaction*, 31–35, 44–46, 236–39.

Hitler and the Nazis were determined to conquer Europe and then establish a global empire.[56] The postwar international system and the European distribution of military power favored their ambitions. The Versailles settlement had much less legitimacy than the Franco-Prussian agreement of 1871. It did not reflect the distribution of industrial or potential military power. World War I had demonstrated that great power wars would turn into exhausting attritional struggles in which victory went to the stronger economic power, and in western Europe that power was Germany.[57] The alleged illegitimacy of the settlement allowed leaders in Germany and Italy to appeal directly to opinion in England and France.[58] Thus the imbalances in the balance-of-power system in Europe all but invited attempts to overthrow it.

By 1939, Germany's economy and war potential far outstripped those of France and Britain. The Nazi army and air force were superior to those of the other European nations and therefore threatened the Low Countries, Paris, and London.[59] Consequently, there was a shift in the balance-of-power system from loose to tight bipolarity between 1936 and 1939. An emerging German-Italian-Japanese entente forced a tightening of the Anglo-French-Polish entente and prompted the English and the Americans to coordinate their policies more frequently in the Far East. The British once again had to concentrate their naval forces near the channel, leaving the Pacific unprotected.[60] In the late 1930s both the Germans and the Japanese established a temporary lead in the arms race and then sought to establish regional hegemony by scoring knockout blows before the United States and the Soviet Union could respond.[61]

In such revolutionary–counterrevolutionary bipolar systems the balance of power was constantly threatened. Both sides competed for allies or at least strove to keep neutrals benevolently neutral. Both sides engaged in arms races, and the system suffered repeated crises as each leading power intervened in the other's sphere or conducted wars by proxy.[62]

---

56 Norman Rich, *Hitler's War Aims*, vol. 1, *Ideology, the Nazi State and the Course of Expansion* (New York, 1973), xi–xlii, 3–10.
57 Kennedy, *Rise and Fall*, 271–74, 296, 303–20.
58 Craig and George, *Force and Statecraft*, 57–58, 71, 87–99.
59 Kennedy, *British Naval Mastery*, 282–83, 286; idem, *Rise and Fall*, 303–20.
60 Stephen E. Pelz, *Race to Pearl Harbor: The Failure of the Second London Naval Conference and the Onset of World War II* (Cambridge, MA, 1974), 2–3; Kennedy, *British Naval Mastery*, 276–79.
61 Kennedy, *Rise and Fall*, 332; Pelz, *Race to Pearl Harbor*, 167–228.
62 Charles W. Kegley, Jr., and Eugene R. Wittkopf, *World Politics: Trend and Transformation* (New York, 1985), 464, 470.

These crises spurred the arms race and stimulated each side to try harder to secure a margin of superiority.[63] Alliances became ideological and inflexible, rather than pragmatic, like the balance system. Eventually a crisis escalated out of hand, and there was a prolonged bipolar war.[64]

Under System II, decision makers in the major powers tended to follow certain rules:

System II: 1793–1815, 1917–45

A. Great power relations with other major powers: Each bloc seeks to conquer and revolutionize its rival in order to expand or legitimize its system

B. Great power relations with small and neutral powers: Each bloc attempts to subvert or crush nearby neutral powers and enroll them in its bloc

C. Conduct of small and neutral powers
   1. Nearby neutral powers usually have to choose sides to avoid being crushed[65]
   2. Distant neutral powers try to stay neutral and exact concessions by threatening to join one side or the other[66]

D. Diplomacy: Each bloc tries to deceive and ruin the other

E. Military action
   1. Each bloc tries to overthrow the balance and impose revolution or counterrevolution throughout the system
   2. Each bloc prefers subversion, economic sanctions, and proxy wars to major wars
   3. Each bloc uses force where it has local superiority
   4. Each bloc fights a major war rather than allow its rival to gain preponderant strength[67]

F. Constraints on the use of force: None, except self-interest (some acts are mutually deterred, such as assassination of political leaders)

G. Military assets, technologies, and doctrines
   1. Economic: Most belligerents rely on extensive national taxes and the levée en masse
   2. Troops: Most belligerents use both volunteers and conscripts
   3. Technology: 1793–1815—most belligerents use large armies, heavy field artillery, and sailing ships of the line; 1917–45—large armies, armor, tactical and long-range strategic bombers, submarines, carriers, and amphibious invasion forces
   4. Strategy: Most belligerents seek annihilation and annihilation through attrition

---

63 Nazli Choucri and Robert C. North, *Nations in Conflict: National Growth and International Violence* (San Francisco, 1975), 114–32, 167–70, 203–18.
64 Russett and Starr, *World Politics,* 114–21.
65 Ibid., 84–85.
66 Ibid., 102.
67 For some similar rules see Kaplan, *Towards Professionalism,* 141–44, 146, 147; and Rosecrance, *Action and Reaction,* 236–39.

H. Ideology: Each bloc appeals to potential dissidents in the rival bloc and among neutral populations
I. Risk taking
  1. The counterrevolutionary bloc chooses defensive policies that increase the likelihood of survival
  2. The revolutionary bloc takes great risks
J. Domestic politics
  1. Elites in each bloc have wide powers to make foreign policy decisions and suppress dissent
  2. Because of the great risks and sacrifices that the bipolar contest requires, the elites take some steps to maintain morale

Between 1793 and 1815, American diplomats followed rule (C)(2). They played the British and the Spanish against revolutionary France and exacted territorial concessions in the Louisiana territory and Florida. The French Revolution ended the Family Compact between France and Spain, thereby opening the Spanish empire to French, English, and American predation, and American diplomats were quick to take advantage of Spanish weakness and France's European difficulties.[68] Napoleon sold Louisiana to the Americans in part because Jefferson threatened to ally with the British if Napoleon continued with his plans to annex it. Thereafter Napoleon threatened English control of the channel twice: from 1803 to 1805 and again from 1812 to 1814. For the British, the need to parry this French threat meant that the new American navy could pose a serious problem for British merchantmen and even for the defense of the British West Indies, where American ships might join the French battle fleet.[69] The hard-pressed British needed the profitable West Indies trade, because they had used their financial resources to offset Napoleon's larger armies and industries.[70] Therefore, they could not interfere with the transfer of the Louisiana territory to the United States. Jefferson's gains from the Louisiana Purchase were great, but realist historians consider the Republicans' policies in defense of trade to be much less commendable. The value of the trade, they argue, did not match the risks of the embargo policy, and eventually Madison led an unprepared nation into a dangerous and unnecessary war. After all, realist historians argue, England and France were still in balance in 1812, and it was to the Americans' advantage to keep them that way.[71]

68 Graebner, *Foundations of American Foreign Policy*, 97–98, 178–79.
69 Bemis, *Diplomatic History*, 94–95, 101–2, 105–7, 110, 120–37; Correlli Barnett, *Bonaparte* (London, 1978), 92–104.
70 Kennedy, *Rise and Fall*, 80, 96, 100.
71 Graebner, *Ideas and Diplomacy*, 82–85; idem, *Foundations of American Foreign Policy*, 118–24, 138–43; Paul A. Varg, *Foreign Policies of the Founding Fathers* (Baltimore, 1963), 70–80, 83–85, 101–14.

Systemic analysis suggests a different explanation for Madison's action as well. In this age of ideological warfare, many in Congress believed that the British wished to crush the American republican experiment and that the United States had therefore to strike a blow against the British. Madison may have had other motives as well. When deciding for war with the English in 1812, he expected Napoleon to conquer the Russians, build up the French fleet, and force the exhausted British to the bargaining table, where they would have to buy peace from both the French and the Americans.[72] Thus Madison may have been following rules (C)(2) and (E)(4) of System II. When he could not deter the British by threatening to join the French, he gambled on war to maintain U.S. independence. We should give Madison more credit than some realist historians do. He had to deal with the new revolutionary and counterrevolutionary rules of System II, and his calculations, though wrong, were not so unreasonable. In any event, the Americans were able, as a distant power, to escape the full consequences of Madison's decision for war, because in 1815 Britain had to concentrate on building a system that would restrain France in Europe.

Realists also give American decision makers low marks for their diplomacy between 1917 and 1941. The collapse of France in 1940, the rise of a worldwide Axis pact, the invention of long-range bombers, and the rise of amphibious and airborne invasion capabilities made the United States a near rather than a distant power. Consequently, most realists would argue that System II required the United States to help the Anglo-French alliance destroy the German threat. Eurasia contained far larger populations and many more natural resources and more industrial strength than the Western Hemisphere, and therefore American diplomats should have tried to keep Europe divided and in balance.[73]

The American reluctance to pursue a policy of Europe first has provoked a fair amount of speculation among realist historians. According to the realists, muddled American policies had especially unfortunate effects in East Asia, where they led to an unnecessary war with Japan. Realists argue that the Americans should have allied with the British to defend Southeast Asia or should have made a deal with Japan at the expense of China, France, and Britain, but instead they did neither. And U.S. decision makers had every incentive to make up their minds, because

---

72 Lawrence S. Kaplan, "France and Madison's Decision for War, 1812," *Mississippi Valley Historical Review* 50 (March 1964): 652–71; Richard Glover, "The French Fleet, 1807–1814; Britain's Problem; and Madison's Opportunity," *Journal of Modern History* 34 (September 1967): 234–51; Kennedy, *Rise and Fall*, 96–100, 137.

73 Spykman, *American Strategy*, 7, 447–48; George F. Kennan, *Realities of American Foreign Policy* (Princeton, 1954), 63–65; Bemis, *Diplomatic History*, 827.

British and Chinese defeats would force the United States to fight a two-ocean war with a one-ocean navy.[74] It is hard to refute the realist analysis of this period.

By 1892 the multipolar balance of power (System I) was ending and the system of nationalistic, bipolar, conventionally armed balances (System III) arose and continued until 1914. Under System III, decision makers had to contend with nationalistic citizens, many of whom had the vote or could achieve influence without the vote through passive resistance, strikes, or revolutionary riots. With the rise of William II to power and with the growing Socialist threat to the monarchy, Germany stopped being a status quo power and challenged England, France, and Russia for hegemony on the Continent and for colonial dominions.[75]

The German threat was substantial. German political and economic unification and railway building led to economies of scale and a rapid shift in the industrial balance of power in Europe. In 1870, Britain had three times the industrial capacity of Germany, but by 1910 Germany had pulled ahead of Britain.[76] The result was a tightening bipolarity and the division of much of Europe into two camps. By 1902, Germany and Austria-Hungary faced a bloc composed of France, Russia, and England. Between 1890 and 1914 the shift from a loose to a tightening bipolarity made it increasingly difficult for neutral powers, such as England and Turkey, to remain nonaligned.[77] The two coalitions were so evenly balanced that they had to try to win over the small Balkan neutrals and paid high prices to prevent defections from their own alliance. Under increasing nationalist pressure, the System I practice of holding regular diplomatic conferences, which had permitted businesslike adjustments of the balance of power, broke down in 1913.[78]

Changes in communications, industrial efficiency, military technology, and military organization also hastened the trend toward bipolarity. All of the nations of continental Europe had adopted conscription and had produced large land forces with many trained reserves. Because citizen soldiers manned the armies, war threats had to be justified at home in drastic terms. Inexpensive newspapers created the images of inveterate

74 Graebner, *America as a World Power*, xiii–xxviii, 1–63, 65–84; Paul W. Schroeder, *The Anglo-American Alliance and Japanese-American Relations, 1941* (Ithaca, 1958); Bemis, *Diplomatic History*, 827.
75 Fritz Fischer, *Germany's Aims in the First World War* (New York, 1967); Holger H. Herwig, *Politics of Frustration: The United States in German Naval Planning, 1889–1941* (Boston, 1976), 13–92.
76 Kennedy, *British Naval Mastery*, 189–90.
77 Russett and Starr, *World Politics*, 102–4, 106, 112–13.
78 Craig and George, *Force and Statecraft*, 40–47; James Joll, *The Origins of the First World War* (London, 1984), 54–56.

enemies and loyal allies. As a result, people began to demand decisive diplomatic victories rather than compromises. Changing military technology also increased tension in Europe and decreased the flexibility of alliances. Improved railroad lines and new military staff systems made surprise attacks and lightning campaigns possible, because they allowed huge armies to move quickly. Staff plans and the telegraph ensured that men, weapons, and supplies arrived on the battlefield together.[79] Britain's power to defend the Low Countries declined drastically, for the British refused to follow the continental powers by adopting conscription. In addition, the continental powers had standing armies that could use the railroads to descend in force on any British expedition that landed on their coasts. And the rise of the submarine, the torpedo boat, and mines made Britain's traditional strategy of close blockade difficult.[80] Because of the widespread fear of surprise attack, once opponents began to mobilize, military strategists insisted that their governments also mobilize and fight, in order to avoid a quick defeat.[81] Many alliance partners and neutral powers also concluded that they had to choose sides quickly and not wait to mediate the dispute, because a war might be over before they could intervene diplomatically or militarily. Gradually, the loose bipolar system lost its flexibility; the time available for diplomacy shrank markedly; and war became more likely.[82]

By 1911 the British had concluded that they would have to send a large army to the Continent if there was a war with Germany.[83] In 1902 the presence of a great German battle fleet just across the North Sea forced the Royal Navy to recall its battleships from the Far East, the Americas, and even the Mediterranean, and the admiralty knew that a British victory would be in some doubt if the fleets clashed.[84] In 1903 the admiralty admitted that the German threat would prevent the dispatch of battleships to defend Halifax and Bermuda and to deal with America's capital ships. Britain had also grown dependent on imports of food (53 percent) and raw materials (85 percent), and the U.S. Navy could help interrupt the delivery of

79   McNeill, *Pursuit of Power,* 185–306.
80   Kennedy, *British Naval Mastery,* 195–202.
81   Rosecrance, *Action and Reaction,* 120–21; Joll, *Origins of the First World War,* 58–91.
82   Patrick J. McGowan and Robert M. Rood, "Alliance Behavior in Balance of Power Systems: Applying a Poisson Model to Nineteenth Century Europe," *American Political Science Review* 49 (September 1975): 862; Russett and Starr, *World Politics,* 102–4, 106, 112–13.
83   Gilpin, *War and Change,* 25; Kennedy, *Rise and Fall,* 209–41, 257–58; idem, *British Naval Mastery,* 198–200, 208–11, 230–31.
84   Kennedy, *British Naval Mastery,* 178–79, 214–29; Arthur J. Marder, *From the Dreadnought to Scapa Flow: The Royal Navy in the Fisher Era, 1904–1919,* vol. 1, *The War Years: To the Eve of Jutland* (London, 1965), 14, 436–40.

such goods if it chose to do so. By 1913 the United States was also producing more than twice as many industrial goods as Britain.[85] The United States was thus the leading candidate to redress the balance of power threatened by Germany and it was in a position to exact a high price from Britain for doing so.

As bipolarity increased in the balance of power, arms races accelerated. Industrialization made it easier for nations to offset the growth of rivals by increasing their own military forces, because growing industrial efficiency reduced the cost of equipping large standing armies with their numerous reserves and masses of artillery. Such heavily armed forces seemed to promise quick victories and the fear of decisive defeat markedly increased tension among European nations. To prevent such defeats, each bloc sought a margin of safety in new alliances or in new weapons. Country A might build forces that provided a comfortable margin of security for itself, but in doing so it inevitably threatened Country B. No matter how strongly A might protest that its intentions were peaceful, A would be unable to convince B that A would not exploit its advantage.[86] Because the decision makers' responsibility for the security of their own country was absolute, they could not permit a major threat to go unanswered if they had the means to deter it. The results were an upward spiral of military spending and an ever-tightening bipolarity in the alliance systems.

To secure political support for the new taxes needed to support increased military spending, leaders on both sides had to blame each other for escalating the competition. The mutual recriminations made a settlement more difficult. With each step up the ladder of arms competition, costs grew geometrically. An all-out arms race began immediately after the Franco-Prussian War. Between 1871 and 1890, Britain increased its military spending 350 percent, France 250 percent, Russia 400 percent, Austria-Hungary 450 percent, and Germany 1,000 percent.[87] After 1915, modern warfare also required that each great power command vast resources to be able to fight a long war of attrition.

As the arms race see-sawed, a series of diplomatic crises occurred. The crises came when superiority was about to pass from one side to the other. Sometimes one or more powers tried to circumvent the quantitative race by choosing to compete qualitatively. If they could build a type of

---

85 Kennedy, *Rise and Fall*, 149, 171, 192–94, 200–202.
86 Samuel P. Huntington, "Arms Races: Prerequisites and Results," in *The Use of Force: International Politics and Foreign Policy*, ed. Robert J. Art and Kenneth N. Waltz (Boston, 1971), 365–76, 385–94; Russett and Starr, *World Politics*, 352–53; Boulding, *Conflict and Defense*, 244–47.
87 Rosecrance, *Action and Reaction*, 254–57.

strategic weapon that rendered all others in its class obsolete, they might overcome a real or threatened quantitative advantage for the other side. Military leaders preferred to develop offensive weapons before defensive weapons, because they thought in terms of winning wars. Such qualitative races were inherently unstable, for they tempted leaders in the arms race to exploit an advantage before rivals could acquire the new technology. Britain's Dreadnought battleships are an example of superweapons designed to overcome quantitative challenges.[88] When serious diplomatic disputes have combined with arms races, they have ended in war 75 percent of the time.[89]

Under the nationalistic, bipolar balance-of-power system, which extended from 1892 to 1914, leaders followed somewhat different rules from those described in Systems I and II.

System III: 1892–1914
  A. Large power relations with other large powers
    1. Each bloc opposes the other's attempts at hegemony
    2. Each power tries to maintain or increase its capabilities, and especially its industrial resources, in order to be able to win an industrialized war
    3. Each bloc engages in quantitative and qualitative arms races in order to maintain the balance
  B. Large power relations with small neutral powers: Each bloc competes for the support of small and neutral powers, with the weaker bloc bidding higher
  C. Conduct of small and neutral powers: Small and neutral powers try to preserve the weaker bloc in order to prevent hegemony
  D. Diplomatic action
    1. Each bloc seeks to construct and maintain the preponderant coalition
    2. The blocs hold diplomatic conferences that readjust the balance of power, but such meetings are confrontational and tend toward zero-sum solutions
  E. Military action: Each bloc risks war rather than allow rivals to expand their power significantly
  F. Constraints on the use of force: None, except self-interest (for example, no assassinations of political leaders)
  G. Military assets, technologies, and doctrines
    1. Economic: Most belligerents rely on national taxes, bond issues, and total mobilization of their manpower and their economies

88 Britain was able to maintain its lead in dreadnoughts until World War I. See Marder, *From the Dreadnought to Scapa Flow*, 3–4.
89 Michael Wallace, "Arms Races and Escalation: Some New Evidence," *Journal of Conflict Resolution* 23 (March 1979): 3–16; J. David Singer, "Accounting for International War: The State of the Discipline," *Journal of Peace Research* 18:1 (1980): 1–18.

2. Troops: Most belligerents use numerous, mobilized conscripts
3. Technology: Most belligerents use repeating rifles, rifled artillery, railroad resupply, steam-driven armored battleships, submarines, and destroyers
4. Strategy: Most belligerents seek annihilation

H. Ideology: Each bloc makes nationalistic appeals to ethnic minorities in the other bloc and to its own people

I. Risk taking
1. When losing in an arms race or in a contest for vital territory, each side has to mobilize and strike a knockout blow before the other side can put all its troops in the field
2. Decision makers take greater risks than under System I, because the stakes are higher in each contest

J. Domestic politics: Decision makers in each bloc try to satisfy domestic interest groups and mass publics, even if doing so entails attempting risky enterprises to satisfy a jingoistic public or forgoing an increase in capabilities to satisfy a pacific public

By 1905 the British and the French were encouraging the United States to hold the balance against Germany, but President Theodore Roosevelt was the only American leader interested in doing so. Most realists would argue that under System III the United States should have shored up the bipolar balance against Germany, and its failure to do so has provided one of the main problems for realist analysis.[90] After their long years of free security, Americans had come to believe that safety lay in geographic isolation. Realist diplomatic historians have also stressed the role that misplaced idealism, public opinion, and politics played in prolonging American isolationism.[91]

Actually, it is not clear that the changing military structure in Europe really required American intervention in World War I, because changes in military technology made the North Americans more secure from attack than at any time in their history. The Americans could seize the major coaling and oiling stations that battle fleets required—the British bases in Jamaica, Bermuda, and Nova Scotia, for example—and then meet any advancing battlefleet with submarines, torpedo boats, and their own capital ships.[92] In the unlikely event that an enemy fleet established a beachhead on the North American continent, railroads would enable the Americans to concentrate overwhelming forces against the invaders. In any event, German domination of Europe

90 Graebner, *Foundations of American Foreign Policy*, xiii–xxxvi, 1–179, 283–311.
91 Kennan, *Realities*, 63–65; idem, *American Diplomacy*, 3–20; Louis J. Halle, *Dream and Reality: Aspects of American Foreign Policy* (New York, 1959), 216–28, 233; Graebner, *Foundations of American Foreign Policy*, 332–33, 351–55.
92 Bourne, *Britain and the Balance of Power*, 313–15.

would not mean German control of the Atlantic, which an Anglo-American alliance could police. It was not until the rise of long-range bombers, amphibious invasion forces, and the Axis pact with Japan in 1940 that the structure of international politics shifted drastically, threatening the Western Hemisphere with a two-front war and possible invasion.

System IV, which we may call the era of nuclear revolutionary dipolarity, lasted from 1949 to 1965.[93] There were two superpowers that were overwhelmingly superior in conventional and nuclear strength to all of the other nations, and each superpower led a bloc of allies. As in System II, where a revolutionary–counterrevolutionary bipolarity prevailed, the superpowers intervened in many nations to establish or maintain governments that would support their bloc. In System II, however, Britain faced France across the channel, whereas in System IV there was a great distance between the two superpowers. That distance made sustained conventional military campaigns near or in each other's homeland difficult, because of the loss of strength gradient.[94] But the development of long-range bombers and missiles rendered both superpowers vulnerable to crippling air attacks. Security became a serious problem for both powers, and levels of tension increased.[95] Consequently, both superpowers conducted a quantitative and qualitative nuclear arms race that was highly unstable at first, because each superpower feared a decisive nuclear first strike.[96] Decision makers in each nuclear superpower were compelled to try to convince their opponents that they did not fear the consequences of a first strike by the other side.[97]

Consequently, the leaders of each superpower risked strategic nuclear war in order to maintain their claim to having a first-strike capability. Soviet and American leaders demonstrated their willingness to risk war during the second Berlin crisis and again during the Cuban missile crisis. When the Russians achieved a degree of nuclear strength, the Americans feared that they would exploit the approaching nuclear stalemate by using their superior conventional military forces in Europe. To forestall that possibility, the Americans rearmed Germany, but in doing so they provoked a conventional arms race and paved the way for the

---

93 Russett and Starr, *World Politics,* 389–90. For periodization see Kennedy, *Rise and Fall,* 357–95.
94 John Lewis Gaddis, *The Long Peace: Inquiries into the History of the Cold War* (New York, 1987), 225–26, 231–37. See the U.S. war plan OFFTACKLE, JCS 1844/46, 8 December 1949, Records of the United States Joint Chiefs of Staff, Record Group 218, CCS 381, USSR (3–2–46), sec. 41, National Archives, Washington, DC.
95 Scott, *Functioning of the International System,* 24–25.
96 Jervis, "Security Regimes," 190–91.
97 Bruce M. Russett, "Cause, Surprise and No Escape," *Journal of Politics* 24 (February 1962): 3–22.

deployment of theater nuclear weapons in Europe and around the world.[98]

The existence of nuclear weapons may have restrained the Soviet-American conflict to some degree, but the struggle between the two superpowers was a real one. Because the Americans were the status quo power after 1945 and because they were appreciably stronger than the Soviets, the system avoided a central war.

The rules of System II and System IV (the early Cold War period) have a great deal in common. Between 1945 and 1949, as their rivalry developed into a full ideological confrontation, the leaders of the United States and the Soviet Union followed the rules of System II. Each bloc used military force to set up friendly regimes in areas where it had local superiority, such as Italy, Eastern Europe, East and West Germany, Japan, and Korea. The Office of Strategic Services, the Central Intelligence Agency, and the Communist Information Bureau (Cominform) also appealed to dissidents in the East and the West. What Stalin lacked in ideological fervor, Mao supplied. In Indochina and Korea, the superpowers encouraged proxies to fight while avoiding direct confrontation. Eventually, each of the powers achieved a secure second-strike capability. With the onset of mutual assured destruction around 1965, both superpowers reduced their risk-taking behavior drastically. After 1965 they shared a strong incentive to act very cautiously, for escalation to the strategic nuclear level promised unacceptable levels of damage to both powers.[99] No overseas interests were worth risking such destruction, and therefore the status quo power had a great advantage in areas of vital interest, because the threats of the revisionist power were not credible.[100]

The quantitative and qualitative arms competition continued. The onset of the era of mutual assured destruction did not end the contest for the lead in the nuclear arms race. Diplomacy was almost impossible in the first-strike era, but became somewhat more practicable in the later period.[101] Nuclear weapons were easy to hide, though, and comprehensive arms control agreements were very difficult to achieve. The bloc leaders also vied for a conventional military lead and tried to gain or maintain numerous alliances in key areas of the world in order to demonstrate their ideological superiority and to deter attacks that might escalate to the strategic nuclear level. Maintenance of this conventional balance required the locally weaker power to make plans for theater

98 Kennedy, *Rise and Fall*, 376–80.
99 Ibid., 383–88, 395–413.
100 Scott, *Functioning of the International System*, 24–25.
101 Jervis, "Security Regimes," 191–92.

nuclear war in some of its spheres of interest. The theater nuclear war plans and the proliferation of nuclear weapons made the nuclear balance increasingly difficult to calculate and made crises potentially much more difficult to control. Consequently, the superpowers had a very strong incentive not to let conventional incidents escalate or to allow their allies to gain access to a nuclear trigger. Early in the period the superpowers were able to control their allies diplomatically, as at Suez and the Geneva Conference on Indochina, but they were unable to stop nuclear proliferation or to prevent their allies from becoming increasingly independent as time passed. There were many neutral powers, but in a large majority of cases their adherence to either bloc would not have substantially altered the balance of power. For the same reason, lesser powers shifted between blocs or into neutrality without provoking major crises.[102] Neutral powers and major international organizations tried to prevent strategic, theater nuclear, or proxy wars, but there was little room for diplomacy.[103] The superpowers and middle-range powers found it increasingly difficult to use force cheaply in the less developed countries, many of which were neutral. There were many reasons for this phenomenon. The penetration of communications networks through these areas contributed to the national mobilization of the masses. In addition, both superpowers were willing to provide rapid-firing weapons to their local allies in these regions. Because of the ideological nature of the contest between the blocs, however, a gain for one side was still considered a loss for the other, in spite of the fact that the nuclear stalemate guaranteed the national security of each bloc leader. Each superpower continued to use modern communications to support the propaganda and subversion efforts in its opponent's territory, in its spheres of influence, and in neutral territory.[104] There were some proxy wars, but because of the danger of escalation, the superpowers preferred to support national liberation movements, as in Vietnam and Eastern Europe.

There were a number of rules that decision makers tended to follow under System IV:

System IV: 1945–65
    A. Superpower relations with the other superpower
        1. The leaders of each bloc try to avoid nuclear, chemical, or biological war
        2. The leaders of each bloc try to destroy and revolutionize their rivals, within the constraints above
        3. The leaders of each superpower try to maintain or gain a margin of superiority in the nuclear arms race

102 Dougherty and Pfaltzgraff, *Contending Theories of International Relations*, 102.
103 Kaplan, *Towards Professionalism*, 141.
104 Scott, *Functioning of the International System*, 19.

4. Each superpower tends to respect the other's sphere of influence, except when the boundaries are unclear or a proxy regime crumbles

B. Superpower relations with major, small, and neutral powers
1. Each superpower tries to set up institutionalized alliance systems around the globe in order to deter conventional wars that might escalate into nuclear war
2. Each superpower tries to persuade its allies to forego nuclear weapons and to avoid actions that endanger the nuclear peace[105]
3. Each superpower allows lesser powers to shift from its alliance or from neutrality to the other alliance

C. Conduct of medium, small, and neutral powers
1. Medium, small, and neutral powers try to play the superpowers against each other in order to maintain their independence and to exact concessions
2. Nations close to a superpower usually have to enroll in one bloc or the other

D. Diplomatic action
1. Bargaining is a zero-sum game that is protracted and often fruitless
2. Each bloc seeks to wear down the other
3. Bargaining often has to take place while military action goes on
4. Truces usually occur after mutual exhaustion in limited wars

E. Military action
1. The superpowers use their forces to deter their opponents, to prevent a shift in the perceived nuclear balance, and to maintain and expand their blocs
2. Each superpower intervenes to prop up failing proxies in its own area of conventional military superiority[106]
3. Each superpower prefers subversion, economic warfare, and proxy wars to military action by its own forces
4. During the first-strike era, bloc leaders threaten major wars and endure nuclear crises but shrink from using nuclear weapons
5. During the mutual second-strike era, decision makers in each superpower mobilize nuclear weapons only as a last resort in a crisis[107]

F. Constraints on the use of force
1. Nuclear, chemical, and biological warfare are too expensive to use for any territorial, economic, or ideological gain
2. Because nuclear, chemical, and biological warfare are unappealing, both superpowers maintain limits on the geographic areas they will penetrate and the amounts of force they will use
3. Threats to use force are more effective in deterring advances than in exacting concessions

105 Dougherty and Pfaltzgraff, *Contending Theories of International Relations*, 102; Kenneth N. Waltz, "International Structure, National Force, and the Balance of World Power," *Journal of International Affairs* 21:2 (1967): 229.
106 See also Kaplan's rules in *Towards Professionalism*, 141–44.
107 Gaddis, *Long Peace*, 238–41.

G. Military assets, technologies, and doctrines
   1. Economic: Most belligerents rely on high and extensive taxes and large military industries
   2. Troops: Most belligerents use professionals and conscripts
   3. Technology: Each side has the ability to impose unacceptable damage on the other via strategic air and missile power, tactical nuclear weapons, mobile armies with great firepower, and carriers and submarines
   4. Strategies: The powers have an assortment of plans for preemption, annihilation, and peoples' wars
H. Ideology
   1. Each superpower makes ideological appeals to dissidents in the other bloc
   2. Each superpower uses ideological campaigns to repress dissidents within its own bloc
I. Risk taking
   1. During the first-strike era, bloc leaders are willing to risk major wars to prevent shifts in the perception of the nuclear balance
   2. During the mutual second-strike era, bloc leaders are reluctant to risk full conventional or nuclear war
J. Role of domestic politics
   1. The elite in the West has to pay a great deal of attention to domestic interest groups and mass opinion
   2. The elite in the East has to spend modest sums to shape domestic opinion and maintain morale

Realist historians are also unhappy with American diplomacy between 1942 and 1965. They believe that the United States could have moderated the Cold War by recognizing a Soviet sphere of interest in Eastern Europe. Instead, American decision makers pushed for national self-determination in an area where the United States had little interest. Realist historians also argue that the United States overreacted to the rise of Communist China and missed many chances to exploit Sino-Soviet friction. Although the policy of containment made some sense in Europe, realist historians consider it to have been inappropriate in much of the Third World, where unrest stemmed from nationalist revolutions. Thus, they believe that the United States entered the conflicts in Korea and Vietnam unnecessarily.[108] Realist historians have underestimated the degree of tension and the amount of bipolar inflexibility that the nuclear revolution created, and

---

108 Graebner, *Ideas and Diplomacy,* 631–43, 711, 716–21; idem, *America as a World Power,* 107–45, 147–63, 165–83, 215–48; George F. Kennan, *Memoirs, 1925–1950* (Boston, 1967), 314–24; Stephen Pelz, "U.S. Decisions on Korean Policy, 1943–1950: Some Hypotheses," in *Child of Conflict: The Korean-American Relationship, 1943–1953,* ed. Bruce Cumings (Seattle, 1983), 93–132; Hans J. Morgenthau, "We Are Deluding Ourselves in Vietnam," *New York Times Magazine,* 8 April 1965.

they may have underestimated the viciousness of the bipolar ideological contest as well.

We can conclude that realist diplomatic historians are correct in stressing the importance of analyzing the nature of international systems. It is one of the first places the diplomatic historian should look in seeking explanations. On the other hand, realist diplomatic historians should stop using the rules and norms of System I as criteria for analyzing and judging the decisions of American leaders in eras whose characteristics are very different from those of System I. Revolutionary eras challenged the legitimacy of the international systems and threatened the existence of many states participating in those systems. The addition of nuclear weapons to a revolutionary bipolar rivalry heightened tensions still further. Consequently, the stakes of diplomacy rose in these periods, options narrowed, alliances became much less flexible, and the scope for negotiations shrank.

Realist diplomatic historians should also consider more carefully the military factors that changed the calculations of decision makers in each era. The rise of conscript armies, industrialized warfare, and especially intercontinental delivery systems for nuclear weapons changed systemic incentives and disincentives drastically. To justify using volunteer and conscript armies, statesmen had to promise total victory, not neat little wars of adjustment. In addition, it is unrealistic of the realists to expect modern leaders to use force as a surgical political tool under such circumstances. The nationalization and industrialization of warfare in the twentieth century made escalation into long wars of attrition all too likely among the great powers. Nor should realists assume that power in the modern age inheres solely in the armies and the industries that nations can mobilize. In the era of modern communications and mass movements, powerful ideological appeals cross political boundaries.

Finally, realist diplomatic historians would do well to pay attention to those factors that transform one system into another. They need to be able to judge how well American leaders adjust to changes from system to system, because the rate of change appears to have accelerated in the twentieth century.[109] Through much of the nineteenth century, the North American subsystem stood outside the main European international system. And when a global system arose and the United States had to play a part in it, the rise of industrialized warfare, nuclear weapons, and Maoist peoples' wars drastically changed the incentives to use force. Only by comparing the incentives and disincentives in each international system can we understand these changes. I would suggest that both diplomatic

109 Scott, *Functioning of the International System,* 24.

historians and international relations specialists can profit from midlevel generalizations like the ones I have suggested, because such generalizations take into account changing historical circumstances.[110] If a sufficient number of us are willing to test some such generalizations, we can then look forward to more systematic and realistic analysis of the structural elements in U.S. diplomatic history.

110   Holsti, Hopmann, and Sullivan, *Unity and Disintegration in International Alliances*, 219–25.

9

Bureaucratic Politics

J. GARRY CLIFFORD

In the mid-1960s, when members of the Harvard Faculty Study Group on Bureaucracy, Politics, and Policy began to write their scholarly tomes, their sometime colleague in the mathematics department, the folk singer Tom Lehrer, inadvertently gave song to what came to be called the "bureaucratic politics" approach to the study of U.S. foreign policy. In his ballad about a certain German émigré rocket scientist, Lehrer wrote: "Once the rockets are up / Who cares where they come down? / That's not my department! / Said Wernher von Braun."[1] Lehrer's ditty, by suggesting that government is a complex, compartmentalized machine and that those running the machine do not always intend what will result, anticipated the language of bureaucratic politics. The dark humor also hinted that the perspective might sometimes excuse as much as it explains about the foreign policy of the United States.

The formal academic version of bureaucratic politics came a few years later with the publication in 1971 of Graham T. Allison's *Essence of Decision*. Building on works by Warner R. Schilling, Roger Hilsman, Richard E. Neustadt, and other political scientists who emphasized internal bargaining within the foreign policy process, and adding insights from organizational theorists like James G. March and Herbert A. Simon, Allison examined the Cuban missile crisis to refute the traditional assumption that foreign policy is produced by the purposeful acts of unified national governments. Allison argued that instead of resembling the behavior of a "rational actor," the Kennedy administration's behavior during the crisis was best explained as "outcomes" of the standard operating procedures followed by separate organizations (the navy's blockade, the Central Intelligence Agency's U-2 overflights, and the air force's scenarios for a surgical air strike) and as a result of compromise and competition among hawks and doves seeking to advance individual and organizational

Another version of this essay originally appeared in the June 1990 issue of the *Journal of American History*. It is printed here by permission of the *Journal of American History*.

1 Tom Lehrer, *That Was the Year That Was* (Reprise Records RS 6179), recorded July 1965.

versions of the national interest. Allison soon collaborated with Morton
H. Halperin to formalize the bureaucratic politics paradigm.[2] Other
scholars followed with bureaucratic analyses of topics including American decision making in the Vietnam War, the nonrecognition of China,
the Marshall Plan, U.S.-Turkish relations, the Antiballistic Missile (ABM)
decision, and U.S. international economic policy, as well as refinements
and critiques of the Allison-Halperin model. The John F. Kennedy School
of Government at Harvard made bureaucratic politics the centerpiece of
its new public policy program, and Allison became its dean. By the 1980s
his framework was being hailed as "one of the most widely disseminated
concepts in all of social science."[3]

The Allisonian message holds that U.S. foreign policy has become
increasingly political and cumbersome with the growth of bureaucracy
after World War II. Diversity and conflict permeate the policy process.
There is no single "maker" of foreign policy. Policy flows instead from
an amalgam of large organizations and political actors who differ substantially on any particular issue and who compete to advance their own
personal and organizational interests as they try to influence decisions.
The president, while powerful, is not omnipotent; he is one chief among
many. Even when a direct presidential decision is reached, the game does
not end because decisions are often ignored or reversed. Jimmy Carter

2 Allison, *Essence of Decision: Explaining the Cuban Missile Crisis* (Boston, 1971). See
   also idem, "Conceptual Models and the Cuban Missile Crisis," *American Political
   Science Review* 63 (September 1969): 689–718; Richard E. Neustadt, *Presidential
   Power: The Politics of Leadership* (New York, 1960); Samuel P. Huntington, *The
   Common Defense: Strategic Programs in National Politics* (New York, 1961); Roger
   Hilsman, *To Move a Nation: The Politics of Foreign Policy in the Administration of
   John F. Kennedy* (Garden City, 1967); Warner R. Schilling, "The H-Bomb Decision:
   How to Decide without Actually Choosing," *Political Science Quarterly* 76 (March
   1961): 24–46; James G. March and Herbert A. Simon, *Organizations* (New York,
   1958); and Allison and Halperin, "Bureaucratic Politics: A Paradigm and Some Policy
   Implications," *World Politics* 24 (Spring 1972): 40–80. This essay combines Allison's
   "organizational process" model and "governmental politics" model into one paradigm.
3 Halperin, "The Decision to Deploy the ABM: Bureaucratic and Domestic Politics in
   the Johnson Administration," *World Politics* 25 (October 1972): 62–96; idem, *Bureaucratic Politics and Foreign Policy* (Washington, 1974); I. M. Destler, *Presidents,
   Bureaucrats, and Foreign Policy: The Politics of Organization Reform* (Princeton,
   1974); David J. Alvarez, *Bureaucracy and Cold War Diplomacy: The United States
   and Turkey, 1943–1946* (Thessaloniki, 1980); Stephen D. Cohen, *The Making of
   United States International Economic Policy* (New York, 1977); Jerel A. Rosati, "Developing a Systematic Decision-Making Framework: Bureaucratic Politics in Perspec-
   tive," *World Politics* 33 (January 1981): 234–51; Hadley Arkes, *Bureaucracy, the
   Marshall Plan, and the National Interest* (Princeton, 1973); Leslie Gelb, *The Irony of
   Vietnam: The System Worked* (Washington, 1979); James C. Thomson, "On the Mak-
   ing of U.S. China Policy, 1961–1969: A Study in Bureaucratic Politics," *The China
   Quarterly* 50 (April–June 1973): 220–43; Robert P. Haffa, Jr., "Allison's Models: An
   Analytic Approach to Bureaucratic Politics," in *American Defense Policy*, ed. John E.
   Endicott and Roy W. Stafford, Jr., 4th ed. (Baltimore, 1977), 224.

may have thought he had killed the B-1 bomber, but a decade later the weapon was still being produced and its utility still being debated. Because organizations rely on routines and plans derived from experience with familiar problems, those standard routines usually form the basis for options furnished the president. Ask an organization to do what it has not done previously, and it will usually do what the U.S. military did in Vietnam: It will follow existing doctrines and procedures, modifying them only slightly in deference to different conditions.

Final decisions are also "political resultants," the product of compromise and bargaining among the various participants. As Allison puts it, policies are "*resultants* in the sense that what happens is not chosen... but rather results from compromise, conflict, and confusion of officials with diverse interests and unequal influence; *political* in the sense [of] ... bargaining along regularized channels among individual members of government." Similarly, once a decision is made, considerable slippage can occur in implementing it. What follows is hostage to standard operating procedures and the interests of the implementers. Even when a president personally monitors performance, as John F. Kennedy tried to do with the navy's blockade during the missile crisis, organizational repertoires and hierarchies are so rigid and complex that the president cannot micromanage all that happens. Kennedy's own naval background notwithstanding, he did not know that antisubmarine warfare units were routinely forcing Soviet submarines to the surface, thus precipitating the very confrontations he so painstakingly tried to avoid.[4]

The bureaucratic politics perspective also suggests that intramural struggles over policy can consume so much time and attention that dealing effectively with external realities becomes secondary. Strobe Talbott's extraordinarily well informed accounts of arms control policy during the Carter and Reagan years confirm the truism that arriving at a consensus among the various players and agencies within the government is more complicated, if not more difficult, than negotiating with the Soviets. Ironically, officials who are finely attuned to the conflict and compartmentalism within the American government often see unitary, purposive behavior on the part of other governments. Recall the rush to judgment about the Soviet shooting down of a Korean airliner in 1983 as compared to the tortured ("rules of engagement") justifications that followed the destruction of an Iranian aircraft by the American naval cruiser *Vincennes* in 1988. Wallace Thies has shown that Washington's protracted efforts in the 1960s to coerce North Vietnam by calibrating military pressure and diplomatic signals were doomed from the outset; not only did senior

4 Allison, *Essence of Decision*, 138, 162.

officials assume that the messages received in North Vietnam would be the same as those sent, never realizing that everyday "noise" created by ongoing military operations might drown out the intended signals, but they were oblivious to the fact that Hanoi's revolutionary goals made negotiations on the terms Washington meant to convey impossible.[5]

Several criticisms have been leveled at the bureaucratic politics approach. Some critics contend that ideological core values shared by those whom Richard J. Barnet has called "national security managers" weigh more in determining policy than do any differences attributable to bureaucratic position. The axiom "where you stand depends on where you sit" has had less influence, they argue, than the generational mindset of such individuals as Paul Nitze, John J. McCloy, and Clark Clifford, whose participation in the foreign policy establishment spanned decades and cut across bureaucratic and partisan boundaries. Similarly, the perspective underestimates the extent to which the president can dominate the bureaucracy by selecting key players and setting the rules of the game. The Tower Commission report exposed the flaws of instant bureaucratic analysis when it simplistically blamed the Iran-contra affair on a loose cannon in the White House basement and exonerated a detached president who was allegedly cut out of the policy "loop."[6] The historian must be careful in each case to judge how much of the buck that stops with the president has already been spent by the bureaucracy.

There is also the problem of evidence. Given the pitfalls of getting access to recent government documents, analysts of bureaucratic politics have relied heavily on personal interviews. Indeed, one scholar has stated that if "forced to choose between the documents on the one hand, and

5   Talbott, *Endgame: The Inside Story of Salt II* (New York, 1979); idem, *Deadly Gambits: The Reagan Administration and the Stalemate in Nuclear Arms Control* (New York, 1984); Thies, *When Governments Collide: Coercion and Diplomacy in the Vietnam Conflict, 1964–1968* (Berkeley, 1980), 397–401.
6   See Robert J. Art, "Bureaucratic Politics and American Foreign Policy: A Critique," *Policy Sciences* 4 (December 1973): 467–90; Stephen D. Krasner, "Are Bureaucracies Important (or Allison Wonderland)," *Foreign Policy* 7 (Summer 1972): 159–79; Desmond J. Ball, "The Blind Men and the Elephant: A Critique of Bureaucratic Politics Theory," *Australian Outlook* 28 (April 1974): 71–92; James H. Nathan and James K. Oliver, "Bureaucratic Politics: Academic Windfalls and Intellectual Pitfalls," *Journal of Political and Military Sociology* 6 (Spring 1978): 81–91; Dan Caldwell, "Bureaucratic Foreign Policy-Making," *American Behavioral Scientist* 21 (September–October 1977): 87–110; Richard J. Barnet, *Roots of War: The Men and Institutions behind American Foreign Policy* (Baltimore, 1972), esp. 48–91; Douglas Little, "Crackpot Realists and Other Heroes: The Rise and Fall of the Postwar American Diplomatic Elite," *Diplomatic History* 13 (Winter 1989): 99–112; and Theodore Draper, "Reagan's Junta: The Institutional Sources of the Iran-Contra Affair," in *The Domestic Sources of American Foreign Policy: Insight and Evidence*, ed. Charles W. Kegley and Eugene R. Wittkopf (New York, 1988), 131–41.

late, limited, partial interviews on the other, I would be forced to discard the documents." In addition to using available documents, James G. Blight and David A. Welch have pioneered a "critical oral history" method whereby participants and scholars meet to reexamine past events such as the Cuban missile crisis.[7] Despite the value of having Robert MacNamara, Dean Rusk, McGeorge Bundy, and others review their roles and answer hard questions for the record, many historians would prefer that the current guardians of national security declassify and transcribe all tape recordings of meetings held by the Executive Committee of the National Security Council during the October 1962 crisis. Just as bureaucratic processes can shape policy, so too can scholarly interpretations be skewed by a research method that permits participants to put excessive spin on the past.

Yet those defects in the bureaucratic politics approach may not hamper historians, who do not need models that predict perfectly. Unlike political scientists, they do not seek to build better theories or to propose more effective management techniques. Because the bureaucratic politics approach emphasizes state-level analysis, it cannot fully answer such cosmic questions as why the United States has opposed revolutions or why East-West issues have predominated over North-South issues. It is better at explaining the timing and mechanics of particular episodes, illuminating proximate as opposed to deeper causes, and showing why outcomes were not what was intended. The bureaucratic details of debacles like Pearl Harbor and the Bay of Pigs invasion are thus better understood than the long-term dynamics of war and peace. As such, to borrow Isaiah Berlin's anthropomorphic analogy, bureaucratic politics provides one of many truths the fox must know as he competes with the single-minded hedgehog.[8] Whether one studies nuclear strategy, the rise of the military industrial complex, or the U.S. alliance with Britain, bureaucratic history provides pertinent pieces to the jigsaw puzzle.

Scholars have made excellent use of the perspective when it fits. In a study of relations between the United States and Argentina during World War II, Randall Bennett Woods shows that an inattentive president and feuding factions within the foreign affairs bureaucracy produced an oscillating "strategy" of treating Argentina as both pro-Fascist pariah and as penitent good neighbor. One of the few efforts to test Allison's model systematically, Lucien S. Vandenbroucke's analysis of the Bay of Pigs affair places much of the blame on officials in the Central Intelligence

---

7 Neustadt, quoted in Allison, *Essence of Decision,* 181; Blight and Welch, *On The Brink: Americans and Soviets Reexamine the Cuban Missile Crisis* (New York, 1989).
8 Berlin, *The Hedgehog and the Fox: An Essay on Tolstoy's View of History* (New York, 1957).

Agency who planned, organized, and sold the operation as a fail-safe version of the 1954 Guatemalan intervention. Vandenbroucke nonetheless concludes that President Kennedy, in his visceral Cold War values, wishful thinking, and discouragement of dissenters from "speaking up in church," was the real father of the fiasco. Jonathan G. Utley and Irvine H. Anderson, in separate accounts of the 1941 decision by the U.S. government to freeze Japanese assets, argue that organizational momentum and excessive zeal by second-echelon officials, most notably Assistant Secretary of State Dean Acheson, transformed the freezing order into a de facto embargo against Japan that neither Franklin D. Roosevelt nor Cordell Hull had intended when he signed it. In a recent study of the end of World War II in the Pacific, Leon V. Sigal demonstrates that both Washington and Tokyo behaved as if "each of their pieces on the board— armies, navies, air forces, diplomats—was acting on its own volition, moving according to its own program. There was, in short, no Pacific Endgame."[9]

Ernest R. May, chairman of the Harvard seminar that inaugurated the bureaucratic politics approach, has utilized it artfully and often. Because "one cannot run the facts of political history through a computer and test whether the outcome would have been different if one variable was changed and the others remained constant," May has been suggestive rather than definitive in studying historical lessons used and misused by bureaucrats and presidents. He has compared Harry S. Truman's decision not to intervene in China with that of John F. Kennedy and Lyndon B. Johnson to do so in Vietnam, and, in a recent collaboration, he and Richard E. Neustadt have shown how decision makers can better use history to "think in time," to "dodge bothersome analogues," and to "place" particular organizations within their own parochial understanding of the past.[10]

9 Woods, *The Roosevelt Foreign Policy and the "Good Neighbor": The United States and Argentina, 1941–1945* (Lawrence, 1979); Vandenbroucke, "Anatomy of a Failure: The Decision to Land at the Bay of Pigs," *Political Science Quarterly* 99 (Fall 1984): 471–91. See also Trumbull Higgins, *The Perfect Failure* (New York, 1987); Utley, "Upstairs, Downstairs at Foggy Bottom: Oil, Exports, and Japan, 1940–41," *Prologue* 8 (Spring 1976): 17–28; Anderson, "The 1941 De Facto Embargo on Oil to Japan: A Bureaucratic Reflex," *Pacific Historical Review* 44 (May 1975): 201–31; and Sigal, *Fighting to a Finish: The Politics of War Termination in the United States and Japan, 1945* (Ithaca, 1988), 283.

10 May, *The Truman Administration and China, 1945–1949* (Philadelphia, 1975), 49. See also idem, *"Lessons" of the Past: The Use and Misuse of History in American Foreign Policy* (New York, 1973); and Ernest R. May and Richard E. Neustadt, *Thinking in Time: The Uses of History for Decision Makers* (New York, 1986). May's study of the Monroe Doctrine, which stressed the primacy of ambition and electoral politics in explaining the actions of President James Monroe and his cabinet in 1823, did not elicit universal acceptance from historians. Perhaps bureaucratic politics, as

Greater application of the bureaucratic politics framework presupposes solid monographs on the foreign affairs bureaucracies and good biographies of key players. Indeed, May has urged "quasi-anthropological research just to establish who ought to be the personae in our narratives."[11] Thus far the historical literature, as might be expected, is fullest on the period before 1945. Building on the organizational synthesis of Robert H. Wiebe and Louis Galambos, historians have done fine work in charting the growth of the State Department and U.S. Foreign Service, analyzing the collective worldview at the State Department, and studying its regional experts. Philip Baram is particularly effective in combining the bureaucratic politics approach and an understanding of Open Door ideology to account for the State Department's pro-Arab policies during World War II.[12] Similar studies of the State Department and other agencies after 1945 have perforce been more impressionistic, as the proliferation of documentary sources and interagency vagaries regarding declassification have compartmentalized much of the historical writing on post–World War II foreign policy. Recent efforts to integrate national security themes and to rescue intelligence history from the espionage buffs should, however, encourage more rigorous bureaucratic analysis of Cold War policymaking.[13]

When can the perspective be most helpful? Because organizations func-

---

an interpretive framework, has greatest utility for the modern bureaucratic era. See Ernest R. May, *The Making of the Monroe Doctrine* (Cambridge, MA, 1975); Harry Ammon, "The Monroe Doctrine: Domestic Politics or National Decision?" *Diplomatic History* 5 (Winter 1981): 53–70; and Ernest R. May, "Response to Harry Ammon," *Diplomatic History* 5:71–73.

11 May, "Writing Contemporary International History," *Diplomatic History* 8 (Spring 1984): 110.

12 Wiebe, *The Search for Order, 1877–1920* (New York, 1967); Galambos, "The Emerging Organizational Synthesis in Modern American History," *Business History Review* 44 (Autumn 1970): 279–90; Waldo H. Heinrichs, Jr., "Bureaucracy and Professionalism in the Development of American Career Diplomacy," in *Twentieth-Century American Foreign Policy*, ed. John Braeman, Robert H. Bremner, and David Brody (Columbus, 1971), 119–206; Richard Hume Werking, *The Master Architects: Building the United States Foreign Service, 1890–1913* (Lexington, KY, 1977); Robert D. Schulzinger, *The Making of the Diplomatic Mind: The Training, Outlook, and Style of United States Foreign Service Officers, 1909–1931* (Middletown, 1975); Baram, *The Department of State in the Middle East, 1919–1945* (Philadelphia, 1978).

13 Barry Rubin, *Secrets of State: The State Department and the Struggle over U.S. Foreign Policy* (New York, 1985); John Ranelagh, *The Agency: The Rise and Decline of the CIA* (New York, 1986); Rhodri Jeffreys-Jones, *The CIA and American Democracy* (New Haven, 1989); Charles E. Neu, "The Rise of the National Security Bureaucracy," in *The New American State: Bureaucracies and Policies since World War II*, ed. Louis Galambos (Baltimore, 1987), 85–108; Anna Kasten Nelson, "The 'Top of Policy Hill': President Eisenhower and the National Security Council," *Diplomatic History* 7 (Fall 1983): 307–26; John Lewis Gaddis, "Intelligence, Espionage, and Cold War Origins," *Diplomatic History* 13 (Spring 1989): 191–212.

tion most predictably in a familiar environment, major transformations in the international system (wars and their aftermaths, economic crises, the Sino-Soviet split) require the analyst to study how institutional adjustments in U.S. policies resulted from the changes. Similarly propitious are transitions that bring in new players pledged to reverse the priorities of their predecessors, and particularly those administrations in which the president, deliberately or not, encourages competition and initiative from strong-willed subordinates. Fiascos like the American failure to fend off the attack on Pearl Harbor and the Iran-contra affair not only force agencies to reassess procedures and programs but, even better, often spawn official investigations that provide scholars with abundant evidence for bureaucratic analysis. Budget battles, weapons procurement, coordination of intelligence, war termination, alliance politics—in short, any foreign policy that engages the separate attentions of multiple agencies and agents should alert the historian to the bureaucratic politics perspective.

Consider, for example, the complex dynamics of American entry into World War II. Looking at the period through the lens of bureaucratic politics reveals that FDR may have had more than Congress and public opinion in mind when making his famous remark: "It's a terrible thing to look over your shoulder when you are trying to lead—and to find no one there." The institutional aversion to giving commissioned naval vessels to a foreign power delayed the destroyers-for-bases deal for several weeks in the summer of 1940, and only by getting eight British bases in direct exchange for the destroyers could Roosevelt persuade the chief of naval operations, Admiral Harold Stark, to certify, as required by statute, that these destroyers were no longer essential to national defense. According to navy scuttlebutt, the president threatened to fire Stark if he did not support what virtually every naval officer opposed and the admiral agonized before acquiescing.[14] Similarly, the army's initial opposition to peacetime conscription, FDR's dramatic appointment of Henry L. Stimson and Frank Knox to head the War and Navy departments in June 1940, his firing of Admiral James O. Richardson for his opposition to basing the Pacific fleet at Pearl Harbor, the refusal of the army and navy to mount expeditions to the Azores and Dakar in the spring of 1941, the unvarying strategic advice not to risk war until the armed forces were better prepared—all suggest an environment in which the

---

14 For Franklin D. Roosevelt's remark see John E. Wiltz, *From Isolation to War, 1931–1941* (New York, 1968), 63; John Callan O'Laughlin memorandum of telephone conversation with Herbert Hoover, 16 August 1940, O'Laughlin Papers, box 45, Library of Congress, Washington, DC; and William R. Castle, Jr., diary, 20 September 1940, Houghton Library, Harvard University, Cambridge, Massachusetts.

president had to push hard to get the bureaucracy to accept his policy of supporting the Allies by steps short of war. Even the navy's eagerness to begin Atlantic convoys in the spring of 1941 and the subsequent Army Air Corps strategy of reinforcing the Philippines with B-17s were aimed in part at deploying ships and planes that FDR might otherwise have given to the British and the Russians.[15]

Bureaucratic opposition also revealed itself in leaks. Colonel Truman Smith, an intelligence officer on the General Staff with close ties to Charles Lindbergh and other isolationists, told former President Herbert Hoover in June 1941 that "no member of the General Staff wants to go to war. . . . Out of fifteen members in his section of the General Staff . . . no one could see any point of our going to war." When the chairman of the American First Committee made a speech the following July predicting the occupation of Iceland while American forces were still at sea, War Department lawyers considered the leak a violation of the Espionage Act of 1917 (even though the landing took place without incident). The more notorious leak of the Joint Army-Navy Board's RAINBOW-5 war plans to the *Chicago Tribune* just a few days before Pearl Harbor led the Federal Bureau of Investigation to trace the source to someone close to Army Air Corps chief General Henry H. ("Hap") Arnold, perhaps Arnold himself.[16] This is not to argue that the German military attaché was correct in boasting to Berlin that pro-Nazi officers on the American General Staff would block U.S. intervention. It does affirm, however, that in steering the country toward war in 1940 and 1941, President Roosevelt could not move any faster than the armed forces were prepared to go. A zigzag course became inevitable.

In sum, this essay should be read as a modest plea for greater attention to bureaucratic politics. The perspective can enrich and complement other

15 J. Garry Clifford and Samuel R. Spencer, Jr., *The First Peacetime Draft* (Lawrence, 1986); J. Garry Clifford, "A Connecticut Colonel's Candid Conversation with the Wrong Commander-in-Chief," *Connecticut History* 28 (November 1987): 25–38; David A. Haglund, "George C. Marshall and the Question of Military Aid to England, May–June 1940," *Journal of Contemporary History* 15 (December 1980): 745–60; Mark A. Stoler, "From Continentalism to Globalism: General Stanley D. Embick, the Joint Strategic Survey Committee, and the Military View of National Policy during the Second World War," *Diplomatic History* 6 (Summer 1982): 303–21; Waldo H. Heinrichs, *Threshold of War: Franklin D. Roosevelt and American Entry into World War II* (New York, 1988), 42–44, 144.

16 Herbert Hoover memorandum of conversation with Truman Smith, 1 June 1941, Post-presidential Individuals Files, box 509A, Hoover Papers, Herbert Hoover Library, West Branch, Iowa; Grenville Clark memorandum to Henry L. Stimson, 18 July 1941, Clark Papers, Baker Library, Dartmouth College, Hanover, New Hampshire; Thomas Fleming, "The Big Leak," *American Heritage* 38 (December 1987): 64–71; James V. Compton, *The Swastika and the Eagle: Hitler, the United States, and the Origins of World War II* (Boston, 1967), 105–24.

approaches. By focusing on internal political processes we become aware of the conflict within government before arriving at the cooperative core values posited by the corporatists or the neorealists. In its emphasis on individual values and tugging and hauling by key players, bureaucratic politics makes personality and cognitive processes crucial to understanding who wins and why.[17] Although bureaucratic struggles may be over tactics more than over strategy, over pace rather than direction, those distinctions may matter greatly when the outcome is a divided Berlin and Korea, a second atomic bomb, an ABM system that no one really wanted, or the failure of last-minute efforts to avert war in the Pacific. Too easily dismissed as a primer for managing crises that should be avoided, the bureaucratic politics perspective also warns national security managers that when "governments collide," the machines cannot do what they are not programmed to do. Rather than press "delete" and conceptualize policy only as rational action, it is incumbent on historians to know how the machines work, their repertoires, the institutional rules of the game, and how the box score is kept. The processes are peculiarly American. The British ambassador Edward Lord Halifax once observed that the foreign policy establishment in Washington was "rather like a disorderly line of beaters out shooting; they do put the rabbits out of the bracken, but they don't come out where you would expect."[18] Historians of American foreign relations need to identify the beaters and follow them into the bureaucratic forest because the game is much bigger than rabbit.

17 Even attitudes toward sex become central if we examine, say, the vicious infighting from 1940 to 1943 that arose over charges of homosexuality against Undersecretary of State Sumner Welles, which eventually led to his resignation. See Irwin Gellman, *The Welles Connection* (forthcoming).

18 Lord Halifax to Sir John Simon, 21 March 1941, Hickleton Papers, reel 2, Churchill College, Cambridge University, Cambridge, England.

10

Psychology

RICHARD H. IMMERMAN

Was Richard M. Nixon mad when he assumed responsibility for U.S. foreign policy? The attention paid to his personality, particularly after the Watergate break-in, suggests that many people believed him to be so, or close to it. In one context Nixon evidently preferred it that way: Although he possessed no secret plan to end the war in Vietnam, he intended to persuade Hanoi that it must either agree to a quick peace or, according to H. R. Haldeman, face the consequences of a madman cocking the trigger on the American nuclear shotgun. "They'll believe any threat of force Nixon makes because it's Nixon," the president reportedly confided to his White House chief of staff. "I want the North Vietnamese to believe I've reached the point where I might do *anything* to stop the war. We'll just slip the word to them [that we] can't restrain him when he's angry . . . and Ho Chi Minh himself will be in Paris in two days, begging for peace."[1]

Whether Nixon sincerely sought to portray himself as a madman, was mad to think he could, or was just plain mad cannot be determined from

Another version of this essay originally appeared in the June 1990 issue of the *Journal of American History*. It is printed here by permission of the *Journal of American History*. The author received instruction in political psychology while a Social Science Research Council/MacArthur Foundation fellow in International Peace and Security Studies. He thanks Fred I. Greenstein and Robert Jervis for their patient guidance. He also wants to thank Professors Greenstein and Jervis, along with Thomas Paterson, George Herring, J. Garry Clifford, and Robert McGlone, for their helpful comments on earlier drafts.

1 The quality varies, but the most obvious examples of personality-oriented studies of Nixon are Bruce Mazlish, *In Search of Nixon: A Psychohistorical Inquiry* (New York, 1972); Fawn Brodie, *Richard Nixon: The Shaping of His Character* (New York, 1981); James David Barber, *The Presidential Character: Predicting Performance in the White House*, 2d ed. (Englewood Cliffs, 1977), 345–442, 457–84; and, most dramatically, Bob Woodward and Carl Bernstein, *The Final Days* (New York, 1976); and Arthur Woodstone, *Nixon's Head* (New York, 1972). In addition, "classics"—such as Garry Wills, *Nixon Agonistes: The Crisis of the Self-Made Man* (Boston, 1970); and Theodore H. White, *Breach of Faith: The Fall of Richard Nixon* (New York, 1975)—should not be ignored. A recent illustration of how Nixon-watchers cannot avoid considering his personality is Joan Hoff-Wilson, "Richard Nixon: The Corporate Presidency," in *Leadership in the Modern Presidency*, ed. Fred I. Greenstein (Cambridge, MA 1988), 165–98. For the "madman" theory see H. R. Haldeman, *The Ends of Power* (New York, 1978), 82–83.

the available evidence. What is more, because Haldeman was reconstructing from memory a conversation that occurred some ten years earlier, he could have distorted the president's words or manufactured the incident to serve his own purposes.[2] Yet Haldeman alleges the conversation did take place, and it is plausible. It is also instructive.

Accounts such as Haldeman's invite us to consider and explore the relationship between psychology and the history of American foreign relations. On the other hand, the episode speaks directly to the influence of a policymaker's personality on his policies. Nixon need not have been mad for his predispositions, attributes, identifications, and emotions to have affected his strategies and tactics, not only toward Vietnam but toward the Middle East, Chile, Bangladesh—everywhere. On the other hand, regardless of the condition of Nixon's mind, he wanted the North Vietnamese to *think* he was mad. This objective suggests another dimension of psychology that bears on foreign relations: cognitive psychology. Here we are concerned with perceptions, beliefs, the encoding and retrieval of information, memory, and other mental processes. Based on his assumptions about the North Vietnamese, Nixon wanted to send a particular signal that he expected to be interpreted in a particular way. Cognitive theories hold that this tactic was vulnerable to error.

Skeptics may judge Nixon and his alleged madman theory too atypical to serve as normative illustrations. Granted that the incident was unusual, the characterization does not negate the argument that psychology is integral to the study of diplomatic history in general. Quite the contrary. Because highly abnormal or unpredictable behavior such as that of Nixon or Woodrow Wilson is not easily explained by situational variables, it is the most accurate barometer of the saliency of personality factors. Personality disorders, moreover, can most readily become consequential. The suitability of a psychological approach, however, is not limited to when individuals appear to act irrationally or erratically.

The history of American foreign relations is punctuated with fascinating individuals: Benjamin Franklin, Thomas Jefferson, John Quincy Adams, William H. Seward, Theodore and Franklin D. Roosevelt, George F. Kennan, James V. Forrestal, John Foster Dulles, John F. Kennedy, Lyndon B. Johnson, Ronald Reagan—the list is endless. Their personalities alone did not determine policy—environmental and situational variables are always influential and frequently decisive. But predispositions, attributes, motives, affects (or emotions), and other elements that

---

2   Fred I. Greenstein raises a number of reasons for being skeptical in his review of *The Price of Power* by Seymour M. Hersh. See Fred I. Greenstein, "A Journalist's Vendetta," *The New Republic,* 1 August 1983, 30–31.

constitute personality, broadly defined, played a role. A secretary of state less self-confident, audacious, or stubborn than John Quincy Adams might have failed to orchestrate the transcontinental treaty of 1819 with Spain or might have settled for a joint Anglo-American declaration of policy toward the Western Hemisphere instead of for the Monroe Doctrine. The impact of Ronald Reagan's personality on his administration's foreign relations was palpable if ambiguous. At a minimum, psychological variables serve as mediators between the environment and human activity. Behavior, therefore, is the product of the *interaction* between the individual and the situation in which he finds himself.[3]

An individual's cognitions, the processes by which he perceives and evaluates his physical and social environment, likewise contribute to his conclusions and recommendations. How else, for example, does he interpret the data he collects on the threat posed by an adversary or assess the potential for a diplomatic initiative? What are the bases for inferences about the normally and oftentimes deliberately ambiguous behavior of others? It has become almost axiomatic that the assimilation and interpretation of information, the grist for the policymaking mill, does not occur in a contextual vacuum. Decision makers frequently rely on the "lessons of history," drawing analogies with historical precedents in order to define a situation or identify a phenomenon. Psychological theories can help to explain how and why decision makers act in this manner, and in the process they can provide clues for locating errors in judgment or perception. They can also alert us to conditions, such as stress or anxiety, that can affect the deliberations and their outcomes.[4]

3   Fred I. Greenstein, *Personality and Politics: Problems of Evidence, Inference, and Conceptualization* (Princeton, 1987), 7; Robert Jervis, "Political Decision Making: Recent Contributions," *Political Psychology* 1 (Summer 1980): 98; George and George, *Woodrow Wilson and Colonel House: A Personality Study* (New York, 1964), xxii.

4   On the lessons of history see Ernest R. May, *"Lessons" of the Past: The Use and Misuse of History in American Foreign Policy* (New York, 1973); Richard E. Neustadt and Ernest R. May, *Thinking in Time: The Uses of History for Decision Makers* (New York, 1987). For the benefits of psychological insights compare these works with, for example, Robert Jervis, *Perception and Misperception in International Politics* (Princeton, 1976), 217–87. See also John D. Steinbruner, *The Cybernetic Theory of Decision: New Dimensions of Political Analysis* (Princeton, 1974); and Yuen Foong Khong, "From Rotten Apples to Falling Dominoes to Munich: The Problems of Reasoning by Analogy about Vietnam" (Ph.D. diss., Harvard University, 1987). On stress and anxiety see Ole R. Holsti and Alexander L. George, "The Effects of Stress on the Performance of Foreign Policy-makers," in *Political Science Annual*, vol. 6, *1975*, ed. Cornelius P. Cotter (Indianapolis, 1975), 255–319; Alexander L. George, "The Impact of Crisis-Induced Stress on Decisionmaking," in *The Medical Implications of Nuclear War*, ed. Frederic Solomon and Robert Q. Marston (Washington, 1986), 525–52. The potential impact of unusual conditions has long preoccupied students of decision making. See, for example, Alexander L. George, *Presidential Decisionmaking in Foreign Policy: The Effective Use of Information and Advice* (Boulder, 1980), 25–53; Irving L. Janis,

The very nature of psychology leads us to associate it with abnormal behavior, distorted perceptions, compromised processes, and the like. For explanatory purposes, therefore, its value would seem to be limited to extraordinary situations, such as Wilson's monumental struggle for the League of Nations. Actually, psychology's relationship to foreign policy is so pervasive as to be unexceptional. Deterrence, brinkmanship, credibility, commitment, risk, threat—these and many more conventional entries in the historian's lexicon are essentially psychological concepts. Central to each are perceptions, fears, wants, values, and parallel mental phenomena. The "psychology of foreign relations" has become more pronounced in the nuclear age as the function, perhaps the raison d'etre, of these weapons has been progressively divorced from the military sphere and associated with diplomatic and political solutions. To illustrate, as defined by Richard Ned Lebow, deterrence "consists of manipulating another actor's assessment of his interests and seeks to prevent any specified behavior by convincing the actor who may contemplate it that its costs exceed any possible gain."[5] The psychological implications are evident. Lebow might have added that experimental evidence suggests that a decision as to what policy best serves the national interest may depend on how decision makers frame their discussions. For example, individuals are more likely to accept greater risks if they perceive the potential outcome as a loss than if they perceive it as a gain.[6]

Conclusions from experiments, of course, do not necessarily generate universal certainties, nor do they generally take into account cultural or temporal differences. When the historian looks at the failures of U.S. policy in Vietnam or the postures of both Washington and Moscow during the Cuban missile crisis, however, the psychological literature on risks and the framing of decisions can prove illuminating. So can the concept of a security dilemma, which is likewise rooted in psychology. The foundation of the security dilemma is the generalization that efforts to increase the security of one nation frequently decrease the security of another. Consider all the historical analyses that emphasize the failure of antagonists to distinguish between offensive and defensive weapons and postures and that show how such spirals of misunderstanding and

Groupthink: Psychological Studies of Policy Decisions and Fiascoes, rev. ed. (Boston, 1982); and Irving L. Janis and Leon Mann, *Decision Making: A Psychological Analysis of Conflict, Choice, and Commitment* (New York, 1977).

5 Lebow, *Between Peace and War: The Nature of International Crisis* (Baltimore, 1981), 83. See also Alexander L. George and Richard Smoke, *Deterrence in American Foreign Policy: Theory and Practice* (New York, 1974); and Robert Jervis, Richard Ned Lebow, and Janice Gross Stein, *Psychology and Deterrence* (Baltimore, 1985).

6 Amos Tversky and Daniel Kahnemann, "Rational Choice and the Framing of Decisions," *Journal of Business* 59 (October 1986): S251–S278.

misperceptions fed tensions and conflict. Indeed, much of the literature on the origins of the Cold War accents this phenomenon. To quote John Lewis Gaddis as an example, "It seems likely that Washington policy-makers mistook Stalin's determination to ensure Russian security through spheres of influence for a renewed effort to spread communism outside the borders of the Soviet Union."[7]

Scarcely an element of international relations is devoid of one, two, or several psychological components. What analysis of negotiations, for example, can overlook the psychology of the different actors? Success or failure at the bargaining table depends largely on the chips one holds and usually on domestic factors as well. But outcomes can also turn on the ability of one participant to "read" or even mislead another, the flexibility of the respective personalities, comparative risk-taking tendencies, and parallel attributes and styles. Statesmen adopt negotiating strategies, as a rule, in light of the predicted response they will generate. Carrots and sticks, or sugar and vinegar, are psychological ploys.[8]

Intelligence, which is progressively being recognized as a fundamental aspect of American foreign policy since World War II, is another area that cannot be analyzed without taking psychology into account. The primary responsibility of the Central Intelligence Agency (CIA) is the collection and interpretation of information. No activity depends more on perceptions and inferences, the core concerns of cognitive theory. The CIA, of course, does not confine itself to analyses and estimates; it also engages in such covert operations as propaganda campaigns, political actions, and paramilitary ventures. These activities invariably rely heavily on psychology. In the 1950s, President Dwight D. Eisenhower went so far as to designate C. D. Jackson his special assistant for psychological warfare, and his administration's strategy for overthrowing the Arbenz government in Guatemala, in the words of the CIA, was "dependent

7   Glenn H. Snyder, " 'Prisoner's Dilemma' and 'Chicken' Models in International Politics," *International Studies Quarterly* 15 (March 1971): 66–103; Robert Jervis, "Cooperation under the Security Dilemma," *World Politics* 30 (January 1978): 167–214. Jervis persuasively argues that the distinction between deterrence and the "spiral model" is a function of respective images of an enemy and perceptions of his intentions: *Perception and Misperception*, 58–113. John Lewis Gaddis, *The United States and the Origins of the Cold War, 1941–1947* (New York, 1972), 355. For the argument that the security dilemma continues to plague Soviet-American relations see Raymond L. Garthoff, *Détente and Confrontation: American-Soviet Relations from Nixon to Reagan* (Washington, 1985).
8   For psychologically informed examinations of competing negotiation strategies see Robert Axelrod, *The Evolution of Cooperation* (New York, 1984); and Charles E. Osgood, *Alternative to War or Surrender* (Urbana, 1962). An example of a case study of negotiations that applies psychological theories is Deborah Welch Larson, "Crisis Prevention and the Austrian State Treaty," *International Organization* 41 (Winter 1987): 27–60.

upon psychological impact rather than actual military strength." Successor administrations may not have believed so strongly in "psywar," but it has remained a staple instrument of American policy.[9] If policymakers recognize the seminal relationship between psychology and foreign affairs, so should scholars.

Until recently, however, historians have been skeptical about the utility of psychology for understanding foreign relations. In part this skepticism evolved from the level-of-analysis question: Are the sources of state conduct to be found at the level of the external environment, the domestic situation, or the individual policymaker?[10] Diplomatic history, reflecting realist roots that go back to Thucydides, has traditionally favored the systemic (external environment) level. Policymakers, with a fixed human nature, are seen as rational actors who seek to advance the national interest through cost-benefit analysis. Because psychology introduces a concern about irrationality, it appeared inappropriate—and discomforting.

Historians greeted those who waded into murky psychological waters with open hostility. This probably would have happened under any circumstances. Incompetent to evaluate the diagnoses, uneasy about the sources, and unsympathetic to the approach, historians in general were unwilling to lend much credence to "psychohistories." The publication of Alexander L. George and Juliette George's study of Woodrow Wilson and Colonel Edward House in 1964 exacerbated these doubts and enveloped the entire undertaking in controversy. Using psychoanalytic theory, George and George argued that Wilson's counterproductive behavior, especially his refusal to compromise over the League of Nations, was explicable primarily if not solely by his relationship with his father and his consequent compulsive personality. Although exemplary in its methodology, the George and George book elicited the criticism of Arthur Link, who challenged the data as well as the conclusions. Subsequently, Link conceded a degree of irrationality to Wilson, but he rejected the Georges' psychoanalytical diagnosis. He joined forces with a physician, Edwin Weinstein, to promote a physiological and neurological explanation. A war of words ensued.[11] To this day a consensus remains elusive.

9   Quoted in Richard H. Immerman, *The CIA in Guatemala: The Foreign Policy of Intervention* (Austin, 1982), 161. See John Lewis Gaddis, "Intelligence, Espionage, and Cold War Origins," *Diplomatic History* 13 (Spring 1989): 191–212; and Gregory F. Treverton, *Covert Action: The Limits of Intervention in the Postwar World* (New York, 1987).
10 J. David Singer, "The Level-of-Analysis Problem in International Relations," in *International Politics and Foreign Policy: A Reader in Research and Theory*, ed. James N. Rosenau, rev. ed. (New York, 1969), 20–29.
11 For the exemplary nature of the Georges' methodology see Greenstein, *Personality*

The controversy underscores the problem of collecting and assessing evidence of this kind. The footing appears surer if the historian concentrates on the impersonal influences on policy—the balance of power, economic stakes, even domestic constraints—and avoids trying to penetrate the persons themselves.

Ironically, the charge that the field was "marking time" while other specialties (for example, social and cultural history) were marching forward may also have made historians of U.S. foreign policy gun-shy when it came to incorporating psychology.[12] When the *Annales* school became all the rage and Clifford Geertz became a household word among historians, the profession treated political history, especially the Rankean tradition of international relations, as pedestrian and antiquated. The history of U.S. foreign policy was top-down history of the worst sort. In another context the application of psychology might have been considered a welcome innovation, but in this historiographic climate it was more suggestive of the problem than of the solution. We would be studying the personalities and cognitions of the elite: the leaders and the decision makers. This would not be in accord with the *Annalistes'* fixation with the masses. In fact, the Geertzian emphasis on cultural anthropology and *mentalité* left little room for the individual. Unless historians were going to probe the psychology of groups instead of individuals, prudence dictated that they borrow theories and perspectives from disciplines other than psychology.[13]

Diplomatic historians are beginning to overcome these impediments. At some recent meetings of the Society for Historians of American Foreign Relations (SHAFR), for example, papers that took psychologically informed approaches attracted large audiences, and the editor of *Diplo-*

and Politics, 21, 61–96. See also the research note in George and George, *Wilson and House*, 317–22. The literature reflecting the polemical exchange is extensive. It includes George and George, *Wilson and House*; Edwin A. Weinstein, James W. Anderson, and Arthur S. Link, "Woodrow Wilson's Political Personality: A Reappraisal," *Political Science Quarterly* 93 (Winter 1978–79): 585–98; Edwin A. Weinstein, *Woodrow Wilson: A Medical and Psychological Biography* (Princeton, 1981); Alexander L. George and Juliette L. George, "*Woodrow Wilson and Colonel House:* A Reply to Weinstein, Anderson, and Link," *Political Science Quarterly* 96 (Winter 1981–82): 641–65.

12 The criticisms are legion. My reference is to the most notorious one, Charles S. Maier, "Marking Time: The Historiography of International Relations," in *The Past before Us: Contemporary Historical Writing in the United States,* ed. Michael Kammen (Ithaca, 1980), 355–87.

13 In the Richard Hofstadter tradition, Robert Dallek did just that when he attempted to explain much of America's international behavior as the product of "displacement": Dallek, *The American Style of Foreign Policy: Cultural Politics and Foreign Affairs* (New York, 1983). Although provocative, the examination lacks methodological rigor.

matic History has invited experts in the psychology of international relations to contribute to SHAFR's journal.[14] Most encouraging of all, in sharp contrast to the reception accorded *Woodrow Wilson and Colonel House* in 1964, historians have more recently praised studies of foreign relations that apply psychological theories, studies that combine impressive archival research with methodological sophistication and rigor.[15] This trend indicates that historians are recognizing that a psychologically informed approach to international relations is a valuable complement to those approaches that emphasize broader social developments and situational variables. After all, the history of U.S. foreign policy is the history of choices, and individuals make those choices. Psychology helps us to understand the particular choices that they made.

The field of psychology that historians are least likely to apply is the one that concerns what lies beneath the surface personality—psychoanalytic theory. The time needed to develop the necessary competence militates against venturing out onto a psychoanalytical limb. Without years of training, the Georges could not have identified the symptoms of a compulsive personality, posited a hypothesis, and then modified and revised it to account for the dynamics of Wilson's development.[16] The adequacy of the evidence, moreover, will always be problematic. The Georges spent years immersed in the details of Wilson's life, but the subsequent publication of the more than sixty volumes of Wilson's papers and the revelations about his health indicate there is a lot more to be done. In addition, few policymakers leave the mountains of papers, especially intimate and introspective letters and diaries, required for this type of study. A number of fine psychohistories have been written in recent years. A list of superior biographies includes studies of Atatürk, Richelieu, and the young Joseph Stalin.[17] It does not include one of an American statesman.

14 Mary Jane Hogan, "Frank Church and Inter-American Security, 1956–60" (paper presented at the 1988 annual meeting of the Society for Historians of American Foreign Relations); William O. Walker III, "Decision-making Theory and Drug Control: Implications for Historical Analysis," *Diplomatic History* (forthcoming). See also Ole R. Holsti's Chapter 5 in this volume; and Robert Jervis, "The Military History of the Cold War," *Diplomatic History* (forthcoming).
15 A good example is Deborah Welch Larson, *Origins of Containment: A Psychological Explanation* (Princeton, 1984). I think it revealing that an earlier study, William A. Gamson and Andre Modigliani, *Untangling the Cold War: A Strategy for Testing Rival Theories* (Boston, 1971), was all but ignored.
16 George and George, *Wilson and House*, 317–22.
17 Vamik D. Volkan and Norman Itzkowitz, *The Immortal Atatürk: A Psychobiography* (Chicago, 1984); Elizabeth Wirth Marvick, *The Young Richelieu: A Psychoanalytic Approach to Leadership* (Chicago, 1983); Robert C. Tucker, *Stalin as Revolutionary, 1879–1929: A Study in History and Personality* (New York, 1973).

Notwithstanding the obstacles to using a psychoanalytic approach, the influence of personality on policies must not and need not be overlooked. The literature on political psychology has indicated that there is a correlation between a policymaker's *observable* personality traits and his behavior. Some analysts have gone so far as to postulate relationships among these traits to produce typologies that generate predictions about styles and policies.[18] I find this approach dangerously reductionist, yet certain finite relationships appear plausible. Evidence suggests, for example, that individuals confident in their ability to control events tend toward more activism in foreign affairs and that extroverts advocate better relations with Communists than do introverts.[19] Although the documentation remains inconclusive, an analysis of such contrasts between Johnson's and Kennedy's personalities as their respective power needs and differing styles of dealing with subordinates raises the possibility that, had Kennedy lived, the American experience in Vietnam would have been different. Even if such unprovable counterfactuals are dismissed as useless, the argument that one's character traits can affect one's decisions remains compelling. An archivally based examination of Johnson's Vietnam policy presents credible evidence that his attributes, including his propensity for "we-they" thinking and his passionately personal identification with the cause of the United States, manifested themselves in a diminished capacity to assess information and advice.[20]

Dogmatism, mental complexity or flexibility, and similar attributes likewise affect policymaking and state conduct. They are also elements of the individual's overall personality, but they lead us to focus on cognitive psychology. Because the objective of cognitive psychology is to explain how individuals perceive and interpret their environment, it is

---

18 The best-known case is Barber, *Presidential Character.*
19 Margaret Hermann, "Leadership Personality and Foreign Policy Behavior," in *Comparing Foreign Policies: Theories, Findings, and Methods,* ed. James N. Rosenau (New York, 1974), 201–34; Lloyd S. Etheredge, *A World of Men: The Private Sources of American Foreign Policy* (Cambridge, MA, 1978).
20 Fred I. Greenstein, "Personality in Politics," in *Handbook of Political Science,* vol. 2, *Micropolitical Theory,* ed. Fred I. Greenstein and Nelson W. Polsby, 8 vols. (Reading, 1975), 2–3. The most recent historical examinations of John F. Kennedy and Vietnam argue that Kennedy would have followed the same course as did Lyndon B. Johnson, although he probably would not have committed army divisions. See Thomas G. Paterson, "John F. Kennedy's Quest for Victory and Global Crisis," in *Kennedy's Quest for Victory: American Foreign Policy, 1961–1963,* ed. Paterson (New York, 1989), 21; and Lawrence J. Bassett and Stephen E. Pelz, "The Failed Search for Victory: Vietnam and the Politics of War," ibid., 252. Both of these studies highlight the importance of Kennedy's personality to his policies. For the influence of both Johnson and Eisenhower on decisions in Vietnam, see Fred I. Greenstein and John P. Burke, in collaboration with Larry Berman and Richard Immerman, *How Presidents Test Reality: Decisions on Vietnam, 1954 and 1965* (New York, 1989).

concerned also with misunderstandings and miscommunications, and its utility for students of international relations is palpable. The two theories of cognitive psychology that are probably most valuable for historians are attribution and schema theory.[21] According to attribution theorists, individuals function like "naïve scientists." We explain others' behavior by looking for clues, cumulative evidence; this is a rational process (unless the perceiver's emotions interfere). Schema theorists contend that our ability to assimilate information is limited; as a consequence we are "cognitive misers." We categorize the knowledge we have into schemata, mental or cognitive structures that fit the knowledge into a pattern. In other words, we have preconceived notions, beliefs about how social objects and phenomena relate to one another.

Intricately tied to the concept of schemata is the theory of heuristics. These shortcuts to rationality allow individuals to reduce complicated problem-solving tasks to simple judgments; they are strategies for managing information overload. Typical is the *representative* heuristic, by which people evaluate the extent to which the characteristics of a person, country, or political system—any object—are representative of a category of that same object: Egypt's Gamal Abdel Nasser is another Adolf Hitler. Guatemala's Jacobo Arbenz must be a Communist. If it looks like a duck and acts like a duck, it is a duck. In the *availability* heuristic, we draw inferences based on whatever pattern or frame of reference is most available and therefore most easily comes to mind. A military man such as General Lucius D. Clay is more likely to interpret the Berlin blockade as the first shot in a Soviet offensive than is an official in the State Department.

These theories help to explain how individuals make sense out of the complex world in which they live. They also help to explain why individuals make frequent errors of judgment and inference. Attached to each theory, or explanation for how we perceive and diagnose, are a series of "biases" or common mistakes: We may tend, for example, to overestimate the influence of personal dispositions on behavior and to underestimate the influence of situational influences. Or we may be more influenced by vivid, concrete data than that which is pallid and abstract; a nonevent (the dog that did not bark in the dark; the Soviet intervention that did not occur) may be overlooked altogether. Or because we know

---

21 Kenneth M. Goldstein and Sheldon Blackman, *Cognitive Style* (New York, 1978). For an overview of cognitive theory I recommend Richard Nisbett and Lee Ross, *Human Inference: Strategies and Shortcomings of Social Judgment* (Englewood Cliffs, 1980); Susan Fiske and Shelley Taylor, *Social Cognition* (Reading, 1984); and Richard R. Lau and David Sears, eds., *Political Cognition* (Hillsdale, 1986). Unless otherwise indicated, the following summary is drawn from these works.

our own motives and intentions, we may assume others know them as well. Or we do not always distinguish between the inferences we draw from the data we receive and the data itself. Or we overlook base rate statistics and overestimate the size of the sample we use to generate a heuristic category. There are many other biases, but the point is clear.

Most fundamentally, cognitive psychologists uniformly agree that once we have formed a belief we are reluctant to discard or even qualify it. New evidence will be interpreted to conform to our prior beliefs: If it is consistent with them, it will be accepted; if inconsistent or ambiguous, it will be discredited or ignored. This tendency is most pronounced when the belief is deeply felt and deeply held. Our values are hierarchically ordered, and our beliefs are interconnected to form a system; when incoming information is so discordant that we cannot ignore it, we will revise our least fundamental notions before even questioning our core assumptions. Our most highly valued beliefs are thus minimally disconfirmed. By establishing the parameters of an individual's "particular type of 'bounded rationality,' " belief systems serve as sets "of lenses through which information concerning the physical and social environment is received."[22] No matter how forcefully Mikhail Gorbachev pushed for arms control, he did not alter Secretary of Defense Richard Cheney's estimation of the Soviet threat. Cheney could "explain away" Gorbachev's behavior by attributing it to the success of a "peace through strength" posture, by dismissing it as a tactic to lull the non-Communist world into complacency while the Kremlin regroups and the economy revives, or by acknowledging that Gorbachev is different but will not last. Cheney's core beliefs and images remained unshakable.

Those theories pertain to our strategies for coping with complexity and highlight the influence beliefs have on perceptions and behavior; a growing body of thought concentrates on our wants, needs, and fears. Psychologists who emphasize motivations argue that our judgments are a function of emotions as opposed to mental capacities. Perhaps the most prevalent motivation for human error is the need to reduce the anxiety that an individual experiences when confronting a severe dilemma. This stress can lead to such tactics as bolstering, in which one chooses one option by extolling its virtues and denigrating all alternatives; defensive

22 Alexander L. George, "The Causal Nexus between Cognitive Beliefs and Decision Making Behavior: The 'Operational Code' Belief System," in *Psychological Models in International Politics*, ed. Lawrence S. Falkowski (Boulder, 1979), 103; Ole R. Holsti, "The Belief System and National Image: A Case Study," *Journal of Conflict Resolution* 6 (September 1962): 245. For the concept of "bounded rationality" see Herbert A. Simon, *Administrative Behavior: A Study of Decision-making Processes in Administrative Organization*, 2d ed. (New York, 1957).

avoidance, in which people refuse to acknowledge a threat; or hypervigilance, in which one makes an impulsive commitment, stemming from panic, to the least objectionable alternative.[23] Based on this conflict model of decision making, Irving Janis developed his "groupthink" hypothesis to explain the Bay of Pigs fiasco. According to Janis, in stressful situations members of a decision-making group tend to seek consensus by failing to challenge overly optimistic predictions and by terminating deliberations prematurely. "The concurrence-seeking tendency," Janis writes of the decision to approve the Bay of Pigs invasion, "was manifested by shared illusions and other symptoms [of groupthink], which helped the members to maintain a sense of group solidarity. Most crucial were the symptoms that contributed to complacent over-confidence in the face of vague uncertainties and explicit warnings that should have alerted the members to the risks of the clandestine military operation."[24]

Although cognitive and motivational explanations for behavior are often placed in opposition to one another, they are in fact interrelated. One's beliefs affect one's emotions and vice versa; unmotivated and motivated biases are frequently indistinguishable.[25] Insights drawn from these psychological theories—and my summary is far from exhaustive—can prove illuminating for historians of foreign relations. Anyone who has ever read a State Department situational report, an intelligence estimate, or the memorandums of a National Security Council meeting will profit from an understanding of the normative strategies by which we perceive the world and draw inferences, an awareness of our cognitive shortcomings, and a sensitivity to the possible influence of emotions.

My own work can serve as an example. In *The CIA in Guatemala* I argued that an exaggerated perception of the Communist threat resulted in Washington's decision to intervene in 1954. I arrived at this explanation after analyzing what I described as a "cold war ethos," which pervaded all sectors of American society in the postwar period. I am now convinced that a familiarity with the literature on cognitive psychology and belief systems would have strengthened my analysis. By clarifying the Cold War ethos, schema and attribution theories provide a perspective, a framework that helps to explain how Americans perceived and defined the threat and why they interpreted labor codes, agrarian reforms, and other liberal measures as evidence of Soviet influence. Nothing the Arbenz government could say or do could shake Washington's preexisting

23 Janis and Mann, *Decision Making*, 85–95, 199.
24 Janis, *Groupthink*, 47.
25 Janice Gross Stein, "Building Politics into Psychology: The Misperception of Threat," *Political Psychology* 9 (June 1988): 257; Robert Jervis, "Political Psychology: Some Challenges and Opportunities," ibid. 10 (September 1989): 487.

beliefs. When Arbenz purchased arms from Czechoslovakia in a last-minute attempt to defend the revolution against an impending invasion, Eisenhower's officials jumped to the conclusion that Guatemala's neighbors were in peril. The CIA's later identification of Fidel Castro with Arbenz and its application to Cuba of the covert strategy developed for Guatemala appear illustrative of the representative and availability heuristics: Arbenz was representative of the Communist leadership of Latin America, despite his making up a set of one; and the CIA planners, many of whom had participated in PBSUCCESS, had the covert Guatemalan operation readily available when conceiving the Bay of Pigs intervention.

I am likewise persuaded that my examinations of Eisenhower's policy toward Indochina would have benefited from a psychologically informed perspective. Although the administration's deliberations during the Indochina crisis are better described as multiple advocacy—the vigorous and uninhibited exchange of viewpoints among advisers—more than groupthink, the dilemma posed by the French request for intervention precipitated the procrastination, wishful thinking, and retrospective rationalization that one might expect from the conflict model of decision making. Indeed, psychological theory suggests that John Foster Dulles's testimony on 11 May 1954, four days after the fall of the French fortress at Dienbienphu—"We do not want to operate on what has been referred to as the domino theory"—was more for his benefit than for that of Congress or the public.[26] Similarly, in light of the evidence of a disunited Communist bloc and the ineffectiveness of Ngo Dinh Diem, the postures ultimately adopted by the administration at the 1954 Geneva Conference and during the 1955 sect crisis are suggestive of bolstering on one hand and hypervigilance on the other. Desperate to find a solution when none appeared possible, the administration concluded that the Geneva settlement was the best that could be achieved and then threw its support behind Ngo Dinh Diem, despite its own recognition of his shortcomings. Currently, my investigation of the American response to Stalin's death in 1953 and his successor Georgi Malenkov's "peace offensive" demonstrates the importance of preexisting beliefs and images. Although the evidence suggests that Malenkov was not a clone of Stalin and that he sincerely sought to improve relations with the United States, officials in the Eisenhower administration rejected the possibility that the Soviet zebra had changed its stripes.

For the historian to use psychology effectively, he or she must learn

---

26 Quoted in Richard H. Immerman, "Between the Unattainable and the Unacceptable," in *Reevaluating Eisenhower: American Foreign Policy in the Fifties*, ed. Richard A. Melanson and David Mayers (Urbana, 1987), 145.

it, which means reading more than one or two textbooks. There are alternate theories to consider, and none should be employed mechanically.[27] Further, even after achieving sufficient familiarity with the literature, one must be careful not to get carried away with psychology's explanatory power. One must take care not to be seduced by the temptation to fit the evidence to the theory. Understanding the individual is necessary but not sufficient for understanding the policy. To assume that there is always a direct linkage between beliefs and behavior would be misguided. And even if the historian has developed adequate expertise in psychology, even if he or she is judicious in its application, and even if the documents are available, there remains the problem of practicality. Ideally we should examine the personalities of all those involved in the policy process (after we have identified who they are), determine which attributes appear related to what behavior, investigate their individual belief systems, and take into account the psychological influences on the process itself. This is an ambitious assignment; in addition to the research involved, it requires that one devise a method of weighing relative personalities and beliefs in proportion to their relative influence on the decision. Once that is accomplished, then one must factor in the other domestic and systemic variables that shape and constrain behavior in order to complete the analysis.

Applying psychology to the history of U.S. foreign relations thus represents a challenge. Yet it is one a growing number of historians are striving to meet. As they have progressively come to recognize that differences among statesmen do matter, that decision makers must interpret an ambiguous international environment, and that nonrational influences affect policymaking, the appeal of psychological explanations has increased. What has also increased is historians' confidence: the confidence that they can apply the theory rigorously and the confidence that their concern with the integrity of their sources will serve as a "quality control." Yes, a psychological approach is a challenge; but it is also an opportunity. Now that historians have accepted it, they can exploit it.

27   For the distinction between rote "classification" and informed "diagnosis" see Alexander L. George, "Some Uses of Dynamic Psychology in Political Biography: Case Materials on Woodrow Wilson," in *A Source Book for the Study of Personality and Politics*, ed. Fred I. Greenstein and Michael Lerner (Chicago, 1971), 80.

11

Public Opinion

MELVIN SMALL

As President Lyndon B. Johnson in March 1968 considered raising American troop levels in Vietnam in the wake of the Tet offensive, his desk was piled high with memorandums from advisers. Included were reports from the Joint Chiefs of Staff on military conditions in Southeast Asia, from intelligence agencies on political developments in Hanoi, from State Department officers on diplomatic currents around the world, and from Treasury Department analysts on the state of the economy. Much of what he read led him to believe that he had the North Vietnamese on the run, that they and their Vietcong allies had been crushed by the American and South Vietnamese counterattack after Tet.

The president was compelled to pay attention to other reports as well. Opinion polls, media surveys, and communications from friends suggested that he had lost a battle more crucial than Tet, the battle for public opinion in the United States. This information told the president that Americans would no longer support escalation in Vietnam in the absence of evidence that an end to the war was in sight. In a dramatic speech to the nation on 31 March 1968, the proud Texan who had once said he would not leave Vietnam without the Communist coonskin nailed to the wall reluctantly began the process of American withdrawal.

In few countries has public opinion played such a significant role in the development of diplomatic and military strategies as it has in the United States. In the scores of authoritarian states that have belonged to the international system the public has had little to say about any policy. Even publics in such democratic countries as England and France have been constrained by tradition and law in their attempts to influence their leaders' foreign policies. Many in those countries believed in the axiom that politics stopped at the water's edge. Once a government adopted a diplomatic posture, internal political debate was supposed to end as all factions closed ranks to present a united front to the outside world. President George Washington expected that his new nation would operate according to that approach, but was dismayed to discover that official foreign policies became fair game for rival politicians.

The United States also differed from other countries because of its

unique system of checks and balances. Most foreign ministers and diplomats have generally spoken for the majority party in their parliaments.
American presidents must share their power with legislators who may
have their own international and domestic agendas. As early as the 1830s,
the French political theorist Alexis de Tocqueville worried about the
ability of the new American system to carry out an effective diplomacy.[1]
Foreign relations had to be carried on in secrecy and with dispatch by
unemotional and realistic professionals. To this European observer, it
appeared even then that matters of state had become grist for the political
mills of reckless, chauvinistic legislators and journalists.

Tocqueville has not been the only one to worry about the prospects
for the development of wise national security policy in the United States.
Looking back during the 1920s at the way his country had played its
first several decades of major-league power politics, the journalist Walter
Lippmann charged that American statesmen had pandered too often to
the whims and ignorance of the public when they constructed their foreign
policies. A generation later, as the United States was entering the Cold
War, the diplomat and historian George F. Kennan sounded the same
tocsin.[2] However much realists such as Kennan may lament the public's
role in foreign policymaking, there is little that can be done about it
except to understand the nature of that role and, perhaps, to improve
the quality of the opinion.

At first glance, the concept of "public opinion" appears rather straightforward. Public opinion in the United States is what Americans think
about an issue. But not all Americans have opinions about all issues,
especially when it comes to the often complicated and obscure interactions that make up a good portion of a major power's diplomacy. Although almost all Americans held opinions about their country's posture
toward Germany in the spring of 1917, for example, only a few cared
or even knew about Sumner Welles's decisive intervention in Cuban
politics in 1933.

In addition, there are several publics in the United States whose members shift from issue to issue. At the top of the apex of a pyramid that
might represent all citizens are the opinion makers, a very small coterie
of government officials, respected national leaders and celebrities, editors,
and journalists.[3] Below them is a group called the attentive public that

1   Some of the discussion that follows, including Tocqueville's analysis, appears in Melvin
    Small, "Public Opinion," in *Encyclopedia of American Foreign Policy*, ed. Alexander
    DeConde, 3 vols. (New York, 1978), 3:844–55.
2   Lippmann, *Public Opinion* (New York, 1922); Kennan, *American Diplomacy, 1900–
    1950* (Chicago, 1951).
3   James N. Rosenau, *Public Opinion and Foreign Policy: An Operational Formulation*
    (New York, 1961), chap. 4.

might be as large as 25 percent on some issues. These well-educated and well-read people tend to pay attention to international politics and influence others around them. Finally, more than 75 percent of the population makes up the mass public that usually does not care much about foreign affairs until the United States is in a crisis.

Most historians interested in the impact of public opinion on foreign policy examine the opinions of only some very important Americans. The difference between mass public opinion, as registered in an election or public opinion poll, and elite opinion was illustrated dramatically by Ernest R. May, who wrote two valuable books on American imperialism in the 1890s. In the first, he discussed opinion in a conventional manner, demonstrating how President William McKinley was influenced by popular mood. In the second and more methodologically sophisticated volume, he concentrated upon late nineteenth-century elites, or opinion makers, whose uncharacteristic lack of consensus in their attitudes toward expansion permitted expansionists in the McKinley administration to deviate from traditional American policy.[4]

American leaders have recognized the special significance of the opinion-making and attentive publics. During the Vietnam War, even when the public opinion polls were in their favor, Presidents Johnson and Richard M. Nixon worried about influential members of the American establishment who were jumping off the bandwagon. The president was not comforted when the head of the Selective Service said the administration was having little trouble on most of America's five thousand university campuses and that problems arose only at Harvard, Columbia, Yale, Michigan, Berkeley, and other elite institutions. Johnson knew that he could not long continue his Vietnam policy without the support of those segments of the population that constituted the opinion leaders and, in this case, their families.[5]

The modern study of public opinion and foreign policy began in the years after World War II when the United States emerged from its allegedly isolationist shell into unprecedented activism. Thomas A. Bailey's anecdotal *The Man in the Street* emphasized the role of public opinion in American diplomacy throughout the nation's history and suggested that it often supported wiser policies than those promoted by the pres-

---

4 May, *Imperial Democracy: The Emergence of America as a Great Power* (New York, 1959); idem, *American Imperialism: A Speculative Essay* (New York, 1968). More recently, Ole R. Holsti and James N. Rosenau used a wealth of survey data to explore a similar problem in *American Leadership in World Affairs: Vietnam and the Breakdown of Consensus* (Boston, 1984).

5 Melvin Small, *Johnson, Nixon, and the Doves* (New Brunswick, 1988), 183. On the attitudes of the attentive public during the Vietnam War see also William L. Lunch and Peter W. Sperlich, "American Public Opinion and the War in Vietnam," *Western Political Quarterly* 32 (March 1979): 21–24.

idents. More recently, in *The Public and American Foreign Policy,* Ralph B. Levering has looked at American views of diplomatic issues in a useful survey informed by modern social scientific theory.[6] Levering found that the public's preferences in the international sphere were generally sound on major and recurring problems but that Americans have lacked knowledge about a good deal of their country's other foreign policies. What is more, although presidents have been generally able to lead the public into accepting their portrayals of foreign countries, they have been less successful in matters relating to war or military intervention. Levering supports Bailey's earlier view of a surprisingly prudent public, not the capricious and belligerent Americans feared by Tocqueville, Lippmann, and Kennan.[7]

Despite the growing attention of diplomatic historians to this subject, political scientists like Gabriel A. Almond, James N. Rosenau, and Bernard C. Cohen have contributed most to our understanding of the opinion-policy nexus with their insightful models of opinion formation, transmission, and decision making.[8] Their message has been that public opinion is indeed a crucial variable in America's foreign relations, but that it is a far more complicated subject than historians, who used newspaper editorials and polls for their sources, have represented it to be. Most important, these political scientists argue that we had better study the phenomenon carefully because the issues that were at stake in the Cold War and the nuclear arms race were far more important to the United States and to the entire international system than the influence, for example, of hawkish opinion on James Madison in 1812.

The Cold War era is replete with examples that suggest that public opinion exercised a powerful influence on American decision makers. President John F. Kennedy was unable to open relations with the People's Republic of China because the public was allegedly not prepared for such a démarche. President Gerald R. Ford could not pursue a more activist policy in Angola in 1975 because Americans and their congressional representatives, reeling from the Vietnam debacle, were in a noninter-

6 See Bailey, *The Man in the Street: The Impact of American Public Opinion on Foreign Policy* (New York, 1948); and Levering, *The Public and American Foreign Policy, 1918–1978* (New York, 1978). Levering brought his study up to date in "Public Opinion, Foreign Policy, and American Politics since the 1960s," *Diplomatic History* 13 (Summer 1989): 383–93.

7 Levering is supported by James A. Nathan and James K. Oliver in *Foreign Policy Making and the American Political System* (Boston, 1983), 164–68.

8 Almond, *The American People and Foreign Policy* (New York, 1960); Rosenau, *Public Opinion and Foreign Policy;* Cohen, *The Public's Impact on Foreign Policy* (Boston, 1973). See also Barry B. Hughes, *The Domestic Sources of American Foreign Policy* (San Francisco, 1978), a useful text.

ventionist mood. President George Bush most likely was influenced by public criticism of his earlier caution when he finally decided to invade Panama in December 1989.

It is one thing to assert that public opinion plays an important role in the decision-making process; it is quite another to demonstrate that impact. It is always difficult to identify the many possible influences that lead presidents and their advisers to select one policy over another. Presidents, moreover, claim to ignore domestic politics when developing national security policies. Armed with secret intelligence and surrounded by experts, they say, it would be irresponsible, not to mention unnecessary, if they spent much time evaluating the views of a usually uninformed and often dangerously impassioned public.

Despite what they say, however, it is obvious that American decision makers do think about the public as they develop their diplomatic strategies. Just as a pilot automatically checks the dashboard indicators before he or she decides that the airplane is safe to take off, former Secretary of State Dean Rusk used to make a comparable public opinion check before launching a new program.[9] Yet, rarely does one find evidence in the archives of the public opinion factor *directly* entering the policy process, as was the case when President John Adams monitored opinion during the crisis with France from 1797 through 1800.[10] This does create serious problems for historians that will be addressed below.

Regardless of the woefully fragmentary archival evidence of the public's impact on foreign policy, presidents do assert that their policies reflect the general will of the American people. Their pride in their fealty to the democratic ideal may be justified. In separate studies, Robert Weissberg and Leonard A. Kusnitz found a congruence between public opinion and foreign policy with opinion shifts sometimes immediately preceding major decisions and sometimes immediately following such decisions.[11] Kusnitz is especially convincing in demonstrating the robust correlations between polling data on China and the vagaries of American policy from 1949 through 1979.

Needless to say, with the bully pulpits from which they set the foreign

---

9 Small, *Johnson, Nixon, and the Doves,* 3. One valuable study of the importance of opinion in the making of American foreign policy is Fen Osler Hampson, "The Divided Decision Maker: American Domestic Politics and the Cuban Crises," in *The Domestic Sources of American Foreign Policy: Insights and Evidence,* ed. Charles W. Kegley, Jr., and Eugene R. Wittkopf (New York, 1988), 227–47.

10 Doris A. Graber, *Public Opinion, the President, and Foreign Policy: Four Case Studies from the Formative Years* (New York, 1968), 85–87.

11 Weissberg, *Public Opinion and American Popular Government* (Englewood Cliffs, 1976); Kusnitz, *Public Opinion and Foreign Policy: America's China Policy, 1949–1979* (Westport, 1984).

policy agenda, presidents have a good deal to do with the development
of public support for their programs. In the period since World War I,
radio, newsreels, and then television have enhanced their ability to educate or manipulate their constituents. Using those media as well as more
traditional tools from 1945 through 1948, President Harry S. Truman
skillfully converted initially skeptical American opinion makers and Congress into enthusiastic Cold Warriors through his interpretation of international crises.[12]

The line between education and manipulation is often a thin one. That
line was crossed when presidential aides secretly sponsored a campaign
to have thousands of letters sent to the White House to support Nixon's
Vietnam policies. In *The Rockets' Red Glare: When America Goes to
War,* Richard J. Barnet concluded that presidents from George Washington through Ronald Reagan had attempted to obtain public support
by concealing and distorting information vital to the free play of opinion
in the United States.[13]

Whether or not presidents were successful in molding or even creating
public opinion, its role in the decision-making process cannot be ignored
in any study of American foreign relations. Bernard Cohen, who relied
heavily on interviews with State Department officials in his seminal work
on the subject, suggests that those interested in the relationship between
public opinion and foreign policy should divide their activities into four
research areas: the characteristics and distribution of opinion, the formation and transmission of opinion, the impact of opinion on the policymaker, and the relationship between the causes and consequences of
opinion.[14]

Although all four areas pose problems for diplomatic historians, particularly for periods before the advent of the scientific public opinion poll
in the 1930s, the most challenging is the impact of opinion on policy.
Using media, polls, and elite letters and speeches, many historians
have studied the publics' opinions on foreign policy issues.[15] Few have

12 Thomas G. Paterson, "Presidential Foreign Policy, Public Opinion, and Congress: The
    Truman Years," *Diplomatic History* 3 (Winter 1979): 1–18. See also Michael Leigh,
    Mobilizing Consent: Public Opinion and American Foreign Policy, 1937–1947 (West-
    port, 1976); Richard W. Steele, *Propaganda in an Open Society: The Roosevelt
    Administration and the Media, 1933–1941* (Westport, 1985); and Robert C. Hilder-
    brand, *Power and the People: Executive Management of Public Opinion in Foreign
    Affairs, 1897–1921* (Chapel Hill, 1981).
13 Barnet, *The Rockets' Red Glare: When America Goes to War—The Presidents and
    the People* (New York, 1990).
14 Cohen, *Public's Impact,* 2–3.
15 See, for example, Alfred O. Hero, *American Religious Groups View Foreign Policy:
    Trends in Rank and File Opinion, 1937–1969* (Durham, 1973); James C. Schneiders,
    Should America Go to War: The Debate over Foreign Policy in Chicago, 1939–1941

tackled the more intractable problem of the impact of that opinion on policymakers.

In order to evaluate that impact, historians must sift through the wide variety of opinion analyses that cross the officials' desks and then attempt to assess their relative weight in the decision-making process. Presidents have been confident in their abilities to evaluate public opinion. After all, they could not have become leaders without possessing the political acumen to intuit accurately what their constituents desired.[16] Further, they have known that they generally can count on the support of most citizens in a crisis, or at least that the majority would rally around the flag after a major presidential initiative, even if it fails—as was the case in the Bay of Pigs invasion in 1961 and the attempt to rescue American hostages in Iran in 1980. All the same, even the most confident modern president relies on experts to take the national pulse for him on domestic and foreign policy subjects.

Estimations of the public's opinion on foreign policy reach the Oval Office from six sources, the polls, the media, friends, correspondents, Congress, and interest groups. These sources constitute much of the evidence that historians must employ to study how presidents evaluate opinion. Since the 1930s, presidents have watched the polls, and in recent years, have commissioned their own. Polls, however, are not the most sensitive indicator of opinion and are often unreliable.[17] Rarely have they asked specific questions dealing with sudden crises that confront presidents and later interest their chroniclers. But general public opinion polls such as those conducted by the Gallup and Roper organizations are important in another way. The publication of a poll may itself contribute to the development of opinion favoring the majority view in that poll. For example, had 60 percent of poll respondents been reported as approving of President Dwight D. Eisenhower's handling of foreign relations during the Suez crisis in 1956, the mere publication of that information could have caused another 10 percent to support the president for fear of being out of step with the majority of their fellow citizens. Like the polls, all of the sources the president employs to analyze opinion may both reflect and shape that opinion.

(Chapel Hill, 1989); and H. Schuyler Foster, *Activism Replaces Isolationism: U.S. Public Attitudes, 1940–1975* (Washington, 1975).

16 Elihu Katz and Paul F. Lazarsfeld, *Personal Influence: The Part Played by People in the Flow of Mass Communications* (Glencoe, 1955), 102–3.

17 Leo Bogart, *Silent Politics: Polls and the Awareness of Public Opinion* (New York, 1972); Michael Wheeler, *Lies, Damn Lies, and Statistics: The Manipulation of Public Opinion in America* (New York, 1976). John E. Mueller made excellent use of polls when he compared the Korean and Vietnam wars in *War, Presidents, and Public Opinion* (New York, 1973).

Elections are a sort of opinion poll as well, but they occur too infrequently to be of use to the decision maker. More important, foreign policy rarely has figured significantly in U.S. congressional and even presidential elections.[18] In such contests, even when foreign policy appeared to be the major issue, as in 1844, 1920, and 1968, candidates did not offer voters a clear-cut choice.

Before the advent of the scientific poll in the 1930s, presidents looked first for opinion in editorials and columns from major newspapers. Since World War II, the White House, the State Department, and the Defense Department, among other agencies, have prepared elaborate media surveys for their chiefs. References to the State Department's weekly *American Opinion Survey* and the Air Force's daily *Current News* appear frequently in the files of presidents and their advisers. One of the most revealing sources for the Nixon presidency are his marginal notes on the daily print and electronic media surveys that he read most carefully.[19]

Some media count more than others. In the period since World War II, presidents and their aides have paid the most attention to the three nightly network newscasts, *Time* and *Newsweek,* and the *Washington Post* and the *New York Times.*[20] These sources have been influential in setting the news agenda and shaping editorial slants and news budgets for many other newscasts, magazines, and newspapers.

Friends, family members, and colleagues, a third source of opinion for decision makers, bring to the Oval Office evaluations of the attitudes of members of the establishment outside of government. As some newspapers count more than others, some people do as well.[21] After Henry Kissinger and David Rockefeller repeatedly called their contacts in the Carter administration to recommend the admission of the shah of Iran to the United States for medical care in 1979, the president ultimately heeded their faulty advice.

18 For a valuable survey in this field see Robert A. Divine, *Foreign Policy and U.S. Presidential Elections,* 2 vols. (New York, 1974).

19 See the use made of these notes by Stephen E. Ambrose, *Nixon: The Triumph of a Politician, 1962–1972* (New York, 1989); and Herbert S. Parmet, *Richard Nixon and His America* (Boston, 1990). Johnson's troubled relations with the media are examined in Kathleen J. Turner, *Lyndon Johnson's Dual War: Vietnam and the Press* (Chicago, 1985). John F. Kennedy's much better media relations are studied in Montague Kern, Patricia W. Levering, and Ralph B. Levering, *The Kennedy Crises: The Press, the Presidency, and Foreign Policy* (Chapel Hill, 1983).

20 Other important sources have been prominent columnists like James Reston and Joseph Alsop, the wire services, the *Wall Street Journal,* and, recently, the Cable News Network.

21 According to the two-step-flow theory of opinion transmission, we are influenced more by opinion leaders than we are directly by the media. See Katz and Lazarsfeld, *Personal Influence.*

Americans call their representatives or write to or cable the White House everyday. The daily mail and phone counts offer another indicator of opinion to the foreign policy decision maker. Surprisingly, a variation of sometimes only hundreds of letters over a weekend in a nation of more than 250 million can disturb the president.[22] Presidential aides who compile the totals do try to distinguish between organized letter-writing campaigns, which they tend to discount, and spontaneous outpourings of support or opposition. Almost all letters are answered by underlings in the White House and rarely make it to the Oval Office as anything more than a number in a category. Yet presidents do read representative letters.

Congress constitutes a fifth opinion source. More than the executive branch, it reflects constituency views and pressures. Legislators do not like to be too far ahead of the people in their district on most issues. They may have a bit more leeway to develop their own approach to foreign policies, a subject that is rarely of overriding importance in a congressional election. Indeed, senators' and representatives' votes on foreign affairs have been less congruent with their constituent opinions than has been the case on domestic affairs.[23] All the same, for many presidents, a few phone calls to trusted colleagues on Capitol Hill have provided a useful assessment of popular attitudes toward specific foreign policy issues.

Finally, a variety of economic, political, and ethnic organizations, often through political action committees, have forcefully made their views known in Washington whenever their special interests became an object of American concern. When China began to fall prey to foreign concessionaires during the late 1890s, the new National Association of Manufacturers pressured the McKinley administration to do something about keeping the door open to that potentially vast market. During the 1920s, similarly, the stridently anti-Communist American Legion and American Federation of Labor periodically warned Republican administrations not to recognize the Soviet Union.[24]

Throughout American history, organized ethnic groups have exerted

22 Small, *Johnson, Nixon, and the Doves*, 10.
23 Warren E. Miller and Donald E. Stokes, "Constituency Influence in Congress," *American Political Science Review* 57 (March 1963): 45–56. See also Stephen E. Frantzich, *Write Your Congressman: Constituent Communications and Representation* (New York, 1986).
24 Thomas J. McCormick, *China Market: America's Quest for Informal Empire, 1893–1901* (Chicago, 1967); Peter Filene, *Americans and the Soviet Experiment, 1917–1933* (Cambridge, MA, 1967). For the lobbying activities of a liberal political group see Steven M. Gillon, *Politics and Vision: The ADA and American Liberalism, 1947–1985* (New York, 1985).

a major influence in national foreign policy debates. Ethnic political activism has been a unique problem for diplomats representing the multicultural United States. In the nineteenth century, and even today on the question of Northern Ireland, Irish Americans lobbied for the adoption of anti-British postures. Jewish and Arab Americans have attempted since the 1940s to influence American policies in the Middle East, while African-Americans have demonstrated a growing interest in South African policies. Cuban, Greek, Armenian, and Eastern European Americans, among others, also have attempted to press presidents on policies dealing with their ancestral homes.[25]

The peace movement is another lobby whose interests American policymakers are frequently compelled to address. The United States has been the home of the peace movement in the twentieth century. The movement has enlisted the fervent support of scores of prominent figures and millions of ordinary citizens. Pressures from American peace groups contributed to the founding of the Hague Conference system at the turn of the century, the arbitration treaty movement of the same period, the organization of the League of Nations and the United Nations, the Kellogg-Briand Pact, the Limited Test Ban Treaty, and other arms control and conflict resolution proposals.[26]

One can find messages and reports from such groups, as well as from polls, media, colleagues, mailrooms, and Congress, on the president's desk almost any day. Here is where the difficulty begins for the historian. Most presidents claim to be specialists in assessing public opinion. Often, however, what they take for opinion will not pass the muster of social scientists who write about the subject. For example, an examination of the media clippings available to Franklin D. Roosevelt suggests that the public by and large supported his quarantine speech in 1937 and was prepared to accept a more interventionist posture in the crises of the period. Persuaded by a few salient but unrepresentative cases, however, Roosevelt decided that the public was opposed to his dramatic condemnation of aggression.[27] Similarly, at a time when his influence among American elites had waned, Walter Lippmann was still viewed by Lyndon

25 Louis L. Gerson, *The Hyphenate in Recent American Politics and Diplomacy* (Lawrence, 1964); Edward Tivnan, *The Lobby: Jewish Political Power and American Foreign Policy* (New York, 1987); Brian Jenkins, *Fenians and Anglo-American Relations during Reconstruction* (Ithaca, 1969); Sander A. Diamond, *The Nazi Movement in the United States, 1924–1941* (Ithaca, 1974).
26 Lawrence S. Wittner, "Peace Movements and Foreign Policy: The Challenge to Diplomatic Historians," *Diplomatic History* 11 (Fall 1987): 355–70; Charles DeBenedetti, *The Peace Reform in American History* (Bloomington, 1980).
27 Dorothy Borg, *The United States and the Far Eastern Crisis of 1933–1938* (Cambridge, MA, 1964), 392.

Johnson as one of the most important columnists in America. Consequently the president lavished considerable attention on him and waxed furious when the administration appeared in a bad light in one of Lippmann's syndicated columns.[28]

Thus it is not enough to evaluate the opinion that crosses the president's desk in order to judge its impact on policy. One must also determine how the president evaluated the importance of the variety of reports he received. Above all, opinion that has an impact on policy is what the president determines it to be, not what scholars may demonstrate is scientifically valid opinion.

Whatever their own views of the public, presidents have been concerned that their adversaries abroad might have confused editorials in the *New York Times,* demonstrations in Washington, or the speeches of dissenting senators with a dominant "public opinion." The president knows that such manifestations from the opposition often do not reflect mainstream America, but he fears that foreign leaders may not be so prescient. During the Vietnam War, presidents who claimed that they were not affected by demonstrations worried that Hanoi was, and thus Johnson and Nixon constructed American policy based in part on what they thought were their opponents' misperceptions of American opinion. Of course, when Ho Chi Minh was encouraged by a critical speech from J. William Fulbright (D-AK), even at a time when the senator was a voice crying in the wilderness, the North Vietnamese president was not altogether misreading American opinion. Fulbright's views may not have been in the majority in 1965 and 1966, but they contributed to a growing disaffection of opinion leaders from the war.

Like most presidents, Johnson envied his counterparts in other capitals who did not have to worry about such obstacles to policymaking as dissenting senators and placard-carrying demonstrators. It is the historian's daunting task to determine just how important these and other such activities were in each of literally thousands of foreign policy issues.[29] Because the public opinion factor is ever present but always elusive, students of American foreign relations confront far more complicated problems than their colleagues who write about the foreign relations of countries that have not had a democratic tradition.

Those problems begin with the definition of public opinion, which is not simply what an undifferentiated population thinks about foreign affairs. They are compounded by the absence of scientific polls before

28 Small, *Johnson, Nixon, and the Doves,* 40–41.
29 Robert Dallek, *The American Style of Foreign Policy: Cultural Politics and Foreign Affairs* (New York, 1983), makes a plausible case for domestic mood as the prime determinant in American foreign relations.

the 1930s. Even for the recent period, polls are often too crude an instrument to be used profitably by historians. Yet the determination of the several publics' opinions on specific issues is far easier than the determination of the influence of those opinions on decision makers. Armed with increasingly sophisticated social-scientific models of opinion flow and decision making, however, historians can find evidence in the archives of the way presidents and their advisers evaluated the publics' attitudes toward foreign policy. Although the search will be arduous, the evidence often impressionistic, and the intuitive leaps challenging, one cannot understand American diplomatic history without understanding the central role of public opinion in that history.

12

Mental Maps

ALAN K. HENRIKSON

The term *mental map*, which most people understand quite intuitively, requires definition.[1] In what follows, *mental map* will be taken to mean an ordered but continually adapting structure of the mind—alternatively conceivable as a process—by reference to which a person acquires, codes, stores, recalls, reorganizes, and applies, in thought or in action, information about his or her large-scale geographical environment, in part or in its entirety. Still more briefly, such a map is the cognitive frame on the basis of which historians of international relations, like diplomats and others who think and act internationally, orient themselves in the world.[2] The purpose of this essay is to show how close attention to these mental frameworks can illuminate international decisions and thereby offer historians and other scholars a valuable new perspective on American foreign policy and world history.

The structures of these maps can be highly complex, although they do tend to have a number of common features. Adapting terms from the work of Kevin Lynch, who applied them only on the urban scale, I list the following constituent elements of many mental maps. These maps consist of the *paths*, or channels along which a person regularly travels;

---

1 A familiar example of the popular conception of a mental map is the artist Saul Steinberg's myopic drawing, "View of the World from 9th Avenue," reproduced in Harold Rosenberg, *Saul Steinberg* (New York, 1978), 79.

2 For an elaboration see Alan K. Henrikson, "The Geographical 'Mental Maps' of American Foreign Policy Makers," *International Political Science Review* 1 (October 1980): 495–530. The conception of mental, or cognitive, maps explained therein is strongly influenced by Gestalt psychology, which emphasizes that perception takes place in organized conceptual wholes, not in stimulus-response fashion. The term *cognitive map* was coined by the psychologist Edward C. Tolman, "Cognitive Maps in Rats and Men," *Psychological Review* 55 (July 1948): 189–208. The expression *mental map*, though used somewhat differently by them, has been given currency by Peter Gould and Rodney White, *Mental Maps* (Harmondsworth, England, 1974). For other such studies, none of them applied to really large-scale problems such as the issues of international relations, see Roger M. Downs and David Stea, eds., *Image and Environment: Cognitive Mapping and Spatial Behavior* (Chicago, 1973); and their more popular work, *Maps in Minds: Reflections on Cognitive Mapping* (New York, 1977). In addition see Gary T. Moore and Reginald G. Golledge, *Environmental Knowing: Theories, Research, and Methods* (Stroudsburg, PA, 1976).

the *edges,* or internal and external boundaries that inhibit his movements; the geographical-cultural *districts,* or regions into which he moves or may wish to gain access; the *nodes,* or the intersections on which his activity centers; and the *landmarks,* or signs to which he refers for self-location, and perhaps also for the orientation and the direction of others.[3]

Many concrete, historically known, internationally salient examples can be cited in illustration. A few are given. Mental-map paths might include images of the Silk Route, the Persian Corridor, and the Alaska-Siberia Air Bridge—historical recollections that might be relevant again. Edges might include the Iron Curtain, the Berlin Wall, and the Korean Demilitarized Zone—Cold War vestiges. Districts would include the cases of Tacna-Arica, Ogaden, and Kashmir—that is, disputed territories. Nodes would include such crossroads and meeting places as Jerusalem, Singapore, and Vienna. Landmarks refer to places such as the Rock of Gibraltar, Mount Fuji, and the Brandenburg Gate. None of these reference points, lines, or planes need be thought of consciously, by their names or even by their images, in order to be parts of the cognitive maps of those who orient themselves by them. Often, however, persons do think of these geographical features explicitly, particularly when they are objects of public discussion, perhaps because they are focuses of international tension.[4]

Mental maps often are latent. They may be thought of as "triggered" into use whenever a person is required to make a spatial decision, that is, when he or she confronts a problem that necessitates a choice among alternative real or imagined movements in space. Moreover, mental maps tend to be somewhat narrowly thematic, that is, pertinent to specific kinds of spatial problems, such as military, economic, or political challenges.

The spatial problems in question may be those of a complete observer who tries to intuit and explain the movements of others who are closer to the decisional center of world affairs. To illustrate: Whether the lead-

---

3   Lynch, *The Image of the City* (Cambridge, MA, 1960), 46–49; Henrikson, "Geographical 'Mental Maps,'" 519–20.

4   A very useful synopsis of current international geographical conflicts is Alan J. Day, ed., *Border and Territorial Disputes* (London, 1982). More thematically selective and interpretive works include Michael Kidron and Dan Smith, *The War Atlas: Armed Conflict— Armed Peace* (New York, 1983); Gérard Chaliand and Jean-Pierre Rageau, *Atlas Stratégique: Géopolitique des rapports de force dans le monde* (Malesherbes, France, 1983); and John Keegan and Andrew Wheatcroft, *Zones of Conflict: An Atlas of Future War* (New York, 1986). For an especially authoritative recent treatise on the logic and legalities of formal geographical divisions see J. R. V. Prescott, *Political Frontiers and Boundaries* (London, 1987).

ership of the Soviet Union in 1979 would exploit the turmoil in and around Iran to launch a military drive southward to gain the age-old Russian objective of a warm water port on the Indian Ocean was a question that entailed active, imaginative "participation" in Soviet geostrategic thinking.[5] To try to determine what Moscow might do about a separatist drive by any of its central Asian republics is another vicarious psychogeographical test. The answers to such questions, and the deeper political-geographical understanding that helps to provide such answers, should partially determine the response pattern of officials in Washington and other capitals.

Although geographical mental maps are relatively stable structures, they are by no means fixed. They can be altered radically by technology— the atomic bomb, the ballistic missile, or the orbital spacecraft. Technological progress has caused some writers, such as John H. Herz, to proclaim the demise of the "territorial state." As Herz points out, now that power can destroy power, from center to center, "everything is different."[6] Traditional geographical concepts and complacencies nevertheless sometimes endure. The very factor that made them unrealistic— scientific and technical innovation—also can be used to rehabilitate them. President Ronald Reagan's Strategic Defense Initiative, a highly territorial concept promising a shield over North America, is a leading case in point.

Mental maps also can be changed by adoption of new geostrategies, or "game plans," as they sometimes are called today.[7] The granddaddy of these in international relations is the "containment" concept. Originated by George Kennan, this notion has dominated American thinking throughout the Cold War era. In his influential Mr. "X" article of 1947, Kennan laid down what became a guideline for all future American national security policy. In light of Moscow's outlook and recent behavior, he stated, "it will be clearly seen that the Soviet pressure against the free institutions of the Western world is something that can be contained by the adroit and vigilant application of counter-force at a series

5 See, for example, Selig S. Harrison, *In Afghanistan's Shadow: Baluch Nationalism and Soviet Temptations* (New York, 1981).

6 John H. Herz, *International Politics in the Atomic Age* (New York, 1959), 108. See also some of the essays in Herz's collection, *The Nation-State and the Crisis of World Politics* (New York, 1976). The argument that the historic notion of territoriality—as provider of security—and of the state—as protector of society—was shattered by Hiroshima and Nagasaki is the unstated premise of a work such as Gregg Herken's ironic *The Winning Weapon: The Atomic Bomb in the Cold War, 1945–1950* (New York, 1982).

7 See, for example, Brzezinski, *Game Plan: A Geostrategic Framework for the Conduct of the U.S.-Soviet Contest* (Boston, 1986).

of constantly shifting geographical and political points, corresponding to the shifts and maneuvers of Soviet policy, but which cannot be charmed or talked out of existence."[8]

Although Kennan probably did not intend his concept to become the basis for a highly militarized, global geostrategy resulting in the establishment of bases and the conduct of military operations on virtually all of the sectors of the Soviet bloc's periphery, he was in truth responsible for the policy formulation that suggested such a "strategic monstrosity," as the philosopher-columnist Walter Lippmann then called it.[9] Years later, Kennan indicated that he had agreed with most of Lippmann's critique, lamenting that he had not employed such rigorous analysis himself.[10]

That Kennan did misrepresent his own thinking is supported by John Lewis Gaddis in *Strategies of Containment*. In Gaddis's view, what Kennan actually favored was something like a classical balance of power among continents, to be achieved through close American cooperation with several of the other "vital power centers," particularly Great Britain, Germany, and Japan.[11] The conceptual-geographical map underlying such an idea is very different from that connoted by "containment," which focused Western attention on the periphery rather than on the center.[12]

As this example of Kennan's containment doctrine will serve to illustrate, the geostrategic concepts that enter into political discourse need not be only an individual's. Mental geography need not be the exclusive domain of the private person, the dream wanderings of an idiosyncratic spirit. Although there is no such thing as a geographical group mind, a transcendent group consciousness of space, geographical thinking can be common property, socially shared, as was the case with manifest destiny in the 1840s.

In foreign affairs, owing to the fact that most members of a society never have visited or at least are not closely familiar with distant foreign societies, geographical mental maps tend not to be very detailed or complicated. This is perhaps especially true for the American people, most of whom have geographical mental maps that are fairly general, both in

8   The text of the article is included, under the same title, in George F. Kennan, *American Diplomacy, 1900–1950* (Chicago, 1951).
9   Lippmann, *The Cold War: A Study in U.S. Foreign Policy* (New York, 1947), 18.
10 Kennan, *Memoirs, 1925–1950* (Boston, 1967), chap. 15.
11 Gaddis, *Strategies of Containment: A Critical Appraisal of Postwar American National Security Policy* (New York, 1982), chap. 2.
12 This point is made in Alan K. Henrikson, "America's Changing Place in the World: From 'Periphery' to 'Centre'?" in *Centre and Periphery: Spatial Variation in Politics*, ed. Jean Gottmann (Beverly Hills, 1980), 73–100, esp. 88–89.

the sense of being commonly shared and in the sense of being abstractly formed, if not actually vague.

In fact, Americans historically have tended to think of "foreign" affairs as being transacted through relatively few paths or channels—over the Atlantic (from New York or Washington to London or Paris or maybe Bonn) and across the Pacific (from San Francisco or Los Angeles to Tokyo or Beijing or maybe Singapore). Diplomacy in the strict, official sense is a more narrow-gauged transaction. It is not conducted between countries, but between capital cities. For American officials, unlike their French counterparts, diplomacy is not, geopsychologically, a radiating, or *tous azimuts,* pattern of communication. In the post–Second World War period, of course, the paths and nodes of American diplomatic movement and contact have greatly multiplied. The fabled "globe-hopping" of Secretary of State John Foster Dulles, for instance, considerably widened and sometimes snarled a vast American diplomatic network.

Diplomats' cognitive patterns for organizing space, it should be emphasized, need not be and usually are not "pictures in the head," that is, deliberate visualizations of geographical places or of the documentary maps made of them.[13] Mental maps are dynamic cognitive systems that, somewhat like software programs used in computers, can generate images in the mind's eye, much as on a monitor. But these projections are not the basic, mentally stored data. The mental map itself is the spatial-geographical information that is possessed, not the graphic or technicolor representation of it.

Geographical information can include valuations. A statesman's purely cognitive geographical map often is closely related to his substantive "world view," or weltanschauung. The paths, edges, districts, nodes, and landmarks that constitute his historically shaped mental map usually have positive or negative connotations and other qualitative judgments attached to them. Some places have been considered safe ("Fortress America") and others have been felt to be dangerous ("Spanish Cockpit"). Some lands have been seen as fertile ("Southeast Asian Rice Bowl") and others have been reported as barren ("Nullarbor Plain").

In addition, it should be noted that the inhabitants of geographic places—districts, in Lynch's lexicon—are not (in the perceptual maps of others, and perhaps even those of the subjects themselves), wholly separable from them.[14] Everyone is part of someone else's environment, even

13   The somewhat misleading expression "pictures in our heads" originated with Walter Lippmann in his seminal study *Public Opinion* (New York, 1922). A similarly graphic phrase, "scratches on our minds," was the original title of Harold R. Isaacs's evocative *Images of Asia: American Views of China and India* (New York, 1958).
14   The psychologist Kurt Lewin's concept of "life space" includes even the perceiving

if not as fixedly integral to it as are the physical features of geography. Men and milieux blend. To Lawrence of Arabia, the Bedouins seemed at one with the desert itself. To Vilhjalmur Stefansson, the Eskimos made the Arctic and its vacancies feel "friendly." To American servicemen in Indochina, the Vietcong seemed able to survive on a bowl of rice per day. Part of the reason why the geographic world is valued, in short, is because it is peopled. Mental maps, like the world they reflect, are alive.

Having examined what a mental map is, let us proceed to consider how it can be applied to what is perhaps still the central problem of American diplomacy: how to co-inhabit the earth with the Soviet Union. After studying first the Americans' and then briefly the Russians' historically conditioned mental maps of their respective places in the world, we may then be in a better position to understand their continuing geopolitical deadlock. In order to do that, however, one must be able to determine, with some certainty, what the mental maps of leaders and peoples in the United States, the Soviet Union, and other countries really are. Several methods will be identified that may assist historians in this purpose of psychogeographical discovery.

An understanding of mental maps, as well as of the revolutionary changes that occurred after World War II in the technology of warfare, enables us to see that the United States and the Soviet Union continued in the postwar period to obey more or less the same national and ideological imperatives they always had obeyed, but in a radically altered real and imaginary spatio-temporal context.[15] The respective "spheres of influence" of the two countries, hitherto distant from one another and relatively small, now seemed to overlap—in Europe, in Asia, and even in the Arctic, emerging as a possible air-age Mediterranean. The planet on which the two countries suddenly emerged as superpowers seemed much reduced, indeed shrunken. A Herbert Block ("Herblock") cartoon in the *Washington Post* in 1947 showed a ball-sized earth, labeled "One World," with a towering Uncle Sam on top pointing a finger downward and saying to a similarly gigantic Uncle Joe Stalin facing him, "I'm Here To Stay, Too."[16] Their circumstances affected their consciousness.

As early as the 1830s, the historian recalls, both America and Russia had been marked out by Alexis de Tocqueville and other Europeans as

subject. Lewin, *Principles of Topological Psychology*, trans. Fritz Heider and Grace M. Heider (New York, 1936).

15   This is the argument I advance in "The Map as an 'Idea': The Role of Cartographic Imagery During the Second World War," *The American Cartographer* 2 (April 1975): 19–53.

16   For the cartoon see ibid., 46.

certain one day "to sway the destinies of half the globe."[17] Geostrategically as well as in their political cultures, the two countries have developed very differently. That is our interest here. The United States developed by the mid-twentieth century as a maritime power with transoceanic allies. The Soviet Union became by that time a truly predominant continental power with mostly contiguous satellites.

This distinction became almost axiomatic in American official strategic thinking in subsequent years. "Russia can protect its most important client states or attack all but one of its most likely enemies without going to sea," Admiral Elmo R. Zumwalt, a former chief of naval operations, pointed out a quarter of a century later. "By contrast, the industry and trade of the United States depend on ocean traffic in both directions and most of its important allies are on the far side of the broad oceans as well."[18] On the basis of their different geographies and associated political relationships, the two sides have developed very different military strategies and force structures. This divergence in security policy has generated a sense of "asymmetry" that has greatly complicated the task of trying to arrive at mutually acceptable arms control arrangements.[19] The tradeoffs necessary to agreement were extremely difficult to measure. As two astute American Sovietologists, Helmut Sonnenfeldt and William G. Hyland, noted, Moscow seemed to feel itself continually in need of "compensations."[20]

In the global mental geography of America's naval strategists especially, the United States is, in Admiral Zumwalt's words, "a 'world island' whose

17 Tocqueville, *Democracy in America*, ed. Phillips Bradley, 2 vols. (New York, 1960), 1: 452. The American diplomat-turned-historian Louis J. Halle, in *The Cold War as History* (New York, 1967), argues on the basis of Tocqueville's remarkable prophecy, in part a geographical insight, that "the historical circumstances, themselves, had an ineluctable quality that left the Russians little choice but to move as they did." He likens the two superpowers to a scorpion and a tarantula in a "bottle" (pp. xiii, 10–11).

18 Zumwalt, *On Watch: A Memoir* (New York, 1976), 60.

19 See, for example, U.S. Department of Defense, *Report of Secretary of Defense Caspar W. Weinberger to the Congress on the FY 1983 Budget, FY 1984 Authorization Request, and FY 1983–1987 Defense Programs* (Washington, 1982), 2:12: "We must recognize the global threat to our interests posed by the overall asymmetry in the types of nuclear warheads and the comprehensive coverage and operational characteristics of Soviet nuclear systems." Weinberger particularly noted the steady increase in the number of the Soviet Union's SS-20s, for which there was, in the early 1980s, no obvious NATO counterpart. This indicated a need for deployment in Western Europe of Pershing II and cruise missiles, both as a further deterrent and (although it vigorously was denied) also as possible bargaining counters.

20 Sonnenfeldt and Hyland, *Soviet Perspectives on Security*, Adelphi Paper No. 150 (Spring 1979).

every activity is bound up with use of the seas."[21] This conception has strong antecedents in the American political-geographical tradition, dating back to Alfred Thayer Mahan's *The Influence of Sea Power upon History*.[22] As Mahan understood, during most of its history the United States had been relatively isolated. This isolation had contributed to its security but had also made it difficult to predict how Americans would react to European or other encroachment from overseas. The American people had enjoyed almost a century of "free security," in part owing to the advantage of their remote and resistant geography. They further were privileged during most decades of the nineteenth century by the de facto protection of the British navy, which was never politically or even intellectually acknowledged.[23]

To be sure, there were historical periods when Americans have felt insecure. During the colonial era, as Max Savelle explains, the Anglo-Americans settled on the Atlantic coast feared that they progressively were being "encircled" by a ring of forts and rivers—nodes and routes—in the hinterland. Their tormenters were the Catholic French and their Jesuit-indoctrinated Indian allies.[24] British military operations during the American Revolution also demonstrated the vulnerability of the new country's position. The burning of Washington, DC, during the War of 1812 further traumatized the coast-based nation, giving rise to temporary thoughts of moving the national capital to the Ohio Valley and ultimately perhaps into the Mississippi region. And the movement of Mexican troops in 1846 across the Rio Grande into what President James K. Polk considered American territory demonstrated the country's vulnerability to aggression from the southwestern quarter.

A geopolitical subtext of these various military conflicts, most of them at the margins of the continent, was the American apprehension that a European-style "balance of power" might be established in North America. During the international intrigue on the Texas question in the early

---

21 Zumwalt, *On Watch*, 60.
22 See Mahan, *The Influence of Sea Power upon History, 1660–1783* (Boston, 1890), 42. On Mahan's central part in the formulation of American imperial ideas see Walter LaFeber, *The New Empire: An Interpretation of American Expansion, 1860–1898* (Ithaca, 1963), 80–101.
23 C. Vann Woodward, "The Age of Reinterpretation," *American Historical Review* 66 (October 1960): 1–19; Walter Lippmann, *U.S. Foreign Policy: Shield of the Republic* (Boston, 1943), 16–22.
24 Savelle, with the assistance of Margaret Anne Fisher, *The Origins of American Diplomacy: The International History of Angloamerica, 1492–1763* (New York, 1968), esp. 512–33. Shorter but equally comprehensive works on the contest of imperial strategies on the continent of North America are Richard W. Van Alstyne, *The Rising American Empire* (New York, 1960); and William J. Eccles, *France in America* (New York, 1972).

1840s, French Foreign Minister François Guizot declared: "In America, as in Europe, by reason of our political and commercial interests we need independence, an equilibrium of the several states [*l'équilibre des divers Etats*]. This is the essential idea which ought to determine the policy of France in America." As Frederick Merk has emphasized, this notion of an *"équilibre américain"* was anathema to Polk and most other Americans, who naturally believed that they and their ancestors had come to the New World to escape the deadly balancing of the Old.[25] The mental maps of Americans at that time simply had no room for such a European idea.

The Civil War once again raised the specter of a North American balance. Military or diplomatic intervention by Great Britain and France could mean not merely the permanent breakup of the Federal Union itself but also the fractionizing of the whole continent, including Canada and Mexico, into an international system. The best way to preclude European intervention, it seemed, was to prevent contact between the Confederate States of America and the continental powers by blockading the long Confederate coastline. "Never did sea power play a greater or a more decisive part," as Mahan later proudly proclaimed, "than in the contest which determined that the course of the world's history would be modified by the existence of one great nation, instead of several rival States, in the North American continent."[26]

In the twentieth century, with the United States consolidated and stronger, there have been even fewer challenges to Americans' sense of automatic continental security. The project to construct a canal through Panama did suggest to Mahan and other imaginative strategists a future "Mediterraneanizing" of the Caribbean, but a progressive buildup of American naval strength allayed most such fears.[27] To be sure, President Woodrow Wilson did send U.S. naval units to the coast of Mexico in

25 Merk, with Lois Bannister Merk, *The Monroe Doctrine and American Expansionism, 1843–1849* (New York, 1966), chap. 3. On British imperial strategy in that era and American reactions to it see Kenneth Bourne, *Britain and the Balance of Power in North America, 1815–1908* (London, 1967); and Kinley J. Brauer, "The United States and British Imperial Expansion, 1815–60," *Diplomatic History* 12 (Winter 1988): 19–37.

26 Mahan, *Influence of Sea Power*, 44.

27 Ibid., 33–35. An even more imaginative geographical "analogy" (Mahan's term) is President Theodore Roosevelt's fear of "another Kiaochow," that is, a German-established fortified port, on the coast of Venezuela. See Howard K. Beale, *Theodore Roosevelt and the Rise of America to World Power* (Baltimore, 1956), 400. Here the mental configuration being superimposed upon the complex Caribbean-Central American region is that of the Shantung Peninsula and Gulf of Pechili area in Northeast Asia, where the Germans had gained a concession, including Kiaochow, in 1897. That situation is described in detail in William L. Langer, *The Diplomacy of Imperialism, 1890–1902*, 2d ed. (New York, 1960), chap. 14, map on p. 455.

order to block anticipated European arms shipments, and the interception and release of the Zimmermann telegram in early 1917 did arouse American fears of imperial Germany's support of Mexican irredentist claims. The Pancho Villa raids into Texas and New Mexico, however, already had caused Wilson to authorize General John J. Pershing to carry out a punitive expedition to foreclose such a possibility.

The Japanese attack on Pearl Harbor in 1941 challenged isolationist notions about the impregnability of the Western Hemisphere. As Michigan Senator Arthur H. Vandenberg later admitted: "That day ended isolationism for any realist."[28] Twenty years later, the Soviet Union's military support for the Cuban regime of Fidel Castro, especially the attempted placement of intermediate-range missiles there in October 1962, once again threatened the continental complacency of most North Americans. Besides the direct security threat, it posed a political danger— that the North American environment could become a Europe-like international system. Under these circumstances, Soviet insistence that Cuba had every right to international protection from outside the Western Hemisphere was difficult for American officials to accept.[29]

Despite these dangers, the basic U.S. mental map of North America, unlike that of Soviet Russia, has been one of a continent at peace. Most citizens of the United States believe their country can have unguarded borders with its neighbors—or at least, in the case of Mexico, a border with no more than wire fences.[30] The geographic conditions of American life, as noted by Frederick Jackson Turner, Ellen Church Semple, Ralph

28 Vandenberg quoted in Manfred Jonas, *Isolationism in America, 1935–41* (Ithaca, 1966), 273. See also ibid., 121–34.
29 Secretary of State Dean Rusk proposed, revealingly, during a White House meeting on 16 October 1962 that the United States get word to Castro, perhaps through the Canadian ambassador in Havana, that "this is no longer support for Cuba, that Cuba is being victimized here, and that, uh, the Soviets are preparing Cuba for destruction or betrayal." "White House Tapes and Minutes of the Cuban Missile Crisis: ExComm Meetings, October 1962," *International Security* 10 (Summer 1985): 172. For recent discussion of the missile crisis, in which the defense-of-Cuba theme is recurrent, see James G. Hershberg, "Before 'The Missiles of October': Did Kennedy Plan a Military Strike against Cuba?" *Diplomatic History* 14 (Spring 1990): 163–98; and Bernd Greiner, "The Soviet View: An Interview with Sergo Mikoyan," with commentary by Raymond L. Garthoff, Barton J. Bernstein, Marc Trachtenberg, and Thomas G. Paterson, ibid., 205–56.
30 On geopolitics across the U.S. northern frontier see Richard A. Preston, *The Defence of the Undefended Border: Planning for War in North America, 1867–1939* (Montreal, 1977); and Richard Gwyn, *The 49th Paradox: Canada in North America* (Toronto, 1985). On relations across the U.S. southern border see J. W. House, *Frontier on the Rio Grande: A Political Geography of Development and Social Deprivation* (Oxford, England, 1982); and Alan Riding, *Distant Neighbors: A Portrait of the Mexicans* (New York, 1985).

H. Brown, and others, have been comparatively stable, despite the continuing drama of westward-moving settlement.[31] The journalist Joel Garreau, despite his limning of new and emergent mental-geographical entities in his sensational *The Nine Nations of North America,* freely states, "I do not think that North America is flying apart, or that it should."[32]

Our present ways of thinking about geopolitical relationships, such as that between the United States and the Soviet Union, are not adequate. A particularly dangerous style of argument is that involving the use of geographical analogies. The sociologist C. Wright Mills, for instance, cautioned in *The Causes of World War Three* against the consequences of basing U.S. troops, ships, and airplanes around the Soviet periphery. "It is easy to see why the Russians consider these bases as aggressive and provocative," he argued. "It is as if, from the American viewpoint, Soviet bases of similar type encircled the North American continent."[33]

The general counterargument to such tendentious and possibly misleading comparisons is the anti-"mirror imaging" counsel, which warns Americans against seeing only themselves when they think they are looking at the Soviet Union.[34] False projections of motive and method may be the result. Americans cannot *know* the Soviet geographical mind indirectly, only by reasoning, subconsciously or consciously, from their own feelings regarding their own changing physical-political situation, assumed without thinking to be comparable to the geopolitical predicaments of the Russians. Even experts sometimes resort to slipshod reasoning, in public exposition if not in their own private thinking. Kennan, for instance, while explaining at an informal press conference in August 1950 why it would be unwise to extend military operations north of the 38th parallel in Korea, commented, "I think you can see that if you put the shoe on the other foot and think how it would be with us if Soviet

31 Turner, *The Frontier in American History* (New York, 1947); Semple, *American History and Its Geographic Conditions* (Boston, 1903): Brown, *Historical Geography of the United States* (New York, 1948). Noteworthy among recent such writings are the geographically sensitive works of William H. Goetzmann, including *Army Exploration in the American West, 1803–1863* (New Haven, 1959), *Exploration and Empire: The Explorer and the Scientist in the Winning of the American West* (New York, 1967), *New Lands, New Men: America and the Second Great Age of Discovery* (New York, 1986), and, with his son William N. Goetzmann, *The West of the Imagination* (New York, 1986).

32 Garreau, *The Nine Nations of North America* (Boston, 1981), xvi.

33 Mills, *The Causes of World War Three* (New York, 1958), 107.

34 The term "mirror image" was applied to the U.S.-USSR conflict by Urie Bronfenbrenner in "The Mirror Image in Soviet-American Relations: A Social Psychologist's Report," *Journal of Social Issues* 17:3 (1961): 45–56.

forces began to come within say seventeen miles of Southern California in fighting Mexico."[35] If an accurate sense of another society's behavior space cannot be built up by the comparative or projective geographical imagination alone, how can it be gained?

There are at least three basic ways to acquire such knowledge. One is through the careful, detailed analysis of the cartographic traditions of countries such as the United States and the Soviet Union. Arguably, there is no *better* evidence of their unique cognitive and perceptual worlds than the actual maps they have employed.[36] The progressive movement of the United States on the map—from the margins of the eighteenth-century Atlantic world, to a continental position between Europe and Asia, to a central place on an Arctic-centered global chart—is easy to trace.[37] The Soviet cartographic self-image is not difficult to discern either. Zbigniew Brzezinski is right in *Game Plan* to stress the diplomatic-historical pertinence of the fact that former Soviet Foreign Minister Andrei Gromyko habitually spent hours in his office contemplating a map of the world. This was, of course, the standard Soviet global chart, centered on Moscow with North and South America distinctly peripheralized—and to a rectilinear American eye, badly distorted besides.[38]

One must not assume, of course, that there is a one-to-one correspondence between such physical maps and the minds of those who behold them.[39] A senior U.S. official once mentioned a discussion he and others had in Moscow with Leonid Brezhnev, the Soviet leader at the time. Brezhnev had before him a map of the Soviet Union with red arrows all around it showing many American attack routes converging upon Soviet territory. Brezhnev asked how the U.S. government could expect him to be reasonable (in the current arms-control negotiations) when this was being done to him! As the American official commented, "I didn't know

---

35   Quoted by John Lewis Gaddis, "The Strategic Perspective: The 'Defensive Perimeter' Concept, 1947–1951," in *Uncertain Years: Chinese-American Relations, 1947–1950*, ed. Dorothy Borg and Waldo Heinrichs (New York, 1980), 109.

36   This is the premise of my prefatory essay, "Frameworks for the World," in *Scholars' Guide to Washington, D.C., for Cartography and Remote Sensing Imagery (Maps, Charts, Aerial Photographs, Satellite Images, Cartographic Literature and Geographic Information Systems)*, ed. Ralph E. Ehrenberg (Washington, 1987), ix–xiii.

37   See, for example, the use of map illustrations in Henrikson, "America's Changing Place in the World." Among many excellent cartographic collections focused on the United States in its North American setting, one may consult, for historical cartography, Seymour I. Schwartz and Ralph E. Ehrenberg, *The Mapping of America* (New York, 1980); and, for modern cartography, National Geographic Society, *Atlas of North America: Space Age Portrait of a Continent* (Washington, 1985).

38   Brzezinski, *Game Plan,* 3–8.

39   Brzezinski elides this distinction by labeling a small reproduction of the typical Soviet world map, "The Global View from Moscow." Ibid., 4.

whether those were the maps they really used, or whether it was just put there for me to read upside down."[40]

A second method for determining the way nations view themselves spatially—that is, "reading" their mental maps—is to study the geographical content of their language. This includes the metaphors and analogies used, as well as straightforward geographical terms. In addition to the examples of such explicit geographical comparisons as already have been mentioned, one may cite President Harry S. Truman's likening of the challenge the United States faced in Korea in 1950 to that earlier confronted during the Greek civil war.[41]

In discussing the Indochina conflict, to cite another example, Secretary of State Dean Rusk often compared the Communist threat to Vietnam in the 1960s to the Fascist threat to Czechoslovakia and the rest of Europe in the 1930s. He also drew geopolitical parallels with the immediate postwar period. "Try and imagine a map of the world if it were redrawn as it would have been had we and others not been interested and concerned in what happened in Iran, Turkey, and Greece, and Berlin and Korea," he asked.[42] At the beginning of the 1980s, another geopolitical parallel became popular. Central America, because it appeared to be either the next "domino" or a possible "quagmire," was labeled "another Vietnam."[43] As such examples indicate, statesmen and others frequently think in geographical as well as in historical analogies, reasoning spatially as well as temporally.[44]

One particular geographical metaphor especially important in interpreting the U.S.-Soviet geopolitical contest in the Cold War is Sir Halford Mackinder's "Heartland" concept. "Who rules East Europe commands the Heartland / Who rules the Heartland commands the World Island / Who rules the World Island commands the World," the British geographer hypothesized.[45] Mackinder created a geopolitical image that, some

40 Stated in conversation with author. Compare with Sonnenfeldt and Hyland, *Soviet Perspectives on Security*, 20: "Her [the Soviet Union's] complaints about allied nuclear weapons systems and American forward bases have a tactical rationale in SALT polemics, but it would be surprising if these aspects are dismissed in Soviet military analysis."

41 Quoted in Ernest R. May, *"Lessons" of the Past: The Use and Misuse of History in American Foreign Policy* (New York, 1973).

42 Quoted in Thomas J. Schoenbaum, *Waging Peace and War: Dean Rusk in the Truman, Kennedy, and Johnson Years* (New York, 1988), 424.

43 See Thomas G. Paterson, "Historical Memory and Illusive Victories: Vietnam and Central America," *Diplomatic History* 12 (Winter 1988): 1–18.

44 Richard E. Neustadt and Ernest R. May, *Thinking in Time: The Uses of History for Decision-Makers* (New York, 1986).

45 Quoted in W. H. Parker, *Mackinder: Geography as an Aid to Statecraft* (Oxford, 1982), 184–85. Here the most pertinent of Mackinder's writings are *Democratic Ideals and Reality*, with additional papers, ed. Andrew J. Pearce (New York, 1962), and

have argued, conceptually inspired the American policy of containment. It is somewhat disconcerting that the Heartland idea, supposedly a master concept for explaining Soviet geopolitical behavior in the world, was scarcely known in Moscow at the start of the Cold War and did not correspond with how the Russians organized their geographical space.[46] To the extent, therefore, that the containment policy was based on the Heartland concept and to the negligible degree that the Heartland notion corresponded with actual Soviet thinking, the American encirclement posture was based on an illusion.

A third way to try to understand better the geographical mentality of countries such as the United States and the Soviet Union is to travel to and through them—physically to stand and to walk where Americans and Russians have been, as they made policy decisions and participated in historical events. This point is (literally) pedestrian, but no less sensible for that. The tradition of such travel is an honored one. From Tocqueville and Kennan to historians and politicians today, America and Russia have been thoroughly "tramped" by observers attempting vicariously to share the national experiences and to discover the national viewpoints of those countries. In the maritime realm (and perhaps in the field of historical exploration generally), Samuel Eliot Morison holds pride of place. Introducing his study of Christopher Columbus, whose routes Morison personally resailed, the historian sharply comments: "Most biographies of the Admiral might well be entitled 'Columbus to the Water's Edge.' "[47] The same might be said of much diplomatic history, perhaps especially American diplomatic history. Diplomacy, like hiking and sailing, should be considered an open-air and also a worldwide sport. Its field, as Secretary of State Dean Acheson liked to say, is nothing less than "the vast external realm."[48]

A visit to the West Coast of the United States, for example, will help the diplomatic historian to appreciate the possible meanings—commercial, cultural, and political—of repeated declarations by American leaders that the United States is a "Pacific" as well as an "Atlantic" power. A journey to the Soviet Union, especially for the first time, can also prompt

---

"The Round World and the Winning of the Peace," *Foreign Affairs* 21 (July 1943): 595–605. It is not well known that Mackinder first conceived of the Eurasian "Heartland" as merely a central drainage area, that is, having no outlet to any sea or ocean.

46 These points are demonstrated in a paper by Ladis K. D. Kristof, "Mackinder's Concept of Heartland and the Russians," Symposium K5: History of Geographical Thought, 23d International Geographical Congress, Leningrad, 22–26 July 1976.

47 Morison, *Admiral of the Ocean Sea: A Life of Christopher Columbus* (Boston, 1942), xv.

48 Acheson, *Present at the Creation: My Years in the State Department* (New York, 1969), 728.

important revelations.[49] A fundamental aspect of this typical experience is the physical reorientation that is involved. One naturally learns the distances and directions that are pertinent to the new locale. Walking on Nevsky Prospekt in Leningrad, for instance, one gains a new, more geography-based outlook on "the West"—the occidental mirage that Peter the Great and his modernizing successors alternately admired and resented. Standing before the Kremlin on Red Square in Moscow, one can more easily imagine sharing the view—a dimension of which is the physical angle of vision—that Brezhnev and other Soviet leaders might have had in 1979 when they sent an invasion force into Afghanistan. One better "sees" from that prospect the proximity of Afghanistan to the People's Republic of China, with a large Muslim element presumably interested in the fate of their Afghan coreligionists. By contrast, on a conventionally oriented north-south American newspaper map of that area, Afghanistan seems to neighbor mainly Iran, Pakistan, and the Soviet Union. The Chinese angle is easy to miss.

It is, of course, never enough for the historian to have "been there," merely to have stood in the Russians' or anyone else's shoes. That experience, however, may be an essential condition of coming to share another nation's geopsychological perspective. The historian must go far beyond this purely spatial awareness to learn the substantive relationships between geography and culture. Only by learning the contents—the facts and not merely the frames—of other nationals' mental cartography can the historian truly be said imaginatively to be traveling by *their* mental maps, rather than his or her own. Only thus can the scholar pass through the "mirror."

The mental maps of nations are not equivalent or interchangeable. Although these representations of geography may have some major characteristics in common, they usually are specific in no less important ways. If both the United States and the Soviet Union, for instance, are continental countries with monolithic attitudes, opposing fissiparous territorial tendencies and rejecting "balance of power" maneuvers within their regions, they nonetheless are fundamentally different in geopolitical outlook. The United States has long been relatively secure. Therefore, it may paradoxically be even more intolerant of encroachments and disruptions at its margins. The overthrow in 1989 of General Manuel Noriega in Panama, however richly deserved by that dictator, does suggest the pervasive influence of American intolerance of local disorder—belying the

---

49 Urie Bronfenbrenner described his trip to Russia in the summer of 1960, a few months after the U-2 incident, as "a deeply disturbing experience." See Bronfenbrenner, "Mirror Image," 45.

impression of geopolitical complacency that Americans give. The Soviet Union, having repeatedly been invaded in the twentieth century and for the past forty years having been militarily "contained," certainly has reason to feel insecure. Nonetheless, this very reality may have "accustomed" Soviet leaders and peoples to their condition, which (unlike that of Americans) has been inescapable. They may have a kind of operational code, or a cognitively and culturally based set of practical rules, for coping with it.[50] In other words, their mental maps may allow them to live with a degree of insecurity.

The current Soviet government seems even willing to accept American participation, through continuation of a limited U.S. military presence in Europe, in securing what it could not secure by itself: a neutralized buffer of Eastern European states, formerly controlled as satellites. The Soviet emphasis now is on "common security" in all its aspects, rather than on independent or mutually exclusive security. Stated differently, it purports to favor one mental map, not several separate or even overlapping ones. "For all the contradictions of the present-day world, for all the diversity of social and political systems in it, and for all the different choices made by the nations in different times," as Mikhail Gorbachev emphasizes in *Perestroika*, "this world is nevertheless one whole. We are all passengers aboard one ship, the Earth, and we must not allow it to be wrecked. There will be no second Noah's Ark."[51]

In this essay, I have attempted to show how careful attention to a nation's geographical mental maps, especially those of the United States, can illuminate past, present, and even future decision making in the field of foreign policy. Historians, like statesmen, can profit from such analysis. After all, it is not merely the multiplicity of state jurisdictions that makes the study of international relations distinctive among political subjects, it is also the huge earthly expanse within which diplomacy takes place. The ways of diplomacy are, in part, geographical paths, sometimes open and sometimes blocked. These configurations, both on the land and in the mind, are complex. They must be traced in order to know how the world moves. Historians, in other words, should think through space as well as time.

50 The "operational code" concept, which has not been applied systematically to geographical thinking and conduct, is discussed in Alexander L. George, "The 'Operational Code': A Neglected Approach to the Study of Political Leaders and Decision-Making," *International Studies Quarterly* 13 (June 1969): 190–222.

51 Gorbachev, *Perestroika: New Thinking for Our Country and the World*, new, updated ed. (New York, 1988), xiv. In its geographical aspects, Gorbachev's "new thinking" has venerable Russian antecedents. It was, for instance, a Russian, V. I. Vernadsky, who developed "biosphere" in modern scientific thought. See Lynton K. Caldwell, *In Defense of Earth: International Protection of the Biosphere* (Bloomington, 1972), 45.

13

Ideology

MICHAEL H. HUNT

Ideology is the proper concern of all diplomatic historians. Its relevance rests on a simple proposition of fundamental importance: To move in a world of infinite complexity, individuals and societies need to reduce that world to finite terms. Only then can they pretend an understanding of their environment and have the confidence to talk about it and the courage to act on it. Policymaking, like any other individual or collective activity, requires that simplifying clarity. Policymakers get their keys to "reality" in the same ways that others in their culture do. Policymakers are formed by a socialization that begins in childhood and continues even as they try to retain those keys or to discard them as a result of experience in making decisions.

Thus, every diplomatic historian, like it or not, constantly comes in contact with the problem of ideology. Those intent on a better understanding of its importance and complexity may turn to a rich, suggestive body of literature. Part of that literature comes from political scientists preoccupied with the problem of definition. Their work catalogs the senses in which *ideology* is used (some twenty-seven according to one count) and sorts through the variations in meaning. Historians will find these writings particularly helpful in formulating a working definition with the greatest utility and applicability to their concerns.[1] Those who think of the concept of ideology as unproblematic will see the importance of being explicit about what it is and what it does, while anyone inclined to downplay the role of ideas or to regard them as freestanding may well reconsider after encountering definitions with clear interpretative promise.

Another version of this essay originally appeared in the June 1990 issue of the *Journal of American History*. It is printed here by permission of the *Journal of American History*. The author owes thanks to Susan Armeny, Michael Hönicke, John Kasson, Lloyd Kramer, Thomas Paterson, and David Thelen for their thoughtful comments.

1 For helpful essays in definition see Willard A. Mullins, "On the Concept of Ideology in Political Science," *American Political Science Review* 66 (June 1972): 498–510; and Malcolm B. Hamilton, "The Elements of the Concept of Ideology," *Political Studies* 35 (March 1987): 18–38. For a succinct, critical, clear-headed introduction see David S. McLellan, *Ideology* (Minneapolis, 1986).

Of the many possible definitions, I favor one that identifies ideology as "an interrelated set of convictions or assumptions that reduces the complexities of a particular slice of reality to easily comprehensible terms and suggests appropriate ways of dealing with that reality." Foreign policy ideologies are thus sets of beliefs and values, sometimes only poorly and partially articulated, that make international relations intelligible and decision making possible. This broad notion launches diplomatic historians on a quest for ideas that give structure and meaning to the way policymakers see the world and their country's place in it. That this definition corresponds closely to that reached independently by two other recent examinations does not make it correct, but it at least suggests that the understanding is plausible and worth testing against other definitions.[2]

Arriving at a definition is an important step, which immediately alters the frame of reference for studying policymakers. The question becomes "not whether they have an ideology but to what ideology they subscribe; not whether ideology makes a difference but what kind of difference it makes for the shaping of their intentions, policies, and behavior."[3] The basic premise that ideology matters and that it is neither simple nor rigid leaves us with a question of overriding importance. What fundamental notions (for example, about human nature, the constituents of power, and national mission) do policymakers carry in their heads? The search for an answer can go in a variety of directions. It can lead us to look at the mindsets of individuals or collectives. Biographical studies dealing with formative, early years are invaluable for the former, while prosopographical techniques are indispensable for the latter, especially as we attempt to identify commonalities or divergences within or between groups, even generations.[4] It can alert us to the need for greater sensitivity to language and especially to the meaning embedded in key words such as "progressive change," "terrorism," or "free world" in our reading of conventional diplomatic documentation and personal correspondence. It asks us to examine rhetoric in a more sophisticated way, and to extend

2   Michael H. Hunt, *Ideology and U.S. Foreign Policy* (New Haven, 1987), xi. For similar definitions see Mullins, "On the Concept of Ideology in Political Science," 510; and Hamilton, "Elements of the Concept of Ideology," 38.
3   Seweryn Bialer, "Ideology and Soviet Foreign Policy," in *Ideology and Foreign Policy: A Global Perspective*, ed. George Schwab (New York, 1978), 86.
4   As examples of biographies see Edmund Morris, *The Rise of Theodore Roosevelt* (New York, 1979); and John M. Mulder, *Woodrow Wilson: The Years of Preparation* (Princeton, 1978). Anyone who doubts the relevance of personality to an understanding of ideology in foreign policy should read M. Brewster Smith, Jerome S. Bruner, and Robert W. White, *Opinions and Personality* (New York, 1956); and Robert Jervis, "Political Psychology—Some Challenges and Opportunities," *Political Psychology* 10 (September 1989): esp. 487–92. See also Lawrence Stone, "Prosopography," in *Historical Studies Today*, ed. Felix Gilbert and Stephen R. Graubard (New York, 1972), 107–40

our scrutiny to symbols and ceremonies that can reveal much about the form and content of ideology that conventional sources usually leave implicit.[5]

Writings about cultural systems further broaden our understanding. They tell us (in the words of anthropologist Clifford Geertz) that ideology springs from those "socially established structures of meaning" associated with culture.[6] As long as cultures create meaning, there will be ideologies that can be understood only by entering into those cultures and decoding their meanings. But a system of culture can seem sprawling and amorphous and far too static to suit the needs of historians.

Neo-Marxist writings can help overcome such limitations, providing insights into causation and process. Their clear focus on class and the hegemonic ideology associated with the dominant class has provided an attractive way of making culture more comprehensible and analytically manageable. Their attention to conflict between different social groups injects a dynamic element missing in the concerns of anthropologists and warns against treating ideology as a unitary or finished product. Neo-Marxist studies also show that ideology is closely tied to patterns of privilege and the exercise of power. Finally, they offer a conception of the relationship between the system of production and consciousness that is complex and indirect, not simple and straightforward. The consciousness of elites may have but a tenuous relationship with the economic system on which their power ultimately rests.[7]

What has been called the new cultural history can also contribute to our enlightenment and help us guard against an overly superficial and

5 On decoding see Daniel T. Rodgers, *Contested Truths: Keywords in American Politics since Independence* (New York, 1987). On rhetoric see Hunt, *Ideology and U.S. Foreign Policy*, 15–16. On symbols and ceremonies see Wilbur Zelinsky, *Nation into State: The Shifting Symbolic Foundations of American Nationalism* (Chapel Hill, 1988).
6 Geertz, "Thick Description: Toward an Interpretive Theory of Culture," in Geertz, *The Interpretation of Cultures* (New York, 1973), 12. Most pertinent here is his classic, "Ideology as a Cultural System," in *Ideology and Discontent*, ed. David E. Apter (London, 1964), 47–76. The deep impact of cultural anthropology on intellectual history can be gauged in the instructive essays in John Higham and Paul K. Conkin, eds., *New Directions in American Intellectual History* (Baltimore, 1979). For the broader impact see Ronald G. Walters, "Signs of the Times: Clifford Geertz and the Historians," *Social Research* 47 (Autumn 1980): 537–56. For a reassessment see Aletta Biersack, "Local Knowledge, Local History: Geertz and Beyond," in *The New Cultural History*, ed. Lynn Hunt (Berkeley, 1989), 72–96.
7 See Raymond Williams, "Base and Superstructure in Marxist Cultural Theory," in Williams, *Problems in Materialism and Culture* (London, 1980), 31–49; Jorge Larrain, *Marxism and Ideology* (London, 1983); and T. J. Jackson Lears, "The Concept of Cultural Hegemony: Problems and Possibilities," *American Historical Review* 90 (June 1985): 567–93. Antonio Gramsci has won a following on the basis of fragmentary observations, available in *Selections from the Prison Notebooks of Antonio Gramsci*, ed. and trans. Quinton Hoare and Geoffrey Nowell Smith (New York, 1971).

schematic notion of ideology. It offers not a model or paradigm, but an argument that alerts students of ideology to linguistic and philosophical complexities. The proponents and practitioners of this approach urge scholars to look beneath the explicit meanings texts convey to the deeper structures of language and rhetoric that both impart and circumscribe meaning. Those structures will help us understand what policymakers can and cannot say about the world. No diplomatic historian will be able to regard evidence in quite the same way after reading the new cultural historians on the relations of language to knowledge and power, the complexity of reading a text and relating it to context, and the creation of meaning through discourse. Although the new cultural history is sometimes couched in convoluted and obscure language, the approach remains an important source for a sophisticated conception of ideology.[8]

Ideology cannot be understood apart from cultural context, relationships of power, and the creation, transmission, and interpretation of meaning. Once this becomes clear, it is no longer possible to treat, however tacitly, policy as autonomous. What goes on in the heads of policymakers is inseparable from the social setting broadly understood. This perspective on the state's policymaking function prompts a series of questions about ideology. How do policymakers' systems of belief relate to those of the broad public or the small portion of it keenly interested in foreign affairs? How do ideologies held by policymakers and the public relate to the patterns of privilege and structures of power in the society? How do fundamental policy assumptions and core ideas assume their meaning, and how does that meaning shift depending on time and context? How does change, even crisis, within society alter ideological formulations?

Those questions, whether applied to a particular policymaker or a particular decision, should induce diplomatic historians to step more often out of the archives and to explore the broader literature of American history dealing with the cultural values and concerns that sustain ideas and give them meaning. Interpretative guidance and inspiration can be found in topics and themes in American history as diverse as the influence

8   See Lynn Hunt, "Introduction: History, Culture, and Text," Patricia O'Brien, "Michel Foucault's History of Culture," and Lloyd S. Kramer, "Literature, Criticism, and Historical Imagination: The Literary Challenge of Hayden White and Dominick LaCapra," all in Hunt, ed., *New Cultural History*, 1–22, 25–46, 97–128; and John E. Toews, "Intellectual History after the Linguistic Turn: The Autonomy of Meaning and Irreducibility of Experience," *American Historical Review* 92 (October 1987): 879–907. For an account that offers a helpful introduction to the "linguistic turn" but does not demonstrate precisely how it might contribute to historiographical or historical understanding see Frank Ninkovich, "Interests and Discourse in Diplomatic History," *Diplomatic History* 13 (Spring 1989): 135–61.

of economic systems and economic interests, the role of social class and ethnicity, the impact of regional identity and national political culture, the process of nation and state building, and even the constraints of gender, as Emily Rosenberg reminds us in her contribution to this volume.[9] To establish the intellectual context of policymaking, our research must become more wide-ranging, imaginative, and ingenious.

The notion of ideology as a complex structure with potentially far-reaching influence and with intimate links to social and economic conditions builds on and offers advantages over older approaches dominant in the field. Diplomatic historians have been slow in coming to terms with ideology, preferring to consider ideas in a somewhat disembodied form. On the one hand, the impact of ideas on policy was often only implied or impressionistically developed. On the other hand, ideas were frequently left free floating, divorced from economic or social processes or needs. "Realists" during the early Cold War tried for the first time to clear room for ideology. But their conception of it as an intellectual deformity characteristic of totalitarian states converted the United States into a special case, thus nullifying the value of the breakthrough. According to the realists, U.S. policymakers, as the leaders of the "free world," had shown a lamentable tendency to fall under the sway of such pernicious influences as moralism and idealism, but they were not ideological.[10]

Finally, in the 1960s and 1970s, an explicitly ideological treatment of U.S. policy came into its own thanks to William Appleman Williams and like-minded historians associated with the New Left.[11] Their critics' pas-

9 See, for example, Robert Kelley, "Ideology and Political Culture from Jefferson to Nixon," *American Historical Review* 82 (June 1977): 531–62; Tennant S. Mc-Williams, *The New South Faces the World: Foreign Affairs and the Southern Sense of Self, 1877–1950* (Baton Rouge, 1988); and Geoff Eley, "Nationalism and Social History," *Social History* 6 (January 1981): 83–107.

10 For a stark example of the neglect of the function and origin of ideas characteristic of much of the early diplomatic history literature see Albert K. Weinberg, *Manifest Destiny: A Study of Nationalist Expansionism in American History* (Baltimore, 1935). For a classic exposition, itself strikingly ideological, see George F. Kennan, *American Diplomacy, 1900–1950* (Chicago, 1951). This denigrative notion of ideology informs the entry by Edward Shils in *International Encyclopedia of Social Science*, ed. David L. Sills, 18 vols. (New York, 1968), 7:66–76; it lingers in Paul Seabury, "Ideology and Foreign Policy," in *Encyclopedia of American Foreign Policy: Studies of the Principal Movements and Ideas*, ed. Alexander DeConde, 3 vols. (New York, 1978), 2:398–408.

11 William Appleman Williams, *The Tragedy of American Diplomacy* (Cleveland, 1959). For a thoughtful appraisal see Bradford Perkins, "The Tragedy of American Diplomacy: Twenty-five Years After," *Reviews in American History* 12 (March 1984): 1–18. Walter LaFeber, *The New Empire: An Interpretation of American Expansion, 1860–1898* (Ithaca, 1963), is an early and impressive attempt to demonstrate the importance of ideology to policymaking.

sionately held Cold War convictions, however, trivialized the discussion of ideology and overshadowed abstract considerations of method and theory. Those critics, most of them open or closet realists, summarily dismissed as absurd the suggestion that Open Door ideology or any other ideology had fundamentally influenced U.S. policy.[12]

Over the past decade and a half, with the cooling of controversy over the origins of the Cold War, a new concern with ideology has infiltrated the field from a variety of directions. Of the various clusters of scholarship concerned with ideology, corporatism, discussed in this volume by Michael J. Hogan, is the most intimately connected to U.S. diplomatic history. By highlighting how organizational forms articulate economic needs and change the mentality of policymakers, corporatist historians have built on earlier efforts to link the economy to dominant policy conceptions. The resulting literature, much of it devoted to the 1920s, shows how a society dominated by corporate institutions and values gives rise to a corporatist outlook in foreign policy.[13]

Other clusters of work incorporating the concept of ideology fall on the margins of the field; scholars associated with these various clusters think of themselves as peripheral to, if not completely outside, the field of U.S. diplomatic history. Writings issuing from political and intellectual history have used the theme of republicanism to illuminate early American foreign policy. This work has helped break free of the older views of early foreign policy as a battle between "idealism" and "realism" or the expression of clear-cut marketplace needs. The work of specialists in American culture wrestling with the meaning of the Vietnam War has uncovered ties between the interventionist impulse and American society that the specialists, locked in the archives, were missing.[14]

12   A striking instance is the comments of Richard Pipes and Andrew Ezergailis, "Communications," *American Historical Review* 75 (December 1970): 2158–59. The comments were in response to Les Adler and Thomas Paterson, "Red Fascism: The Merger of Nazi Germany and Soviet Russia in the American Image of Totalitariansim, 1930's–1950's," ibid. (April 1970): 1046–64.
13   For a broad application of the corporatist approach see Emily S. Rosenberg, *Spreading the American Dream: American Economic and Cultural Expansion, 1890–1945* (New York, 1982). For key appraisals of corporatism see Thomas J. McCormick, "Drift or Mastery? A Corporatist Synthesis for American Diplomatic History," *Reviews in American History* 10 (December 1982): 318–30; John Braeman, "The New Left and American Foreign Policy during the Age of Normalcy," *Business History Review* 57 (Spring 1983): 73–104; and Michael J. Hogan, "Corporatism: A Positive Appraisal," *Diplomatic History* 10 (Fall 1986): 363–72.
14   On republicanism see Drew R. McCoy, *The Elusive Republic: Political Economy in Jeffersonian America* (Chapel Hill, 1980); and Thomas R. Hietala, *Manifest Design: Anxious Aggrandizement in Late Jacksonian America* (Ithaca, 1985). On the Vietnam War the prime example is Loren Baritz, *Backfire: A History of How American Culture*

Other work, also peripheral to the field, has issued from area studies with its multidisciplinary basis and strong orientation toward the study of culture. As the area studies approach has grown in range, resources, sophistication, and influence, it has encouraged U.S. diplomatic historians touched by it to reflect on the seemingly self-evident beliefs and long-hidden assumptions of their country and culture. Nowhere has the resulting attention to culturally grounded world views, both elite and popular, been more marked than in American–East Asian relations.[15]

A fifth cluster of relevant work comes from political scientists who examine the policymaking process and contemporary international relations. This work has shown a fascination with the intellectual underpinnings of U.S. Cold War policy and with the post–Vietnam War breakdown of foreign policy consensus.[16] A last identifiable cluster is associated with British and British Commonwealth historians, who have the advantage of both distance from and familiarity with the United States. Those informed outsiders have brought into sharp relief racial thought, nationalist ideas, and imperial attitudes familiar from the earlier British experience. Shy on theory, these works have been notably strong in exploiting comparisons.[17]

If a concern with ideology has developed within diplomatic history, resistance remains—for good reasons as well as bad. Some diplomatic historians are troubled by concerns that have long worried intellectual historians. Any attempt to assign ideology its proper influence and to anchor it in a specific social and economic context is attended by a

Led Us into Vietnam and Made Us Fight the Way We Did (New York, 1985). See also John Hellman, *American Myths and the Legacy of Vietnam* (New York, 1986).

15 John W. Dower, *War without Mercy: Race and Power in the Pacific War* (New York, 1986); Michael H. Hunt, *The Making of a Special Relationship: The United States and China to 1914* (New York, 1983). Training in area studies provided much of the impetus for Hunt, *Ideology and U.S. Foreign Policy*. On the rise of area studies see Robert A. McCaughey, *International Studies and Academic Enterprise: A Chapter in the Enclosure of American Learning* (New York, 1984); and Paul M. Evans, *John Fairbank and the American Understanding of China* (New York, 1988).

16 Robert A. Packenham, *Liberal America and the Third World: Political Development Ideas in Foreign Aid and Social Science* (Princeton, 1973); D. Michael Shafer, *Deadly Paradigms: The Failure of U.S. Counterinsurgency Policy* (Princeton, 1988); Ole R. Holsti and James N. Rosenau, *American Leadership in World Affairs: Vietnam and the Breakdown of Consensus* (Boston, 1984); Enrico Augelli and Craig Murphy, *America's Quest for Supremacy in the Third World: A Gramscian Analysis* (London, 1988).

17 Thorne, *Allies of a Kind: The United States, Britain, and the War against Japan, 1941–1945* (New York, 1978); Phillip Darby, *Three Faces of Imperialism: British and American Approaches to Asia and Africa, 1870–1970* (New Haven, 1987); David McLean, "American Nationalism, the China Myth, and the Truman Doctrine," *Diplomatic History* 10 (Winter 1986): 25–42.

daunting array of pitfalls. Reductionism is the most frequently mentioned. Stressing one complex of ideas, the anxious contend, not only will fail to illuminate the complexity of policymaking but may also divert attention from other, more eligible kinds of explanations.

Although these concerns are justified, diplomatic historians should take them not as a deterrent but (as they have proved for intellectual historians) as a spur to try fresh approaches and rethink old ones. Historical writings that take risks in order to analyze ideological assumptions and structures deserve to be judged by the standards that we usually apply, in other words (as one intellectual historian has put it), according to "the clarity, the ingenuity, and the soundness and spread of documentation with which the argument is advanced."[18] The best test of an interpretation is not whether it can withstand a sweeping dismissal but whether it can help illuminate specific cases, perhaps even by revealing complexities not previously recognized.

Yet other critics of efforts to study ideology in U.S. foreign policy have reacted with barely disguised hostility, prompted by a well-founded sense that important interpretative notions face vivisection under the knife of ideology. "Power politics," "international realities," "containment," and "geopolitics" are all terms that often assume a privileged interpretative role. But they are also terms with strong ideological dimensions. To recognize those dimensions is to advance revisionism at the expense of the long-dominant view of the Cold War to which most critics of ideology are still attached. By calling into question fundamental categories preferred by historians who identify with the views underlying U.S. policy, the ideological approach threatens to reawaken slumbering Cold War controversies.

Still other historians, wedded to a narrow conception of the policy process and devoted to closely researched archival studies, have proved indifferent, if not averse, to the historical study of ideology. They ask: "What has intellectual history to do with diplomatic history?"[19] Committed to the herculean task of assimilating a mountain of materials from government archives and presidential libraries, such scholars want their job of reconstructing the day-by-day development of policy made simpler, not more complex and time consuming. Among social science approaches, they have chosen those that highlight bureaucratic behavior and decision making, prizing their help in making sense of the mass of paper generated by the Cold War state. A concern with ideology, by

18 Laurence Veysey, "Intellectual History and the New Social History," in Higham and Conkin, eds., *New Directions in American Intellectual History*, 19.
19 This very question was the focus of an inconclusive discussion at a panel at the 1989 annual meeting of the Society for Historians of American Foreign Relations.

contrast, threatens to increase the scholar's burden as archival texts become denser and questions of societal context proliferate.

Whatever objections or misgivings may exist, ideology is likely to remain an important, perhaps even a central preoccupation of diplomatic history for the foreseeable future. The concept is an invaluable tool whose versatility can help expand the concerns and methods of diplomatic historians, whatever their topic or orientation. Ideology forces us, as no other approach does, to focus on the consciousness of policymakers and the cultural values and patterns of privilege that shape that consciousness. Reflecting its broad application, the study of ideology overlaps with several approaches discussed in this book. Its connections to culture, gender studies, and corporatism have been noted. Ideology also encompasses the study of national security, which is an intellectual construct created and defended by bureaucrats and policymakers as well as intellectuals closely identified with them. That study is also a valuable auxiliary to dependency and world systems approaches as they develop the claims to dominion that issue from centers of imperial power alongside the attitudes of collaboration and resistance that spring up in response among subjugated and dependent peoples.

An interest in ideology is likely to persist as much for its relevance to the contemporary world as for its interpretative utility. Historians, who are shaped by their times, have of late watched established ideologies undergo challenge, and they have thereby gained both a distance from and an interest in them. Within the United States the Vietnam experience has given rise to the emotional alienation and intellectual distancing from Cold War constructs that first showed up in New Left writings. Liberal mission and anti-Communist crusading slowly relaxed their grip on diplomatic history, paradoxically revealing just how strong and deep had been their influence on the underlying beliefs, fears, and hopes that drive policymakers. An even more fundamental challenge to old certitudes abroad—in Eastern Europe, the Soviet Union, and China—has reinforced historians' interest in ideology. Watching old state ideologies falter and new visions struggle to take form can only further heighten their sensitivity to both the power and the mutability of ideology. These developments serve as a welcome reminder that ideologies form a universal web in which even American leaders have been entangled.

14

National Security

MELVYN P. LEFFLER

Every year scores of books and hundreds of articles appear on the topic of national security. Yet only recently have historians and political scientists begun to use the concept of national security to develop an overall interpretative framework for studying American diplomatic history or international politics. In the most sophisticated theoretical analysis of the concept of national security, Barry Buzan points out that in the scholarly literature concerns about national security often have been obscured by realists who focus on power and by idealists who dwell on peace. In the most influential syntheses of American foreign policy, security considerations also have been overshadowed either by the emphasis on morality and legality or by the stress on territorial expansion and commercial empire. This is not to say that those interpretations do not deal with security matters; they simply do not make them central to their analyses.[1]

National security policy encompasses the decisions and actions deemed imperative to protect domestic core values from external threats.[2] The national security approach provides an overall interpretative framework for studying foreign policy, because it forces historians to analyze the foreign as well as the domestic factors shaping policy. If the inputs from both sources are faithfully studied, a great divide in the study of American diplomatic history might be overcome. Realist historians believe that diplomatic behavior responds (or should respond) mainly to the distribution of power in the international system; most revisionist and corporatist scholars assume that domestic economic forces and social structures are of overwhelming importance. A synthesis would include study of the dynamic interaction between the two sources of foreign

Another version of this essay originally appeared in the June 1990 issue of the *Journal of American History*. It is reprinted here by permission of the *Journal of American History*.

1 Buzan, *People, States, and Fear: The National Security Problem in International Relations* (Brighton, 1983), 4–9. See, for example, George F. Kennan, *American Diplomacy, 1900–1950* (Chicago, 1951); and William Appleman Williams, *The Tragedy of American Diplomacy* (Cleveland, 1959).
2 This working definition emerges from the writings of P. G. Bock and Morton Berkowitz. See, for example, Bock and Berkowitz, "The Emerging Field of National Security," *World Politics* 19 (October 1966): 122–36.

policy behavior. By relating foreign threats to internal core values, the national security approach facilitates such assessment.

It does more. The national security approach acknowledges that power plays a key role in the behavior of nations and the functioning of the international system. Proponents of that approach believe that a nation's power depends on its political stability, social cohesion, and economic productivity as well as the number of its troops, tanks, planes, ships, missiles, and nuclear warheads. It recognizes that an overarching synthesis must integrate questions of political economy, military policy, and defense strategy. It assumes that fears of foreign threats are a consequence of both real dangers in the external environment and ideological precepts, cultural symbols, and mistaken images.

To be sure, national security, as Arnold Wolfers wrote many years ago, is an ambiguous symbol. Security is used to encompass so many goals that there is no uniform agreement on what it encompasses and hence no universal understanding of the concept. Certainly it involves more than national survival. But just what is involved is often left vague and indeterminate.[3] Although the ambiguity presents formidable problems to policymakers and contemporary analysts, it should not handicap the work of historians. Indeed, it should focus attention on central questions: How have policymakers assessed dangerous threats? How have different executive branch officials, government agencies, legislative committees, political parties, economic interest groups, and ethnic communities defined core values?

External dangers come in many varieties. The historian of U.S. foreign policy must appraise the intentions and capabilities of the nation's prospective foes. But that step is only the beginning. Views of a potential adversary, after all, are heavily influenced by perceptions of other variables such as the impact of technological change, the appeal of one's own organizing ideology, and the structural patterns of the international system itself.[4] Perceptions of the international system, for example, were probably more important in determining the policies of the United States in 1946–47 than were assessments of Soviet behavior. In other words, Daniel Yergin's dichotomy between the proponents of the Yalta and Riga axioms, between those who saw the Soviet Union as just another great power and those who saw it as an aggressive ideological foe bent on revolutionary change, constitutes only part of the perceptual story. The other part was the dangerous connotation imparted by American officials

3 Arnold Wolfers, " 'National Security' as an Ambiguous Symbol," *Political Science Quarterly* 67 (December 1952): 481–502.
4 See Kenneth N. Waltz, *Theory of International Politics* (Reading, MA, 1979), 79–101.

to developments within the international system, like the proliferation of bilateral trade agreements and exchange controls, the political instability within European governments, and the rise of revolutionary nationalist movements, especially in Asia. Soviet actions in late 1946 and early 1947 were no more threatening than in 1945 and 1946, perhaps less so. But the structure of the international system seemed much more ominous nonetheless.[5]

In studying the systemic sources of foreign policy behavior, the national security approach demands that analysts distinguish between realities and perceptions. This task, as simple as it sounds, is fraught with difficulty because it is often harder for historians to agree on what constituted an actual danger than on what was a perceived threat. For example, the very different interpretations of American diplomacy in the 1920s and 1930s between "realists" on the one hand and "revisionists" or "corporatists" on the other hand rests in part on whether or not there were real threats to American security during the interwar years. If there were no real threats before the middle or late 1930s, then contemporary proponents of arms limitation treaties, arbitration agreements, and nonaggression pacts might be viewed as functional pragmatists seeking to create a viable liberal capitalist international order rather than as naive idealists disregarding the realities of an inherently unstable and ominous balance of power.[6]

Perceptions of events abroad are themselves greatly influenced by the core values of the perceiver. The national security approach demands that as much attention be focused on how the American government determines its core values as on how it perceives external dangers. The term *core values* is used here rather than *vital interests* because the latter implies something more material and tangible than is appropriate for a national security imperative. The United States has rarely defined its core values in narrowly economic or territorial terms. Core values usually *fuse* material self-interest with more fundamental goals like the defense of the state's organizing ideology, such as liberal capitalism, the protection of its political institutions, and the safeguarding of its physical base or territorial integrity. N. Gordon Levin, Jr., has beautifully described how, when faced with unrestricted German submarine warfare, Woodrow Wil-

5 Yergin, *Shattered Peace: The Origins of the Cold War and the National Security State* (Boston, 1977); Melvyn P. Leffler, "The American Conception of National Security and the Beginnings of the Cold War, 1945–48," *American Historical Review* 89 (April 1984): 356–78.
6 For a reevaluation of the relative strength and efficacy of American military capabilities in the 1920s and early 1930s see John Braeman, "Power and Diplomacy: The 1920s Reappraised," *Review of Politics* 44 (July 1982): 342–69.

son fused ideological, economic, and geopolitical considerations. Together these factors became core values and influenced his decisions for war, for intervention, and for the assumption of political obligations abroad.[7]

To determine core values, historians must identify key groups, agencies, and individuals, examine their goals and ideas, and analyze how trade-offs are made. Decision makers and interest groups will have different internal and sometimes conflicting internal and external objectives. Core values are the goals that emerge as priorities after the trade-offs are made; core values are the objectives that merge ideological precepts and cultural symbols like democracy, self-determination, and race consciousness with concrete interests like access to markets and raw materials; core values are the interests that are pursued notwithstanding the costs incurred; core values are the goals worth fighting for. Different groups may have different core values or different strategies for pursuing the same core values. The struggle between interventionists and isolationists on the eve of World War II illuminates how groups sharing similar core values could disagree about strategies. Interventionists believed aid to the Allies was essential to protect American liberal capitalism and the territorial integrity of the United States; isolationists believed such aid would aggrandize the powers of the chief executive and the federal government, provoke the Axis powers, and thereby endanger not only the nation's physical safety but also its political institutions and ideology. Explaining how core values are translated into policy requires a careful investigation and a viable theory of the relationship of the state to society.[8]

The effort to show how core values emerge in the policymaking process forces the diplomatic historian to study the importance of foreign policy goals in relation to the officials' other objectives. As they seek to achieve diplomatic aims, officials (and leaders of private organizations) may encounter costs that exceed the value of the goals themselves.[9] For example, much as Republican officials in the 1920s yearned for markets abroad, they were unwilling to forego the protection of the home market; much

7   Buzan, *People, States, and Fear*, 36–72: Levin, *Woodrow Wilson and World Politics: America's Response to War and Revolution* (New York, 1968).
8   One can choose from a variety of Marxist or pluralist approaches. One can see the state acting autonomously or as a captive of particular groups or classes. For some stimulating views and essays see Ralph Miliband, *The State in Capitalist Society: An Analysis of the Western System of Power* (New York, 1969); Charles E. Lindblom, *Politics and Markets: The World's Political Economic Systems* (New York, 1977); Peter J. Katzenstein, ed., *Between Power and Plenty: Foreign Economic Policies of Advanced Industrial States* (Madison, 1978); and Charles Bright and Susan Harding, eds., *Statemaking and Social Movements: Essays in History and Theory* (Ann Arbor, 1984).
9   Robert Gilpin, *War and Change in World Politics* (New York, 1981), 50–105.

as they wanted international financial stability, they were reluctant to cancel the war debts or raise taxes; much as they sought good relations with the Japanese, they were unwilling to eliminate the discriminatory provisions in the immigration laws. In these cases the foreign policy benefits did not seem to outweigh the domestic costs. Hence the diplomatic objectives, significant though they were, never became core values.[10] American history is replete with examples demonstrating a quest for territory, markets, and influence and with examples demonstrating restraint. An interpretative framework for the study of American foreign relations must be able to explain why Theodore Roosevelt sent troops to the Caribbean and Central America and why Franklin Roosevelt did not; why Wilson hesitated to intervene in Europe in 1914–16 but chose to do so in 1917; why the United States resisted the role of hegemon in the interwar years yet assumed it after World War II; why the United States eschewed political commitments and strategic obligations in one era while it welcomed them in another.

The protection and pursuit of core values requires the exercise of power. Power is the capacity to achieve intended results. Power may be an end in itself as well as a means toward an end. In the twentieth century, power (including military power) derives primarily from economic capabilities. Power stems from the scale, vigor, and productivity of one's internal economy and its access to or control over other countries' industrial infrastructure, skilled manpower, and raw materials. Power is relative.[11]

The chief characteristic of twentieth-century American foreign policy has been the willingness and capacity of the United States to develop and exert its power beyond its nineteenth-century range to influence the economic, political, and military affairs of Europe and Asia. This trend has manifested itself in the evolution of the Open Door policy, in the aid to the Allies in both world wars, in the wielding of American financial leverage, in the assumption of strategic obligations, in the deployment of troops overseas, in the provision of economic and military assistance,

---

10 Melvyn P. Leffler, "1921–1932: Expansionist Impulses and Domestic Constraints," in *Economics and World Power: An Assessment of American Diplomacy since 1789,* ed. William H. Becker and Samuel F. Wells, Jr. (New York, 1984), 225–75.

11 This definition of power comes from Bertrand Russell and was used by Paul Nitze's Policy Planning Staff in the Department of State in the early 1950s. See Paper Drafted by the Policy Planning Staff, "Basic Issues Raised by Draft NSC 'Reappraisal of U.S. Objectives and Strategy for National Security,' " n.d. [July 1952], U.S. Department of State, *Foreign Relations of the United States, 1952–1954* (Washington, 1984), 2:61 (hereafter *FRUS*); Gilpin, *War and Change,* 67–68; Paul Kennedy, *The Rise and Fall of the Great Powers: Economic Change and Military Conflict from 1500 to 2000* (New York, 1987); and Klaus Knorr, *Power and Wealth: The Political Economy of International Power* (New York, 1973).

in the undertaking of covert operations, in the huge expenditures on armaments, and in the growth of the American multinational corporation. The national security approach helps to make sense out of these developments. Alterations in the distribution of power, changes in the international system, and developments in technology influence the perception of threat and the definition of core values and impel American officials to exercise power in varying ways.

Notwithstanding the desire of American officials in the 1920s and 1930s to expand markets, stabilize European affairs, pursue investment opportunities, and gain control over raw materials abroad, those goals did not become vital interests worth fighting for until changes in the international system impelled American officials to redefine them as core values. The Axis domination of much of Europe and Asia in 1940 and 1941, for example, endangered markets and investment opportunities.[12] But far more important, Axis aggrandizement enabled prospective adversaries of the United States to mobilize additional resources, coopt other nations' industrial infrastructure, and secure forward bases. Nazi conquests, moreover, raised the possibility that Latin American countries, which had traditionally traded largely with the European continent, would be sucked into the Axis orbit. To deal with autarkic and regimented trade practices abroad and to protect the United States from the growing military capabilities of the adversary, American officials felt they had to mobilize, raise taxes, monitor potential subversives, and prepare to assist or perhaps even take over the export sector of the American economy. Appropriate vigilance against an external threat seemed to require new powers for the state as well as higher taxes and restrictions on personal liberties. Even if the United States had not been attacked, core values were at stake, not because the Axis powers crushed the self-determination of other nations or jeopardized the world capitalist system, but because foreign threats of such magnitude endangered the nation's physical integrity, required a reordering of its domestic political economy, and portended additional restrictions on civil liberties and individual rights.[13]

After World War II the Soviet presence in Eastern Europe, the vacuums of power in Western Europe and northeast Asia, and the emergence of revolutionary nationalism in the Third World created a similar specter. American core values were perceived to be at risk. The Kremlin might have neither the intention nor the capability to wage war effectively

12 For this view see Patrick J. Hearden, *Roosevelt Confronts Hitler: America's Entry into World War II* (DeKalb, IL, 1986).
13 Melvyn P. Leffler, "Was 1947 a Turning Point in American Foreign Policy?" in *Centerstage: American Diplomacy since the Second World War*, ed. L. Carl Brown (New York, 1989), 19–42.

against the United States, but prudence dictated that the United States mobilize and project its own power to protect its core values. If the country did not do so, if it withdrew to the Western Hemisphere, President Harry S. Truman warned that the American people would have to accept

a much higher level of mobilization than we have today. It would require a stringent and comprehensive system of allocation and rationing in order to husband our smaller resources. It would require us to become a garrison state, and to impose upon ourselves a system of centralized regimentation unlike anything we have ever known. In the end, . . . we would face the prospect of bloody battle— and on our own shores. The ultimate costs of such a policy would be incalculable. Its adoption would be a mandate for national suicide.[14]

During the Cold War years, the perception of an external threat to core values inspired American officials to mobilize American power in unprecedented ways. The Marshall Plan and the North Atlantic Treaty Organization (NATO) are two excellent examples. For the first time in American history the U.S. government appropriated billions of dollars for the rehabilitation of European economies and assumed strategic obligations to protect European countries. In the 1920s, Republican policymakers also had been cognizant of the interdependence of the economies of Europe and the United States.[15] Nevertheless they had eschewed long-term governmental aid and security commitments. How does one account for the willingness of American officials to incur such financial sacrifices and strategic commitments after World War II but not after World War I?

According to the national security approach, the answer rests primarily in the ways American officials perceived external threats to core values. In the mid-1940s the political and economic vulnerability of Western European governments, the popularity of Communist parties in France, Italy, and Greece, and the economic and social problems beleaguering Germany adumbrated a possible significant strengthening of the Soviet Union. And if this happened, Truman and his advisers believed, there would be profound repercussions in the way the U.S. government would have to structure its domestic economy and conduct its internal affairs.

---

14 *Public Papers of the Presidents of the United States: Harry S. Truman, 1952–53* (Washington, 1966), 189.
15 Melvyn P. Leffler, *The Elusive Quest: America's Pursuit of European Stability and French Security, 1919–1933* (Chapel Hill, 1979); Michael J. Hogan, *Informal Entente: The Private Structure of Cooperation in Anglo-American Economic Relations, 1918–1928* (Columbia, MO, 1977); Frank Costigliola, *Awkward Dominion: American Political, Economic, and Cultural Relations with Europe, 1919–1933* (Ithaca, 1984).

Because the configuration of power in the international system was profoundly different in the mid-1920s, external developments did not pose as much danger and hence did not justify the allocation of government aid and the assumption of overseas strategic obligations.

Other approaches to American foreign policy, although sophisticated and incisive, do not offer the same synthetic capacity both to interpret change over time and to explain discrete decisions at given moments. In his books, articles, and contribution to this volume, for example, Michael J. Hogan brilliantly shows how business corporations, private-public linkages, and supranational institutions served as policy instruments. Continuities are emphasized; change minimized. But many students of American history believe the Marshall Plan and NATO represented significant change and want to know how to account for it. As splendidly as the corporatist approach elucidates the tactical changes in policy, it is less successful in explaining motivations. I remain unconvinced by the evidence purporting to show that the New Deal coalition had a greater bearing on the formulation of the Marshall Plan than did the drastically altered configuration of power in post–World War II Europe.

Corporatism has the capacity to show *how* American officials hoped to cast a modern, integrated industrial economy. But to be persuasive as an overarching synthesis of American foreign policy, it must address matters of motivation as boldly and provocatively as did an earlier generation of revisionists, and it must cast its net just as widely. Either by self-definition or by practice, corporatist writers have not dealt with threat perception, arms expenditures, military assistance, force deployments, nuclear strategy, military alliances, political commitments, and client states in the Third World—matters central to the study of international diplomacy in the post–World War II era. Much to my own chagrin, because I did not see how the corporatist model could explain many of these developments, I have relegated it to an instrumentalist, rather than interpretative, role in my writing on the Cold War, despite the great relevance that it had to my analysis of American diplomacy in the 1920s.

Because it calls for integrating core values, power, and foreign threats, the national security approach forces historians to study geopolitical and strategic issues in relation to political economy and ideology. Attention is focused on how policymakers linked means and ends and on how they sought to balance commitments and resources. In seeking to accomplish those tasks, scholars can and should use techniques from other interpretative approaches and from other disciplines. In discussing threat perception, psychological approaches will help; in discussing core values, theories of decision making and organizational behavior and an understanding of culture and ideology will be useful; in discussing the exercise of power, corporatist, realist, and world systems approaches will be applicable.[16]

Heretofore the integrative potential of the national security approach has been obfuscated by the fact that it has become so closely linked to debates over revisionism and postrevisionism. John Lewis Gaddis, the founder of post-revisionism, has sought to use the national security approach to reduce the centrality of economic factors and to minimize American responsibility for the Cold War. Gaddis argues that in responding to Soviet threats and to foreign invitations for help, the United States exercised economic power for political purposes, that is, to check Soviet advances, to create independent centers of power, and to fashion a world of diversity. According to Gaddis, containment was motivated neither by ideological nor by economic factors, but by geopolitical considerations. In its most successful stages, containment was infused with a sense of restraint, with a focus on Western Europe, and with an acute awareness of the potential to split Communist parties from the Soviet behemoth.[17]

There is much that is captivating in this interpretation, but it is not the only one that can flow from the national security model. One might wish to develop the perception of threat by stressing not so much Soviet behavior as the interaction between the vulnerabilities of the international system and the perceived capacity of the Kremlin to take advantage of those vulnerabilities. One might discuss core values not simply by alluding to a balance of power, but by elucidating how the configuration of power sought by American officials was inextricably related to their image of the American state and to that state's organizing ideology, political institutions, and physical base. And furthermore, one might conclude that the purposes of power were not balance and diversity, but hegemony and preponderance. When the United States emerged from World War II, American policymakers were intent on fashioning a viable international economy and were willing to have the nation assume the role of hegemon. When Dean Acheson, Robert Lovett, Paul Nitze, and most other influential policymakers (except for George Kennan) talked about power, they meant "preponderant power." And preponderant power, in the words of the

16 See Ole R. Holsti's contribution to this volume, Chapter 5.
17 This too brief summary of Gaddis's stimulating work is based on Gaddis, *Strategies of Containment: A Critical Appraisal of Postwar American National Security Policy* (New York, 1982); idem, *The Long Peace: Inquiries into the History of the Cold War* (New York, 1987); and idem, "The Emerging Post-Revisionist Synthesis on the Origins of the Cold War," *Diplomatic History* 7 (Summer 1983): 171–90.

State Department Policy Planning Staff, was designed to achieve "a hierarchy of objectives, namely: a. strength at the center (Western Europe, West Germany, and Japan); b. strength at the periphery (Southeast Asia, Middle East, and North Africa); c. the retraction of Soviet power and a change in the Soviet system."[18]

Policymakers' belief that it was a vital American interest to integrate core and periphery suggests that there should be a close convergence between the national security approach to understanding American diplomatic history and the world systems model outlined by Thomas J. McCormick in this volume. There are some important distinctions, however. I would agree that the American economy always has functioned as part of the world capitalist system, but only occasionally has its participation in that system dictated critical foreign policy decisions. For example, American officials rejected a hegemonic role for the United States in 1919 and spurned responsibility for the effective functioning of the world capitalist system during the Great Depression. When the United States did assume the role of hegemon in the late 1940s, American policymakers were inspired as much by their concern for America's long-term physical security and for its domestic political freedoms and free enterprise economy as by solicitude for the world capitalist system itself. For although McCormick is right to say that the Truman administration faced a global, systemwide capitalist crisis in early 1950, policymakers nevertheless believed that the foundering of the system would redound to the benefit of the Kremlin. If the Soviet Union could attract part of the periphery or lure Germany or Japan into its orbit, Soviet strength would grow and the power of the Western alliance would erode. Eventually, the Kremlin might gather enough resources, industrial infrastructure, military capabilities, and self-confidence to challenge more vital American interests and to wage war effectively if it should erupt through miscalculation or accident.

According to official Washington, prudence dictated that the United States intervene on the periphery, rearm Germany, and militarize its foreign policy. If the Truman administration did not do so, it might subsequently encounter even greater dangers. It might then have to

18 Policy Planning Staff, "Basic Issues," n.d. [July 1952], *FRUS, 1952–1954* 2:62–63. Although Gaddis borrows heavily from the insights and vocabulary of political scientists, the notion of hegemon, so pervasive in the works of political economy, rarely appears in his interpretation. On hegemony see Charles P. Kindleberger, *The World in Depression, 1929–1939* (Berkeley, 1973); Gilpin, *War and Change*, 173–75; David P. Calleo and Benjamin M. Rowland, *America and the World Political Economy: Atlantic Dreams and National Realities* (Bloomington, 1973), 71–72; and Robert O. Keohane, *After Hegemony: Cooperation and Discord in the World Political Economy* (Princeton, 1984).

multiply its defense expenditures, raise taxes, interfere in the operation of the marketplace economy, and infringe on individual rights in ways that far exceeded the possibilities contemplated in NSC 68 and the worst excesses of the McCarthy era. The real threat therefore emanated not from the malfunctioning of the capitalist system, but from the Kremlin's ability to capitalize upon it; the core values that were endangered were not markets, raw materials, and overseas investment opportunities, but political liberty and free enterprise at home. Truman, Acheson, and Nitze wanted to integrate core and periphery, as McCormick incisively argues, but for more complex reasons (related to strategy, geopolitics, and ideology) than the world systems approach allows for.

Preponderance and hegemony, as Paul Kennedy and Robert Gilpin have written, confer advantages and impose costs. If threats are exaggerated and commitments overextended, if one's credibility is vested in the achievement of too many goals, one's relative power will erode and one's core values may become imperiled. There is an ominous dynamic influencing the behavioral patterns of great powers.[19] Whether or not the United States will succumb to it will depend on whether groups, bureaucracies, and individual policymakers can find a means of restoring a viable equilibrium among threats, core values, and the exercise of power.

The national security model can and should serve as a framework for studying the history of American foreign policy in the eighteenth and nineteenth centuries as well as in the twentieth. For although changing perceptions of space and time caused by technological change made it imperative to integrate policy in a more timely manner after World War II, the use of power to overcome threats and defend core values has been an enduring element of the American diplomatic experience. Jefferson and Madison, after all, sought to use economic leverage and then went to war to protect neutral rights, to foster trade, and to demonstrate the viability of the republican form of government. Only recently, however, have several historians begun to apply the national security model to the pre-atomic era.[20] Although that model is not well designed to evaluate and measure the *impact* of American policies on foreign countries, it is eminently well designed to study policy formulation at any given period of time. And it can be used in a comparative framework to study the behavior of foreign governments as well as that of the United States. Not

---

19   Gilpin, *War and Change;* Kennedy, *Rise and Fall of the Great Powers.*

20   Thomas H. Buckley and Edwin B. Strong, Jr., *American Foreign and National Security Policies, 1914–1945* (Knoxville, 1987); James Chace and Caleb Carr, *America Invulnerable: The Quest for Absolute Security from 1812 to Star Wars* (New York, 1988).

the least of the advantages of the national security model is that it encompasses diverse variables, allows for different weights to be assigned to them, and constitutes the basis for synthesis without imposing rigidity and uniformity.

15

Culture and
International History

AKIRA IRIYE

In July 1989, President George Bush visited Poland on his way to the Paris economic summit. On the eleventh, he delivered an address at the Solidarity workers' monument in Gdansk. Referring to Poland as the place where World War II had started fifty years earlier, he praised that country's "freedom fighters" for playing "a major role" in winning the war. Bush went on to commend the recent political and economic reforms in Poland, assuring his listeners: "You can see a new and prosperous Poland in your lifetime." He talked of "the kinship of an ancient dream ... the dream of freedom" that united Americans and Poles. "Because Americans are so free to dream," he said, "we feel a special kinship with those who dream of a better future."[1]

An event such as Bush's visit to Poland can serve as an excellent text for the study of diplomatic history and may be analyzed on a number of levels. The president's visit was part of a cautious redefinition of the relationship between the Atlantic alliance and the Soviet bloc, designed, as the president said, to "end the division of Europe." It was also a move toward strengthening economic ties between Poland and the United States, as well as other Western nations, and the ways to achieve this goal would be discussed at the Paris summit. On a third level of analysis, however, Bush's visit to Poland and his speech at Gdansk can be seen as cultural events. They pointed out the dreams shared by Poland and the United States, especially the vision of liberty with which the United States identified and which it saw as an expression of universal aspirations.

The cultural approach to diplomatic history stresses this third level of analysis, examining international affairs in terms of dreams, aspirations, and other manifestations of human consciousness. There is no definition of culture that is completely satisfactory for the study of international

Another version of this essay originally appeared in the June 1990 issue of the *Journal of American History*. It is printed here by permission of the *Journal of American History*.

1 *New York Times*, 12 July 1989.

affairs. Nor does there exist a good theoretical work that serves as the point of departure for the application of the concept of culture to diplomatic history.[2] A number of studies described below do, however, demonstrate how this concept may be profitably employed.

Culture in the study of international relations may be defined as the sharing and transmitting of consciousness within and across national boundaries, and the cultural approach as a perspective that pays particular attention to this phenomenon. Theoretically, at least, this emphasis distinguishes the cultural approach from the conceptualizations most commonly used in the field: the power and economic approaches. The concepts of power and economy are as elusive concepts as culture, but in the study of diplomatic affairs one may define power as a nation's ability to defend itself and economy as its production and exchange of goods and services. Culture, in contrast, is the creation and communication of memory, ideology, emotions, life styles, scholarly and artistic works, and other symbols.

Of course, power, economy, and culture may be so defined as to become interchangeable. For instance, national security—a power phenomenon—may be comprehended as an idea or a world view, which is a cultural product; political scientists even use "strategic culture" as a conceptual framework to examine the cultural underpinnings of a given strategy. Economic activities may likewise be examined in terms of the cultural equipment (education, technology, or work ethic) with which those activities are pursued. But there is little to gain by mixing up the three, or by developing an overarching, anthropological definition of culture so broad that it includes every human phenomenon. A loose cultural determinism is no more helpful than power determinism (seeing international affairs only as geopolitical interplays—the "realist" construction) or economic determinism (viewing foreign policy as an expression of certain domestic interests—the "self-interest" school of interpretation).

Rather, it would be useful to start by recognizing the obvious. Nations, like individuals, sometimes use force to protect themselves and often engage in selfish pursuits to enrich themselves but they also develop visions, dreams, and prejudices about themselves and the world that influence their relationships. A good example of this tripartite distinction was a statement Secretary of State James Baker made before the House Foreign Affairs Committee in June 1989 concerning U.S. policy toward China. He noted that human rights were the keystone of the American

---

2 One excellent attempt, an exception to the statement made here, is Frank Ninkovich, "Interests and Discourse in Diplomatic History," *Diplomatic History* 13 (Spring 1989): 135–61.

approach to that country, but that the United States also had to take into consideration geopolitical and economic factors.[3] What Baker implied was that the United States and China related to one another as potential allies (or antagonists) in the regional security system, as trading partners (or competitors), and as ideologically compatible (or conflicting) nations. To reduce these three aspects to a single factor would be too simplistic. U.S.-Chinese relations in 1989 and 1990, for instance, were clearly incompatible ideologically, but that did not prevent the growth of trade between the two countries, and Washington was reluctant to punish Beijing too severely for its transgression of human rights lest China's geopolitical importance in the Asian balance of power be compromised. What this suggests is that the United States, China, and all countries are definable as powers, as economic systems, and as cultures, and that they can behave differently in these various modes. The cultural approach to diplomatic history attempts to take account of this fact by considering nations as cultures when looking at their international affairs.

Leslie White's analysis of "cultural systems" may be useful in this connection. There are, he says, intrasystemic and extrasystemic types of behavior. The former refers to movements and developments within the cultural system and the latter to those between one cultural system and another.[4] Historians of international relations must, then, concern themselves both with the formation and preservation of cultural products within nations and with their interactions with their counterparts elsewhere. Ultimately, moreover, it will be necessary to inquire into the existence (or absence) and transformation of a global cultural system. In other words, the cultural approach consists of three levels of analysis: national, cross-national, and global. Of course, the same would be true of the power or economic approaches. But what is most fascinating, as well as most frustrating, about the cultural approach is that it forces the historian to recognize simultaneously qualitative differences among cultural traditions and vocabularies and determine whether some universal "structures of meaning" (to use Clifford Geertz's phrase) might result from direct or indirect contact among the representatives of different cultures.[5] The power and economic approaches, in contrast, start by assuming that there exists an international power or economic system in which national entities behave as essentially interchangeable "actors." The international cultural historian cannot make a similar assumption. He or she must accept the existence of and be well versed in various

3 *Asahi*, 24 June 1989.
4 Leslie A. White, *The Concept of Cultural Systems* (New York, 1975), 20.
5 Clifford Geertz, *Interpretation of Cultures* (New York, 1973), 14.

cultures and also have a vision of the world cultural order. This is a tall order, and a far more challenging task than merely reading documents in one language or applying theoretical vocabularies indiscriminately to all nations. Fortunately, there are excellent works that have responded, at least partially, to this demanding task. They may be divided into three categories, corresponding to the three levels mentioned.

First, a growing body of literature explores the ideological or intellectual underpinnings of a nation's behavior toward others. One could call this the intrasystemic approach. It focuses on what Paul Ricoeur calls the "layer of images and symbols which make up the basic ideals of a nation."[6] Fundamental to this approach is the proposition that a nation consists of people with shared memories, dreams, attitudes, and values. Even when their ideas and aspirations are divided, their self-perception prescribes adherence to some "ethico-mythical nucleus" that defines the boundaries within which they exist. One may say that these "core values" make a nation what it is. By focusing on what Bernard Bailyn calls "interior world views—shared attitudes and responses and 'mind-sets' "—it will become possible to raise serious questions about a country's behavior and attitudes toward others.[7] For instance, the question of mutual understanding or antagonism among nations cannot be fully examined so long as one focuses exclusively on security or trade issues; one will also have to consider the mind sets of leaders and people across national boundaries. In a sense, one will then be exploring the human qualities, not just the geopolitical or economic realities, that define a country's position in the world.

Some notable studies have dealt with the ideological foundations of American diplomacy. Perhaps the most influential has been Felix Gilbert's *To the Farewell Address,* which examines the intellectual equipment of the American leaders in the late eighteenth century. A more recent work, Michael H. Hunt's *Ideology and U.S. Foreign Policy,* points to certain underlying themes that the author asserts have sustained American attitudes toward other countries, such as a sense of superiority, race consciousness, and democratization. Hugh DeSantis's *Diplomacy of Silence* studies the ideas and attitudes held by some key Foreign Service officers who specialized in Soviet affairs during the 1930s and the 1940s.[8]

6 Paul Ricoeur, *History and Truth,* trans. Charles A. Kelbley (Evanston, 1965), 282.
7 Bernard Bailyn, "The Challenge of Modern Historiography," *American Historical Review* 87 (February 1982): 22.
8 Gilbert, *To the Farewell Address: Ideas of Early American Foreign Policy* (Princeton, 1961); Hunt, *Ideology and U.S. Foreign Policy* (New Haven, 1987); DeSantis, *The Diplomacy of Silence: The American Foreign Service, the Soviet Union, and the Cold War, 1933 to 1947* (Chicago, 1980).

218 *Akira Iriye*

As these studies suggest, scholars using the intrasystemic approach must be careful to demonstrate the relevance of ideas and attitudes for public policy. Can certain ideologies be said to have influenced a policy decision more than considerations of national security or economic interests? No blanket answer can be given. Rather, it would be best to say that at certain times and in certain circumstances ideas and assumptions do become crucial. What these times and circumstances are must be studied carefully, providing in itself a fascinating area of inquiry for diplomatic historians.

Another methodological problem with the intrasystemic approach is the issue of hegemony. Are we talking about the ideologies of the elites in society who impose their perceptions on the rest of the population, or can we say something about mass-generated ideas and attitudes? Here again, the only recourse historians have is to empirical research. Certainly, some recent works would seem to indicate that from time to time certain attitudes, even if they may have been fostered by "dominant groups," tend to be magnified and exaggerated by the general public. See, for instance, John W. Dower's *War without Mercy,* a study of American and Japanese prejudices, raw emotions, and instincts during the Second World War, Deborah Welch Larson's *Origins of Containment,* an attempt to psychoanalyze the origins of the Cold War, Paul Boyer's *By the Bomb's Early Light,* a superb examination of popular attitudes toward the atomic bomb in the immediate aftermath of the war, and Spencer R. Weart's *Nuclear Fear,* which traces the same phenomenon over a longer period of time.[9]

Speaking of mass emotions and prejudices raises another important question. Rather than talking of the masses or the general public, should not one examine the nation's diverse "subcultures" and see how they fit into the total picture? This is especially important for a country like the United States, where it would make little sense simply to talk of "public opinion" without exploring how subcategories of the population develop their own self-perceptions and relate themselves to external events. Immigrants, for example, may influence American foreign relations through ties to their kin overseas, through the influence they exert on their children, or, more directly, through their own political action. How such groups develop distinctive perceptions of external affairs, and how their

9 Dower, *War without Mercy: Race and Power in the Pacific War* (New York, 1987); Larson, *Origins of Containment: A Psychological Explanation* (Princeton, 1985); Boyer, *By the Bomb's Early Light: American Thought and Culture at the Dawn of the Atomic Age* (New York, 1986); Weart, *Nuclear Fear: A History of Images* (Cambridge, MA, 1988).

conflicting perspectives are (or are not) reconciled before policies are formulated, are important questions that await extensive investigation.

All of these inquiries are preliminary to the important question of mutual understanding or lack thereof among nations. What do Americans, leaders and the public alike, know about another country? Do they have any understanding of world affairs? Are they, in turn, understood by the people of other countries? What images do they have of one another? Do intellectuals try to educate the masses so that they will have a less distorted image of the world, or do they inculcate more self-centered views? What do schools tell their pupils? Does literacy have anything to do with attitudes toward foreigners? Does a country with a higher level of education necessarily do "better" in international affairs than one with a lower level of literacy?

None of these questions has been explored fully, although numerous monographs exist that deal with cross-national images. The essays in *Mutual Images: Essays in American-Japanese Relations*, edited by Akira Iriye, are good examples. More recent works of note are Sheila Johnson, *The Japanese through American Eyes* and Daniel N. Nelson and Roger B. Anderson's edited volume on *Soviet-American Relations.*[10] A binational, if not a multinational, perspective is a prerequisite for exploring the question of mutual understanding and cross-national communication. Consequently, the historian should at least try to learn something about the culture and society of another country besides his or her own if he or she is to examine how the two understand or communicate with each other. Fortunately, such a need seems to be widely recognized today, which may explain why "diplomatic history" is being increasingly referred to as "international history."

Still, there is a danger that preoccupation with cultures as intrasystemically constituted, in terms of core values, hegemonic ideologies, or whatever, may lead to a myopic or nation-centered view of international relations. There is a temptation to assume the uniqueness of each cultural system and to discuss international relations as an interplay of national ideologies, traditions, emotions, and other cultural productions. The result would be to nationalize international history, an unfortunate development if only because international history is more than a sum total of national histories. In order to understand international relations two related operations are sometimes necessary. In some cases, we must trans-

10 Iriye, ed., *Mutual Images: Essays in American-Japanese Relations* (Cambridge, MA, 1975); Johnson, *The Japanese through American Eyes* (Stanford, 1988); Nelson and Anderson, eds., *Soviet-American Relations: Understanding Differences, Avoiding Conflicts* (Wilmington, DE, 1988).

nationalize our inquiry, that is to say, we must recognize that national cultures do change as they encounter one another. Other cases require denationalization, which shifts the unit of analysis from nations to individuals and groups within those nations that may interact with their counterparts elsewhere not so much as representatives of nations but as fellow humans or as members of some religious, labor, or educational group.

A second kind of cultural study of diplomatic history, the cross-systemic approach, responds to such considerations. Historians of American foreign relations have fruitfully used this approach to study how individual Americans, mostly on private initiative, have reached across national boundaries to engage in commercial, religious, educational, and other activities overseas. After the United States achieved independence, individual traders, missionaries, scientists, teachers, sailors, and travelers were often the first to establish contact with people in other lands, preceding both consuls and naval officers. What they saw, experienced, and reported home constituted a rich legacy of American foreign relations, and it would be no exaggeration to say that until the beginning of the twentieth century these activities defined the nature of American relations with the rest of the world.

There is a rich literature chronicling the activities of Americans overseas, but most earlier accounts were little more than adulatory biographies. Recently, however, fresh works have been published that draw on the insights and methodologies of social history, psychohistory, literary criticism, and other disciplines. Among the most notable are Warren I. Cohen's *The Chinese Connection,* Jane Hunter's *The Gospel of Gentility,* and Robert Rosenstone's *Mirror in the Shrine.* The first examines the careers of three Americans who were among the prewar experts on Asian affairs; the second is a sociological study of female American missionaries in China at the turn of the century; and the third describes the experiences of a missionary, a scientist, and a novelist from America who found in nineteenth-century Japan an outlet for their energies and a milieu for achieving psychological satisfaction.[11] Perhaps it is no accident that these works all deal with American-Asian interactions, for cross-cultural relations are nowhere more fascinating than in the meeting of Americans, imbued with a sense of mission and proud of the best legacies of Western civilization, and Asians with their own traditional heritage. A few studies

11 Cohen, *The Chinese Connection: Roger S. Greene, Thomas W. Lamont, George E. Sokolsky, and American-East Asian Relations* (New York, 1978); Hunter, *The Gospel of Gentility: American Women Missionaries in Turn-of-the-Century China* (New Haven, 1984); Rosenstone, *Mirror in the Shrine: American Encounters with Meiji Japan* (Cambridge, MA, 1988).

that have been published on Chinese and Japanese encounters with Americans confirm this.[12]

Going beyond individual encounters, it is important to consider how American goods, ideas, and ways of life spread to and influence other societies. Through the export of American goods, the activities of missionaries and educators, and the showing of movies and art works, American culture penetrates other cultures. The phenomenon of cultural transmission and diffusion has been studied more extensively by anthropologists and art historians than by historians, but notable exceptions exist. Among the most successful attempts is Frank Costigliola's *Awkward Dominion*, a study of American economic and cultural influence in Europe during the 1920s. Costigliola documents not only the well-known infiltration of European theaters by Hollywood movies but also more intangible influences such as the spreading of the ideas of efficiency, business rationalism, and capitalist internationalism. The converse phenomenon of foreigners making an impact on American life and thought has been described in such works as H. Stuart Hughes's *The Sea Change*, Laura Fermi's *Illustrious Immigrants,* John Diggins's *Mussolini and Fascism,* and James T. Kloppenberg's *Uncertain Victory*.[13] Studies of this sort remind us that the cross-systemic approach is a fruitful way of coming to grips with deeper layers of international relations as they are transformed by contact among peoples, their ideas, and their products.

Cultural exchange in the ordinary sense also falls into this category. It refers to programs for sending students abroad and for inviting foreign scholars to the United States, to hosting tours by overseas artistic and musical groups, and to holding international symposiums and the like. The historical significance of such enterprises, as well as less structured activities such as tourism, has not been well researched. But in the long run these exchanges may prove to be of decisive importance in changing the ways peoples view one another. Similarly, only recently have historians begun to turn their attention to the intermingling of people of diverse nationalities in different parts of the world. For example, the occupation of Japan can be seen as a cultural phenomenon as well as a military and political act. The consequences of the massive intermingling of Americans and Japanese are yet to be fully assessed.

12 See Paul Cohen, *Between Tradition and Modernity: Wang Tao and Reform in Late Ch'ing China* (Cambridge, MA, 1974); and Haru Reischauer, *Samurai and Silk: A Japanese and American Heritage* (Cambridge, MA, 1986).
13 Hughes, *The Sea Change: The Migration of Social Thought. 1930–1965* (New York, 1975); Fermi, *Illustrious Immigrants,* 2d ed. (Chicago, 1971); Diggins, *Mussolini and Fascism: The View from America* (Princeton, 1972); Kloppenberg, *Uncertain Victory: Social Democracy and Progressivism in European and American Thought, 1870–1920* (New York, 1986).

The American occupation of Japan suggests that not all cultural exchanges take place through private initiatives, and that some individual encounters and cross-cultural interactions go beyond the informal level. Often the state interposes itself in the process, to promote cultural exchange as part of its diplomatic efforts or to define a framework in which interpersonal relations with foreigners take place. The U.S. government has been far less prone to undertake such intervention, but it nevertheless has been interested in the phenomenon. As Emily S. Rosenberg's pioneering study *Spreading the American Dream* demonstrates, from the 1890s onward official Washington took a great deal of interest in what Americans did abroad and sought to steer their activities in such a way as to promote national interests, especially by creating a world environment conducive to the extension of American trade and investment. Frank Ninkovich's *The Diplomacy of Ideas,* in contrast, deals with cultural policy as an explicitly defined aspect of State Department policy since the 1930s. During the early Cold War, he notes, even overseas artistic exhibitions had to conform to certain foreign policy objectives. Thus the relationship between the informal and formal, or the private and public, spheres of cultural activities is an intricate one; it is nothing less than the relationship between a nation's self-definition as a culture and as a power (or as an economic system).[14]

The third form of cultural history, what may be termed the global approach, builds on these works and attempts to relate national cultures and their interactions to the larger international system, thereby raising the question of global consciousness: whether there exist worldwide concerns that transcend national boundaries. International affairs take place within a world that is defined geopolitically and economically, but the global approach posits that there may also be a world of shared conceptions, dreams, and problems. Just as historians write about the rise and fall of the great powers or the emergence and erosion of a world economic system, they should also ask whether there may develop global cultural trends and countertrends. It is often said, for instance, that contemporary Japan is a global power economically but is isolated culturally. But to speak of cultural isolation assumes that there is an international cultural order in terms of which a nation is judged to be isolated.

Is there in fact such an order? Here is an exciting area of inquiry for students of international history. They will need to draw on the insights and methodologies of anthropologists, sociologists, and practitioners of

14 Rosenberg, *Spreading the American Dream: American Economic and Cultural Expansion, 1890–1945* (New York, 1982); Ninkovich, *The Diplomacy of Ideas: United States Foreign Policy and Cultural Relations, 1938–1950* (New York, 1981).

other disciplines who have long been interested in the phenomenon of cultural diffusion and transformation. The perspectives of such scholars will be invaluable for historians attempting to trace the forces that make for, or militate against, the formation of an international cultural order. International cultural historians—those who study international relations as intercultural relations—will therefore have much to contribute because of their awareness of the need to transcend narrowly defined national histories.[15]

Examples of recent works that discuss global consciousness or shared concerns include Wesley T. Wooley's *Alternatives to Anarchy* and Alan K. Henrikson's edited volume, *Negotiating World Order*. The former relates post–1945 American supranationalism to its European counterpart, while the latter contains essays on multinational cooperation in such areas as health and communications. Both books suggest that these themes cut across national boundaries and contribute to developing a shared consciousness in the world community.[16] Certainly, recent events in China and Eastern Europe and in Indonesia and Brazil, no less than in the United States and Western Europe, would seem to suggest that freedom, human rights, health care, the protection of the environment, and the like know no national boundaries, and that it is never possible to study these issues merely in national or even regional frameworks. The world, it would appear, is fast transforming itself culturally, even faster than it is changing geopolitically or economically. It is the responsibility of historians everywhere to chronicle this striking phenomenon.

It may be asserted that just because some recent developments suggest the emergence of a global cultural awareness, one should not automatically transpose that pattern onto the past. After all, have not power realities and economic interests been fundamental determinants of national and international affairs? Merely to propose that international relations are intercultural relations may be no more than an act of faith or a methodological statement.[17] But that would be true of the "realist," "self-interest," or any other school of thought. What historians can do is examine the evidence to see whether it may be said that in certain periods of history cultural issues do become critically important, even as in other periods security or trade may overshadow other factors.

---

15 See Akira Iriye, "The Internationalization of History," *American Historical Review* 94 (February 1989): 1–10.

16 Wooley, *Alternatives to Anarchy: American Supranationalism since World War II* (Bloomington, 1988); Henrikson, ed., *Negotiating World Order: The Artisanship and Architecture of Global Diplomacy* (Wilmington, DE, 1986).

17 See Akira Iriye, "Culture and Power: International Relations as Intercultural Relations," *Diplomatic History* 3 (February 1979): 115–28.

In retrospect, for instance, it may appear that no matter how culturally related France and Germany were at the beginning of the twentieth century, these ties were not sufficient to overcome forces, basically related to security and territorial questions, that made for conflict. Likewise, neither the superficiality of cultural contact between Americans and Russians nor their ideological antagonism prevented them from joining together in a military alliance during World War II. Cultural affinity has been no safeguard against serious trade disputes among European nations. At the same time, international relations during the 1920s may be said to have been characterized as much by cultural as by military or economic affairs. The sociologist Robert Park may have prematurely asserted, in 1926, that modern civilization was "steadily bringing all the peoples of the earth measurably within the limits of a common culture and a common historical life" so that there was already evidence of "the existence of an international society and an international political order."[18] Within a few years a catastrophic economic crisis would destroy this incipient world political order, and a series of aggressive wars and atrocities would belie any sense of common culture across nations. But that would not negate the crucial roles culture played in the international affairs of the 1920s.

In a somewhat similar vein, it may be possible to argue that for several decades after the 1930s, security, strategic, and geopolitical issues were at the forefront of international relations, overshadowing all other concerns, and that from the 1970s on such economic questions as natural resources, balances of payment, gold reserve, and rates of exchange steadily grew in importance. Indeed, the vogue of books like Paul Kennedy's *The Rise and Fall of the Great Powers* and David P. Calleo's *Beyond American Hegemony* indicated an increasing awareness that national power was fundamentally determined by economic resources and performance, and that international relations would increasingly come to reflect this.[19] Opinion polls were showing that a majority of Americans no longer considered security vis-à-vis the Soviet Union to be the critical foreign policy question; rather, the public was far more concerned about economic competition with allies, notably Japan.

It seems possible to go a step farther and anticipate that at the end of the twentieth century, if these trends continue, cultural questions will become increasingly important. In fact, they may already have come to overshadow purely economic issues. After all, economic competition en-

18 Robert Park, *Race and Culture* (Boston, 1945), 144, 148–49.
19 Kennedy, *The Rise and Fall of the Great Powers: Economic Change and Military Conflict from 1500 to 2000* (New York, 1987); Calleo, *Beyond American Hegemony: The Future of the Western Alliance* (New York, 1987).

tails work habits, rates of domestic consumption and saving, levels of spending on basic research, and standards of education. These are cultural matters. But beyond such obvious areas, there seems to have been an accelerating tempo of cross-national population movements through tourism, multinational business enterprises, educational exchanges, and, above all, democratization movements symbolized by the razing of the Berlin Wall. At the same time, nations of the world have begun in earnest to cooperate in such matters as the control of drug abuse, the search for a cure for AIDS, the battle against terrorism, the protection of endangered species, and the creation of a global telecommunications network. Under such circumstances, culture may become as crucial a concept of international affairs as security and trade. Historians would seem to have an obligation to recognize this trend and to reexamine the past with the new perspective in mind.

16

Corporatism

MICHAEL J. HOGAN

The challenge for diplomatic historians is to construct an analytical framework that illuminates the internal and external sources of policy. Scholars may disagree over which set of sources is more important or begin at different ends of the chain of causation. They may see American leaders as responding to the demands of a domestic system that opens outward to the world, thereby shaping the basic thrust and particular goals of diplomacy, or as reacting to imperatives embedded in the global environment. But wherever they start, the explanatory power of their work will be diminished if one set of sources is ignored or treated as clearly peripheral to the long-term pattern of American diplomacy. In the 1960s, for example, revisionist historians highlighted the domestic economic and ideological influences on policy without elaborating the geopolitical considerations that also figured in the thinking of American leaders. More recent studies have tended to reverse this emphasis. Post-revisionist scholars concentrate on policymaking elites in the government and on the structure of the international system, including external threats to the state, shifts in the balance of power, and various strategies to contain aggressors and promote security. Although their approach bridges the gap between diplomatic history and political science, it adds to the impression that specialists in foreign policy are isolated from the main currents of historical scholarship. They fail to explore the nature of the American system or its influence on diplomacy, and thus fall short of a coherent synthesis. Still needed is a framework that accommodates national and international imperatives, whatever the point of departure, and borrows as much from the literature on domestic processes as from the perspectives of political science.

The latest effort to meet this need comes from a group of diplomatic historians whose work deals with the interaction of national systems in the world arena. Tracing this interaction dictates a concern with many of the international factors at the center of postrevisionism, with the

Another version of this essay originally appeared in the June 1990 issue of the *Journal of American History*. It is printed here by permission of the *Journal of American History*.

policies and objectives of other states, for example, and with global balances, threat perception, deterrence strategy, and alliance politics. At the same time, however, these factors become part of an interpretative approach that begins with the nature of the domestic system—the American system, in my case, though different national systems have been studied by other scholars. Like the revisionism of an earlier day, this new approach analyzes the domestic economic, social, and ideological influences at work on diplomacy. But it also describes the organizational dimension of decision making, focuses on the role of functional elites rather than governing classes, and traces the connection between foreign policy and ongoing changes in the industrial and political structure. Although adaptable to the interpretative slant that marked revisionism, it offers a more layered analysis and draws its inspiration from the corporatist model employed by recent scholars of the American political economy.[1]

These scholars use the terms *corporatism* or *associationalism* to describe an American system that is characterized by certain organizational forms, by a certain ideology, and by a certain trend in the development of public policy. Organizationally, corporatism refers to a system that is founded on officially recognized functional groups, such as organized labor, business, and agriculture. In such a system, institutional regulating and coordinating mechanisms seek to integrate the groups into an organic whole; elites in the private and public sectors collaborate to guarantee stability and harmony; and this collaboration creates a pattern of interpenetration and power sharing that often makes it difficult to determine where one sector leaves off and the other begins. Ellis W. Hawley defines corporatism in these terms, his work building on the insights of historians, such as Alfred D. Chandler and Robert H. Wiebe, who have identified the organizational revolution and the search for order as major themes in recent American history.[2]

---

1 This essay draws on my earlier work, especially Michael J. Hogan, "Corporatism: A Positive Appraisal," *Diplomatic History* 10 (Fall 1986): 363–72. For another discussion of the corporatist synthesis as applied to diplomatic history, see Thomas J. McCormick, "Drift or Mastery?: A Corporatist Synthesis for American Diplomatic History," *Reviews in American History* 10 (December 1982): 318–30. See also Ellis W. Hawley, "The Discovery and Study of a 'Corporate Liberalism,'" *Business History Review* 52 (Autumn 1978): 309–20. McCormick's essay shows how revisionist scholars might adapt corporatism to their own needs and purposes, pointing out that adaptability is one of the concept's virtues. Hawley's essay enumerates some of the differences, other than those noted in the text, in the way revisionists and nonrevisionists use the concept.
2 Hawley, "The Discovery and Study of a 'Corporate Liberalism' "; Wiebe, *The Search for Order, 1877–1920* (New York, 1968); Chandler, *Strategy and Structure: Chapters in the History of the Industrial Enterprise* (Cambridge, MA, 1962); idem, *The Visible Hand: The Managerial Revolution in American Business* (Cambridge, MA, 1977).

Still other scholars have delineated the ideology and public policies of the associative state and its champions among progressive political leaders and their counterparts in labor, industry, agriculture, and the professions. They have uncovered a body of liberal thought that celebrated such virtues as voluntarism, enlightened cooperation, efficient administration, and managerial expertise. They have explored the many programs to promote social welfare, tame the business cycle, and nurture growth. And they have shown how these programs often sought to contain the state by entrusting much of the responsibility for public policy to semiautonomous agencies, to supposedly nonpartisan experts, and to collaborative systems of economic planning and voluntary regulation. According to the most recent studies, those who championed the associative system saw it as a "middle way" between the laissez faire capitalism of a bygone day and the paternalistic statism of an Orwellian nightmare. In this system, partisan politics would give way to managerial expertise, public legislatures would yield some of their functions to private forums, and redistributive battles would dissolve in a material abundance in which all could share.[3]

The portrait drawn in this scholarship is fluid rather than static; the relative weight assigned to various components of the corporative system, particularly to public versus private power, varies according to historical circumstances. While corporatism is therefore a useful model for describing American society at any particular moment, it is best perceived and most fruitfully employed as an analytical device for explaining important, long-term trends in politics, the economy, and public policy. By using it in this way, historians have discovered hitherto obscure lines of continuity running throughout the twentieth century. But they have done so without slighting the significance of new ideas and scientific adaptations and without substituting consensus theory for one that takes account of political struggles. On the contrary, they have focused on efforts to contain group conflict through strategies of growth and through organizational structures that could harmonize differences. They have also talked of competing political coalitions and have sought to integrate important economic and political transformations into the unfolding history of

---

3   For a sample of Hawley's work see "Herbert Hoover, the Commerce Secretariat, and the Vision of an 'Associative State,' 1921–1928," *Journal of American History* 61 (June 1974): 116–40. See also Joan Hoff-Wilson, *Herbert Hoover: Forgotten Progressive* (Boston, 1975); Robert M. Collins, *The Business Response to Keynes, 1929–1964* (New York, 1981); Kim McQuaid, *Big Business and Presidential Power: From FDR to Reagan* (New York, 1982); and Robert Griffith, "Dwight D. Eisenhower and the Corporate Commonwealth," *American Historical Review* 87 (February 1982): 87–122. For a discussion of corporatism, its connections to organizational history, and the relevant literature see Hawley, "The Discovery and Study of a 'Corporate Liberalism.'"

American corporatism. My own work, for example, describes how the Great Depression of the 1930s combined with changes in the industrial structure to produce the New Deal coalition, an alliance of interests that defeated conservative opponents and elaborated the corporative design envisioned by Republican leaders a decade earlier.[4]

If corporatism has illuminated important trends in domestic history, it has been no less helpful to a new group of diplomatic historians. As these historians realize, American leaders seldom compartmentalize their vision, thinking one way about the American system, another about the international system. On the contrary, they have sought throughout this century to build a world order along lines comparable to the corporatist order taking shape at home. Their global design became more elaborate as time passed and as circumstances changed, just as the same process evolved in the United States, and much of what we know of this design emerges from scholarship on American foreign policy in the 1920s.

Although rejecting the League of Nations and other collective security arrangements, Republican policymakers were heirs to a long tradition of expansionism and dollar diplomacy. They built on this tradition, on the internationalism of the war period, and on such venerable shibboleths as the Open Door, joining forces in many cases with industrial and financial institutions that had a growing stake in the global economy. My early work focused on their efforts to reconstruct the international system in the wake of World War I. Similar contributions have come from Carl P. Parrini, Joan Hoff-Wilson, Burton I. Kaufman, Melvyn P. Leffler, Emily S. Rosenberg, and Frank Costigliola.[5]

---

4 Michael J. Hogan, "Revival and Reform: America's Twentieth-Century Search for a New Economic Order Abroad," *Diplomatic History* 8 (Fall 1984): 287–310; idem, *The Marshall Plan: America, Britain, and the Reconstruction of Western Europe, 1947–1952* (New York, 1987), 1–25. My argument about the formation of the New Deal coalition borrows from Thomas Ferguson, "From Normalcy to New Deal: Industrial Structure, Party Competition, and American Public Policy in the Great Depression," *International Organization* 38 (Winter 1984): 41–94.

5 Parrini, *Heir to Empire: United States Economic Diplomacy, 1916–1923* (Pittsburgh, 1969); Hoff-Wilson, *Herbert Hoover;* idem, *American Business & Foreign Policy, 1920–1933* (Lexington, KY, 1971); Kaufman, *Efficiency and Expansion: Foreign Trade Organization in the Wilson Administration, 1913–1921* (Westport, 1974); Michael J. Hogan, *Informal Entente: The Private Structure of Cooperation in Anglo-American Economic Diplomacy, 1918–1928* (Columbia, MO, 1977); Leffler, *The Elusive Quest: America's Pursuit of European Stability and French Security, 1919–1933* (Chapel Hill, 1979); Rosenberg, *Spreading the American Dream: American Economic and Cultural Expansion, 1890–1945* (New York, 1982); Costigliola, *Awkward Dominion: American Political, Economic, and Cultural Relations with Europe, 1919–1933* (Ithaca, 1984). See also Ellis W. Hawley, *The Great War and the Search for a Modern Order, A History of the American People and Their Institutions, 1917–1933* (New York, 1979). This list does not include the contributions by specialists in European diplomatic history, especially Charles S. Maier, some of whose articles are cited in subsequent notes.

These studies differ in chronological coverage, topical focus, and point of view, but all share elements of the corporatist synthesis. The ideology of American diplomats, as they elaborate it, echoes the ideology of the associational movement in the United States. For Republican policymakers, they argue, state trading, national autarky, and unregulated international rivalries posed a threat to global peace and stability comparable to the threat that paternalistic government, class conflict, and the unbridled pursuit of self-interest posed to liberal capitalism and democracy at home. And if the dangers were similar, so were the safeguards. According to these historians, the Republicans saw economic growth as the way to eliminate autarky and integrate national economies into a world capitalist order. Growth could be achieved by unleashing private initiative and normal market forces, steps best arranged through most-favored-nation treaties, convertible currencies, the reduction of international indebtedness, and the export of private capital and technical know-how. Government would play a positive role in promoting these initiatives and in organizing the private sector for overseas expansion. But in the international arena, as on the home front, the major emphasis was on scientific administration, not political management, and on voluntary self-regulation by cooperating private elites.

Guided by their associational vision, these historians argue, Republican leaders touted a "scientific" settlement of war debts and tariff rates by nonpartisan "experts" and semiautonomous commissions. They joined forces with the financial community to regulate foreign loans, tried to reconcile the differences between private groups with a stake in foreign trade, and sought to bring bankers and manufacturers together in collective programs to expand the world economy. In an era dominated by economic problems, Republican policymakers also fostered an international network of cooperating central banks. They relied on private commissions to modify the reparations settlement imposed on the defeated Germans, and they sanctioned the organization of multinational groups to underwrite development, manage resources, and expand communications. Their goals were peaceful growth and integration without destabilizing competition or excessive intervention by the state. And to achieve these goals, the Republicans tried to forge a new order in which market forces and cooperating private groups worked in tandem to regulate the global economy.

While analyzing the New Era vision and the programs that resulted, the historians of American corporatism also describe the imperfect internationalism that contributed to the collapse of world peace and prosperity after 1929. They have noted the failure of Republican leaders to control public opinion, ameliorate group differences, and overcome bureaucratic obstacles. In surveying the complicated negotiations between the United States and other governments, they have pointed out the limits inherent in the Republican design as applied to trade and tariff disputes, debt-funding agreements, loan policies, and collective security arrangements. In addition, Leffler has combined his discussion of economic diplomacy with a careful scrutiny of such issues as strategic commitments, neutrality rights, and naval limitations. Costigliola has focused attention on the expansion of American technology and mass culture, as well as American business, while Rosenberg has done much the same in a volume that traces the evolution of American diplomacy from the late nineteenth century through World War II.[6]

Corporatist works put to rest forever what William Appleman Williams called the legend of isolationism.[7] They revise substantially the older textbook interpretation of the New Era as a decade of unmitigated reaction, marked by a rigid and ethnocentric diplomacy, and they make it possible to see important connections between the search for order at home and abroad. In addition, the best of these works show convincingly that a corporatist analysis can be combined with a searching examination of state-to-state relations and the influence exerted by party politics, congressional pressures, and public opinion. Like postrevisionist scholarship, they note the important role of government elites in shaping foreign policy. But they do not divorce these elites from the domestic system in which they operated. Nor do they ignore the private groups that helped to formulate policy, the organizational structures through which they interacted, and the compromises hammered out—including compromises that tended to limit or undo the corporative design that guided diplomacy. These same works integrate the economic influences identified by revisionists into a larger, multidimensional analysis that takes account of other internal imperatives as well as geopolitical considerations. Something similar can be said of their treatment of bureaucratic determinants. While drawing heavily on bureaucratic theory, including its emphasis on elite leadership and hierarchical patterns of power, corporatist historians have talked about nongovernmental and governmental bureaucracies alike and about the mechanisms established to harmonize their interests. Their innovative discussion of informal diplomacy, cultural expansion, and ideology also suggests a potential link

6 See the citations to Leffler, Costigliola, and Rosenberg in footnote 5.
7 Williams, "The Legend of Isolationism in the 1920s," *Science and Society* 18 (Winter 1954): 1–20.

to recent works by Akira Iriye and other scholars, whose stress on the connection between power and culture parallels the corporatists' emphasis on the fusion of public and private sectors.[8]

Although corporatist historians have concentrated on the 1920s, virtually all of the works noted above see patterns that link Republican diplomacy to the foreign policy of the Progressive Era, notably the Wilson administration, and to New Deal diplomacy in the 1930s. In addition, Richard Hume Werking and William H. Becker have described the late nineteenth- and early twentieth-century efforts of American business leaders to establish essentially "quasi-corporative" organizations, such as the U.S. Chamber of Commerce, that could protect their interests at home and abroad. They have uncovered the linkages that business groups tried to forge with public policymakers, particularly in the State and Commerce departments, who were devising their own plans to make government more efficient and to improve their connections with the private sector. They have also shown how the search for private gain, including career goals and bureaucratic advantage, often coincided with the promotion of national interests and with the larger themes of professionalism, scientific management, and national efficiency that characterized the period as a whole.[9]

Other works extend the corporatist analysis from the interwar period to the 1940s and 1950s. David S. Painter does so for oil diplomacy in an impressively researched monograph that devotes particular attention to the close collaboration between public policymakers and company officials.[10] Burton Kaufman's study of economic diplomacy in the 1950s lends weight to Robert Griffith's important article on the domestic and diplomatic aspects of Eisenhower's "Corporate Commonwealth."[11] In addition, Charles S. Maier and I have used corporatism to analyze the

8   Iriye, *Power and Culture: The Japanese-American War, 1941–1945* (Cambridge, MA, 1981); idem, "Culture and Power: International Relations as Intercultural Relations," *Diplomatic History* 3 (Spring 1979): 115–28; idem, "War as Peace, Peace as War," in *Experiencing the Twentieth Century*, ed. Nobutoshi Hagihara, Akira Iriye, Georges Nivat, and Philip Windsor (Tokyo, 1985), 31–54.

9   Werking, *The Master Architects: Building the United States Foreign Service, 1890–1913* (Lexington, 1977); idem, "Bureaucrats, Businessmen, and Foreign Trade: The Origins of the United States Chamber of Commerce," *Business History Review* 52 (Autumn 1978): 321–41; Becker, *The Dynamics of Business-Government Relations: Industry & Exports, 1893–1921* (Chicago, 1982). The phrase "quasi-corporative" is taken from Hawley, "The Discovery and Study of a 'Corporate Liberalism.'"

10   Painter, *Oil and the American Century: The Political Economy of U.S. Foreign Oil Policy, 1941–1954* (Baltimore, 1986). Painter's is the last of several books on oil diplomacy, all of which provide support to those looking for a corporatist synthesis of American foreign policy.

11   Kaufman, *Trade and Aid: Eisenhower's Foreign Economic Policy, 1953–1961* (Baltimore, 1982); Griffith, "Dwight D. Eisenhower and the Corporate Commonwealth."

evolution of European and American diplomacy from the end of World War I through the early Cold War. My contribution revises conventional interpretations that rely on external factors alone, particularly on the Soviet menace of the early Cold War, to explain the triumph of internationalism in American diplomacy. It sees this triumph stemming as well from the rise of the New Deal coalition in the United States, a coalition that prevailed against Robert Taft and other conservatives whose anti-Communist strategy ruled out many of the economic and military innovations of the Roosevelt and Truman administrations.[12]

As the preceding discussion points out, the recent work of corporatist historians describes how internal and external developments (domestic politics and Soviet expansion) led Cold War policymakers to elaborate the associational formulations of the New Era. Through the General Agreement on Tariffs and Trade, as well as the reciprocal trade agreements, they added multilateral ingredients to the Open Door prescriptions of the first postwar period. Through technical assistance schemes they extended Hoover's earlier efforts to export the American way. Through government aid programs, including the Marshall Plan, they enlarged the design for a corporative world order envisioned by their predecessors. And through new alliances and military assistance programs they committed the United States to collective security arrangements that would safeguard this design against potential aggressors. There were organizational innovations too, including the World Bank and the International Monetary Fund, which tended to formalize the mechanisms of economic coordination that had taken shape during the Republican ascendancy. As in the 1920s, moreover, Cold War diplomacy was often a by-product of close collaboration between public policymakers and private elites. At times this collaboration took the form of frequent consultation or the appointment of private leaders to public positions, phenomena described by Painter in his study of oil diplomacy. At times, as my book on the Marshall Plan points out, cooperation was institutionalized in new agencies that operated as a bridge between the public and private sectors.[13]

These works illustrate again how a corporatist analysis can take account of political pressures, bureaucratic rivalries, and geopolitical strategy. Painter integrates these factors into his investigation of oil diplomacy, as does Griffith in his overview of the Eisenhower administration. My

---

12 Hogan, "Revival and Reform"; idem, *The Marshall Plan;* Maier, "The Politics of Productivity: Foundations of American International Economic Policy after World War II," *International Organization* 31 (Autumn 1977): 607–33; idem, "The Two Postwar Eras and the Conditions for Stability in Twentieth-Century Western Europe," *American Historical Review* 86 (April 1981): 327–52.
13 Painter, *Oil and the American Century;* and Hogan, *The Marshall Plan.*

book on the Marshall Plan details the bureaucratic wrangling between the administrative agencies involved and outlines the critique of the plan mounted by conservatives in Congress. It also argues that economic aid became a vehicle for reconstructing the elements of a viable balance of power on the Continent, first by reconciling Franco-German differences in the West, then by bringing the participating countries into a unit of sufficient strength and coherence to contain the Soviet bloc in Eastern Europe. Economic policy reinforced geopolitical goals, just as military policy, particularly the North Atlantic Treaty and the military assistance program, sought to reinforce the corporative design for a new European order that inhered in the Marshall Plan.[14]

From the works on the interwar era, and those on the 1940s and 1950s, we now have the rudiments of a corporatist view covering a substantial portion of recent history. This interpretation places key events within a framework that emphasizes ongoing transformations and that connects the national and international sources of American diplomacy. Critics have charged that corporatism is marked by conceptual fuzziness, that it ignores important discontinuities, and that historians have applied the model only to those topics, areas of the world, and periods suited to their purpose.[15] To be sure, the past is prologue in a corporatist analysis, which stresses how historical forces limit the choices available to decision makers and how change usually comes in evolutionary increments, not at dramatic watersheds. But if used properly, as the discussion of post–World War II diplomacy suggests, corporatism can highlight long-term patterns of policy without ignoring important innovations. Even critics admit that it has proven to be a remarkably fruitful mode of analysis as applied thus far. Further research should enlarge the subjects at its command and expand its chronological horizon.

There are different varieties of corporatism, as Philippe C. Schmitter noted several years ago; their central components may remain the same but the relationship between them and their relative weight vary according to national circumstances and the historical period involved.[16] This variety helps to illustrate that what critics see as corporatism's fuzziness

14 Painter, *Oil and the American Century;* Griffith, "Dwight D. Eisenhower and the Corporate Commonwealth"; Hogan, *The Marshall Plan.*

15 For the most thoughtful critiques see John Lewis Gaddis, "The Corporatist Synthesis: A Skeptical View," *Diplomatic History* 10 (Fall 1986): 357–62; idem, "New Conceptual Approaches to the Study of American Foreign Relations: Interdisciplinary Perspectives," *Diplomatic History* 14 (Summer 1990): 405–23; and Leo Panitch, "Recent Theorizations of Corporatism: Reflections on a Growth Industry," *British Journal of Sociology* 31 (June 1980): 159–87.

16 Schmitter, "Still the Century of Corporatism?" *Review of Politics* 36 (January 1974): 85–131.

others see as its strong suit, namely, its flexibility as an analytical device and its emphasis on historical *process*. These attributes make corporatism particularly useful for explaining change over time and for comparing national systems in an age when different brands of corporatism characterize much of the world. Indeed, one of the most exciting aspects of this concept is the hope it holds for writing what is often termed international history, what might better be called transnational or comparative national history. As Charles Maier was the first to show in his impressive study of the 1920s, corporatism provides a framework for analyzing how different national systems respond to similar forces, both internal and external, and thus for comparing societies that are usually treated separately.[17] In addition, corporatism may enable us to see the international system as not simply a conglomerate of autonomous institutions, competing states, and rival alliances but as a complex defined by imperatives arising from within the complex itself or projected globally by national corporatisms.

If it is useful to resort to such concepts as postrevisionism, then a corporatist approach, as Maier suggests, "might best be described as transrevisionist. It has crossed to new concerns."[18] Corporatism is not for those historians who are content to work with conventional categories of analysis, such as the national interest and the balance of power, or within older interpretative frameworks, such as the realist critique and its recent resurgence among postrevisionist scholars. Nor is corporatism for those who want to concentrate primarily on such familiar topics as military strategy or on such well-worn issues as the question of who started the Cold War. To be sure, a corporatist analysis takes account of the strategic and geopolitical notions that typify traditional diplomatic history. But it is far more concerned with the globalization of economic, political, and social forces; with the connections between state and society and between national systems and foreign policy; and with the interaction of these systems internationally.

As such, corporatism can provide an analytical link between scholars with different interests and points of view. As noted earlier, it is compatible with the approach of international historians who tell their story from the point of view of at least two countries, who use research drawn from both countries, and who are thus less impressed with American perceptions of the world beyond Washington than with the reality of

17 Maier, *Recasting Bourgeois Europe: Stabilization in France, Germany, and Italy in the Decade after World War I* (Princeton, 1975). To my mind, Maier's book is still the best example of transnational or comparative national history.
18 Maier, "American Visions and British Interests: Hogan's Marshall Plan," *Reviews in American History* 18 (March 1990): 102.

that world. In addition, corporatism is adaptable to the analytical needs of scholars who are interested in world systems and dependency theories, in state-centered paradigms, in bureaucratic models, and in the connection between culture and power. Although each of these approaches can explain aspects of policy or policymaking, none can absorb the others in a coherent synthesis. Corporatism, on the other hand, can bring all of them together in an integrated framework, creating the first broad conceptual approach to the discipline in nearly thirty years. In the process, moreover, corporatism can restore the connection between diplomatic historians and their colleagues in other fields. It can overcome what many see as the isolation of diplomatic history and enable its practitioners to rejoin the larger community of scholars who are unraveling the history of modern America.

Index